AMERICAN LABOR IN THE ERA OF WORLD WAR II

AMERICAN LABOR IN THE ERA OF WORLD WAR II

Edited by
Sally M. Miller and Daniel A. Cornford

Westport, Connecticut
London

The Library of Congress has cataloged the hardcover edition as follows:

American labor in the era of World War II / edited by Sally M. Miller
and Daniel A. Cornford.
    p.   cm. — (Contributions in labor studies, ISSN 0886–8239 ;
no. 45)
  Includes bibliographical references and index.
  ISBN 0–313–29074–1 (alk. paper)
  1. Labor—United States—History—20th century. 2. Working class—
United States—History—20th century. 3. Industrial relations —
United States—History—20th century. 4. Industrial mobilization—
United States—History—20th century. 5. World War, 1939–1945.
I. Miller, Sally M. II. Cornford, Daniel A.
III. Series
HD8072.A5136   1995
331'.0973'09046—dc20   94–24570

British Library Cataloguing in Publication Data is available.

A hardcover edition of *American Labor in the Era of World War II*
is available from Greenwood Press, an imprint of Greenwood
Publishing Group, Inc. (Contributions in Labor Studies, Number 45;
ISBN 0–313–29074–1).

Library of Congress Catalog Card Number: 94–24570
ISBN: 0–275–95185–5 (pbk.)

First published in 1995

Praeger Publishers, 88 Post Road West, Westport, CT 06881
An imprint of Greenwood Publishing Group, Inc.

Printed in the United States of America

∞™

The paper used in this book complies with the
Permanent Paper Standard issued by the National
Information Standards Organization (Z39.48–1984).

10 9 8 7 6 5 4 3 2 1

Copyright Acknowledgments

Nancy L. Quam-Wickham, "Who Controls the Hiring Hall? The Struggle for Job
Control in the ILWU during World War II," in *The CIO's Left-Led Unions*, ed. Steve
Rosswurm (New Brunswick, N.J.: Rutgers University Press, 1992). Reprinted by
permission.

James B. Atleson, "Wartime Labor Regulation, Industrial Pluralists, and the Law of
Collective Bargaining," in *Industrial Democracy in America: The Ambiguous
Promise*, ed. Nelson Lichtenstein & Howell John Harris (New York: Cambridge
University Press, 1993). Copyright © 1993 by Cambridge University Press. Reprinted
with permission.

To my sister, Phyllis Miller Borak

To my father, Hugh Cornford

Contents

Acknowledgments

The editors and the various authors represented in this volume have incurred a variety of debts along the way to the completion of this volume. All of them owe, perhaps, their most heartfelt debt to the Southwest Labor Studies Association for holding the conference where the majority of these contributions were first read. Sally M. Miller is especially pleased to acknowledge the association and particularly wishes to thank, for their support and help in a variety of ways, Robert W. Cherny, Lorin Lee Cary, Frank Stricker, and Robert H. Zieger. She also wishes to express her thanks to the University of the Pacific for helping to support the association and to the staff of the university's library for its invaluable assistance, as well as the support staff of its Department of History. Daniel Cornford is grateful for the assistance of Marilynn S. Johnson, Nancy Grey Osterud, and Jeffrey Stine. James B. Atleson acknowledges the fellowship that he received from the National Endowment for the Humanities and the research grant from the State University of New York at Buffalo during the course of his work. He is also pleased to express his appreciation to those who read drafts of his chapter, especially Fred Konefsky, Nelson Lichtenstein, Katherine Stone, and Clyde Summers, and to former students David Woods and Joyce Farrell for their assistance. Marilynn S. Johnson wishes to acknowledge the University of California Press, with which she published a full-length monograph, *The Second Gold Rush: Oakland and the East Bay in World War II*, on the same topic as her work in this volume. Nancy L. Quam-Wickham expresses her gratitude to Jeff Quam-Wickham, Harvey Schwartz, Paula Fass, Steve Rosswurm, Bruce Nelson, Daniel Beagle, Lisa Rubens, and James Gregory for their valuable comments on earlier versions of her chapter. Each of the contributors to this volume, although grateful for assistance from others, assumes responsibility for any errors in his or her own work.

Introduction

Daniel A. Cornford and Sally M. Miller

This volume represents a selection of the most outstanding papers presented at the annual conference of the Southwest Labor Studies Association (SWLSA) in 1991. The SWLSA is one of the oldest in the country, having held its first meeting in 1975, with the association itself organizing in 1978. It, like the Pacific Northwest Labor History Association, the Illinois Labor Historians, and other regional and state associations across the country, is devoted to labor studies, especially history, in the broadest sense.

The association brings together in annual conferences those with an interest in labor — whether activists, teachers, unionists, scholars, or labor history buffs. Accordingly, it is not simply an organization of labor scholars discoursing with each other but one that encourages interaction across the barriers that sometimes exist between workers and those who teach and write about their protagonists' activities and culture. The SWLSA seeks to share the knowledge and concerns of workers and students of labor through the association's conferences, newsletters, and occasional publications.

The SWLSA is regional in scope, focusing particularly on the world of labor in California, Arizona, and New Mexico, as well as some of the surrounding states. Additionally, conference programs always feature sessions that address national and international issues. The theme of the seventeenth annual conference in 1991 was "Labor in the Era of World War II" in observance of the fiftieth anniversary of the entry of the United States into that war. Of the 17 sessions at the conference, more than half focused on aspects and ramifications of the war for American workers. The chapters in this collection are revised versions of papers read by James B. Atleson, Richard Boyden, Alan Derickson, Marilynn S. Johnson, Delores Nason McBroome, Shirley Ann Moore, Nancy L. Quam-Wickham, David Oberweiser, Jr., and Robert H. Zieger. Only the chapters by Nancy L. Quam-Wickham and James Atleson have been previously published, and the chapter by Gretchen Lemke-Santangelo represents a later, invited contribution.

Many of the important issues that arose during World War II had antecedents in the 1930s, and their resolution and implications extended far beyond the war. Therefore, the "war era" is defined broadly in this volume as encompassing the period from the mid-1930s until almost the 1960s. During these years, and especially during the war itself, an unprecedented "recomposition" of the American population occurred;[1] yet, only recently have scholars begun to explore the demographic, cultural, and economic changes in a serious manner. Clearly, it is impossible to understand such phenomena by focusing narrowly on the world of labor. A fuller understanding of this crucial period requires approaches and methodologies that represent all subfields of the new social history.[2]

During World War II alone, approximately 15 million Americans moved from one city, state, or region to another in search of work, while about 13 million Americans donned military uniforms. As Marilynn S. Johnson has noted, relatively little attention has been paid to migration in American history after 1920. She calculates that, between 1940 and 1947, some 25 million people (21 percent of the population) migrated to another county or state, compared with only 13 percent who moved in the period 1935–40, and migration rates were even less during the early 1930s.[3]

The magnitude of this migration alone does not reflect the degree to which the work force was altered. Four and one-half million people moved permanently from the farm to the city, pulled by some old industrial cities like Detroit that benefited from the wartime boom and by the industrial transformation of the Far West and parts of the South.[4] In the course of World War II, 1.6 million blacks and whites left the South, and black employment in agriculture declined from 41 percent to 28 percent. Employment of African-Americans tripled between 1942 and

1945, and their employment in manufacturing grew by 150 percent, rising to 1.25 million in 1944. Approximately 300,000 of this number were black women, many of whom abandoned domestic and agricultural work for wartime employment in manufacturing and services. In addition, the number of blacks employed by all levels of government during the war increased from 60,000 to 200,000.[5]

The war drew millions of women into the work force; their numbers increased by 6 million, or nearly 60 percent. In 1940, women had constituted 25 percent of the labor force, but by 1945, they made up 36 percent. In the airframe industry, they comprised 40 percent of the labor force; the United Auto Workers contained 250,000 female members and the United Electrical Workers, 300,000. Although discriminatory practices and other factors led to a decline in the female labor force participation rate immediately after the war, the trend was not completely reversed, and by 1960, women's labor force participation rate had inched back up to 36 percent.[6]

The war also brought about significant changes in work settings. The exigencies of wartime mass production and the way wartime contracts were awarded stimulated big business at the expense of small. The 56 largest corporations received three-quarters of all federal war contracts, with the ten biggest receiving almost one-third.[7] The number of firms employing fewer than 100 workers fell from 26 percent to 19 percent between 1939 and 1944, while the number of corporations with 10,000 or more workers increased from 13 percent to 30 percent.[8] In the aircraft industry, 100,000 people were employed at Douglas Aviation plants in El Segundo and Long Beach, California; 50,000 at Curtiss-Wright in New Jersey; and 40,000 at Ford's bomber plant at Ypsilanti, Michigan.[9]

The increase in plant size, the massive migration of workers from the countryside to the city, and the interventionist role of numerous federal government agencies during the war accelerated the homogenization of the American working class. At the same time, its recomposition led to some tensions between white male workers and women, minority, and white male migrants of rural and small town origins in the work force.

Offsetting these frictions were a number of factors. They included the waning of ethnic identities among many of the second generation of southern and eastern European background, who as early as 1930 numbered 25 million, making up one-third of the population.[10] Reflecting the assimilation of those newcomers, the rate of naturalization increased dramatically during the war years from an annual average of 148,291 between 1934 and 1939 to an average of 295,872 yearly between 1940 and 1945. At the same time, the number of foreign language radio stations and newspapers fell.[11] As Lizabeth Cohen has argued persuasively, even before the war erupted, a "worker culture that unified workers across race, ethnicity, region, age, and sex" was emerging.[12] This was due in significant part to the homogenizing influence of such organs of mass culture as radio, chain stores, advertisers, and movies. The 27 percent growth of real incomes for workers between 1939 and 1945 further abetted the penetration of mass culture.[13] At the same time, "symbols and language of an insurgent Americanism," which, in Gary Gertsel's view, had played such an important role in the rise of the Congress of Industrial Organizations (CIO) during the 1930s, helped unify the working class as it fought the good war.[14]

Since the early 1980s, a stream of scholarship has appeared on labor in the era of World War II.[15] The recent attention to this period represents a significant shift by labor and social historians. During the 1960s and 1970s the new labor history was much more preoccupied with the 1930s. The initial presumption was that the severity of the Great Depression produced a level of militancy as pronounced as in any other decade of American history. After a half century of old institutional labor history and almost two decades in which consensus historiography reigned supreme, a new generation of labor historians was anxious to recover the American worker from the condescension of posterity at a time when the political foundations of the post–World War II consensus were crumbling.

Some New Left historians, in particular, also hoped that if the sources of the rank-and-file revolt could be discovered, perhaps the sagging fortunes of the contemporary American labor movement could be regenerated. In the words of James Green: "If we can understand the history American workers made during the Depression, we might clearly be able to see the contemporary working class more clearly. We might be able to offer a better explanation for the coincidence of class consciousness and conservatism in some older workers and for the explosive militancy and potential radicalism of many younger workers."[16]

A vigorous debate ensued concerning the nature and extent of the labor upheaval of the 1930s, with David Brody, for example, publishing four important review articles on the subject in *Labor History* during the 1970s.[17] Indeed, no issue divided labor historians more than the nature and extent of rank-and-file militancy in the 1930s and the factors that led to its containment. By the end of the 1970s, something of a consensus emerged that the 1930s may have been, in fact, the "not so turbulent years" and that historians such as Staughton Lynd had overestimated the depth, breadth, and continuity of the rank-and-file revolt.[18]

For the most part, this debate was conducted with relatively little reference to labor during World War II and the late 1940s. This was true for several reasons, especially the assumption by both New Leftists and their critics that, in essence, the die had been cast by the late 1930s as to the fate of the post–World War II labor movement. The consensus was that, for better or worse, following the Wagner Act, the labor movement accepted a highly legalistic system of industrial relations that circumscribed the parameters of collective bargaining and ultimately contained rank-and-file militancy. Additionally, the reforms and political realignments of the New Deal era in general integrated the labor movement into a mid-century liberal capitalist system. On a more mundane level, the absence of a comprehensive and scholarly survey of American labor history of the stature of Irving Bernstein's *The Turbulent Years*,[19] which provided the springboard for many of the debates about labor in the 1930s, deterred scholars from examining the labor history of the 1940s more closely.

To be sure, Art Preis's *Labor's Giant Step* provided the first comprehensive history of the CIO up to its merger with the American Federation of Labor (AFL) in 1955.[20] However, although the book did not pass unnoticed, the Trotskyist sympathies of its author and his relative lack of distance from the events about which he wrote prevented the work from achieving the full recognition that it perhaps deserved. In Robert Zieger's words, it "enjoyed at best an underground reputation."[21]

A 1975 issue of *Radical America* devoted to "American Labor in the 1940s" heralded the advent of a much more serious interest in the period.[22] The editors noted that "while left historians and old militants have begun to reconstruct a critical history of the entire working class in the eventful years of the 1930s, there is still no adequate analysis of the equally significant 1940s." Influenced in part by Preis's book and by unpublished works in progress (notably that of Nelson Lichtenstein), the editors took issue with the view that the history of the working class in the 1940s and later had been foreordained, in some sense, by the struggles and compromises of the 1930s: "The working-class history of the 1940s also shows why the corporations failed to gain complete hegemony over society and the means of production, even under the most favorable of circumstances."[23]

By the late 1970s, important articles by Nelson Lichtenstein and Joshua Freeman on labor during World War II had appeared in *Labor History*, while Melvyn Dubofsky and Warren Van Tine's masterful biography of John L. Lewis shed much light on the nature of the labor movement and collective bargaining, not only during the war but also in the late 1940s and early 1950s — insights that extended, moreover, beyond the role of Lewis and the United Mine Workers.[24]

At virtually the same time, David Brody turned his attention away from the historiographical debates over the nature of militancy in the 1930s to the labor movement during the 1940s and the postwar era as a whole. To an extent, his findings were presaged in his 1976 essay "The New Deal and World War II," but in his two seminal "Uses of Power" essays published in *Workers in Industrial America*, Brody paid special attention to the development of industrial relations during the 1940s. Written by the foremost authority on American twentieth-century labor history, the essays demonstrated such depth and breadth that they stimulated the emerging interest in labor during that decade.[25]

Bemoaning that "we have, in fact, no coherent history for the years since World War II at all comparable to that for the years when labor was struggling for recognition,"[26] Brody was at pains to stress the potential power of the American labor movement by 1945 as total union membership reached 15 million and the union density rate approached 30 percent. More importantly, and not unrelatedly, he emphasized the success of many industrial unions in challenging some of management's prerogatives at the workplace. In focusing on how a system of "workplace contractualism" evolved to contain this "insidious erosion" of management's authority on the shop floor, Brody reaffirmed the criticality of focusing on labor relations during the 1940s and implicitly rejected theories of industrial relations that viewed the 1930s as predetermining outcomes.

When Nelson Lichtenstein's book *Labor's War at Home: The CIO in World War II* appeared in 1982, he confidently proclaimed that the war was as much of a watershed in the history of American labor as were the 1930s: "The NDMB (National Defense Mediation Board) and its successor, the National War Labor Board, were as important as the Wagner Act in shaping the American system of industrial relations."[27] In another important book, published in the same year as Lichtenstein's, Howell Harris made similar claims for the importance of World War II, and, indeed, the whole of the 1940s, in shaping the course of labor relations as he examined them from the perspective and actions of corporate managers: "The relatively unexplored territory of war mobilization emergency and of peacetime prosperity in the first Truman administration seemed to be the critical period in which to search for answers, because many of the distinguishing features of the contemporary American labor movement clearly emerged in those years."[28]

Although the work of Brody, Lichtenstein, and Harris, in particular, signified a shift among the labor history profession to the 1940s, only gradually during the 1980s did labor historians begin to produce scholarship of commensurate quality and quantity with the work on the 1930s. In a major review article on the fiftieth anniversary of the founding of the CIO, Robert Zieger observed that important work had been done on the anticapitalist left during the 1930s and 1940s and that there was a growing body of literature on the leaders of the CIO and on the experience of women and ethnic minorities. However, he lamented that the "CIO's post World War II character as a new center of working class institutional and political expression has remained largely without systematic exploration." Echoing what Lichtenstein had said in a bibliographical note in his book several years earlier, Zieger also observed that the quality of the new social history's contribution to our under-standing of the CIO era was poor by comparison with work on nineteenth-century American workers.[29]

Much of the published work that Zieger reviewed focused on the CIO in the period from 1935 to 1941. However, Zieger also cited a significant number of unpublished works (mainly doctoral dissertations) on the institutional and social history of labor during the 1940s. The tide of labor historiography by the mid-1980s was perhaps shifting more toward the 1940s to a greater extent than Zieger acknowledged. Indeed, as Lichtenstein noted, Zieger's own book, *American Workers, American Unions, 1920–1985*, devoted twice as much space to the 1940s as to the 1930s, even though it drew almost entirely on secondary sources.[30]

When Zieger published a sequel to his 1985 review article on the CIO five years later, he commented that since his first article, work on the CIO "has proceeded apace," and he estimated that 30 book-length monographs had appeared on the CIO and closely related topics in the previous five years.[31] The flourishing state of historiography on the labor movement and its relationship to the political economy of the 1940s was also reflected in the publication of Steven Fraser and Gary Gerstle, editors, *The Rise and Fall of the New Deal Order*.[32] Several of the chapters in this volume summed up or made extensive reference to the state of labor historiography on the 1930s and 1940s while setting the agenda for some of the debates of the 1990s.

Reflecting somewhat of a reaction to the new focus on the 1940s, Steve Fraser argued that, to a great extent, the New Deal order was forged even before the election of Franklin Roosevelt. By the mid-1920s, he argued, the CIO had already appeared: "Most fundamentally, the CIO already existed as an embryonic strategic alliance, its incipient leadership already integrated, via the left wing of the scientific management movement, into the political circles around Frankfurter and Brandeis."[33] However, essays by Alan Brinkley and Nelson Lichtenstein took issue with this interpretation, viewing the 1940s, rather than the 1930s, as the politically formative years of the New Deal order. Lichtenstein, in particular, extended his analysis of labor and the postwar political economy beyond World War II to argue that developments in the years immediately after the war were as important as those during the war itself.[34]

Disagreements persist about the degree of continuity between the 1930s and 1940s and the relative importance of the two decades in shaping the contours of postwar industrial relations. However, there can be no doubt that the era of World War II has, by the mid-1990s, assumed an importance that few accorded it in the early 1980s.

As social and labor historians began to focus less on the institutional history of the labor movement and the cold war's impact on it, the importance of the social, demographic, and economic changes wrought by World War II grew accordingly. In all the debates about the causes, nature, and extent of rank-and-file militancy the implications of the wartime recomposition of the working class were neglected.[35]

Furthermore, the recent decline in the fortunes of the American labor movement in terms of both absolute numbers and union density has been responsible for a heightened interest in the 1940s by labor historians and industrial relations scholars.[36] Union density, which exceeded 30 percent from 1943 to 1960, has fallen to little more than 10 percent in the mid-1990s. Seeking an explanation for this decline, scholars have probed more deeply into the limits of the postwar system of workplace contractualism. As Eileen Boris and Nelson Lichtenstein put it, "The end of liberal, political hegemony and the decline in the fortunes of the union movement have prompted many historians to take a closer and more critical look at the peculiarly American interclass accommodation that jelled in the late 1940s."[37] Paradoxically, some of the very scholars that were critical of labor's postwar accommodations and compromises now view this period as something of a golden age by comparison to what has happened since the mid-1970s. Thus, in reviewing the decline of organized labor from the mid-1970s relative to the power it exercised during the previous 30 years, Barry and Irving Bluestone entitle one of their chapters, "Goodbye to the Glory Days."[38]

Labor historians and industrial relations experts have tended to view the system of workplace contractualism that emerged in the late 1930s and 1940s very critically. Their accounts of the postwar labor-management compromise have stressed the constraining historical circumstances of the postwar era and the misguided policies of the labor movement itself. More specifically, they have stressed the following factors: first, the degree to which the Wagner Act, Taft-Hartley, various legal decisions, and the composition of the National Labor Relations Board straightjacketed the labor movement;[39] second, the extent to which national collective bargaining, entailing, by the early 1950s, multiyear contracts, took power even further away from the hands of rank-and-file workers; third, the fact that the political climate at home and abroad from the late 1930s was not favorable to the expansion of labor's political influence in all realms; fourth, how, in the light of all of the above, most CIO unions became even more bureaucratized and undemo-cratic in their structure, especially as they began to oust Communists in the late 1940s; fifth, the extent to which, given external constraints and the internal failings of unions, labor accommodated itself politically to the "privatization of the welfare state" and to an essentially subordinate role in the "right to manage" at the workplace in return for a measure of security and wage agreements linked to productivity and the cost of living.[40]

The evidence in favor of the above arguments is quite strong. However, their very persuasiveness militated until recently against a closer examination of the system of workplace contractualism and led, at least implicitly, to somewhat facile and unclear assumptions about worker militancy and consciousness. If the postwar union movement was parochial, compliant, and unable, or unwilling, to expand its base, at least it maintained it until the 1970s. Although the strike rate never approached the 1946 peak, from 1947 through 1957, the Bureau of Labor Statistics counted an average of 370 major strikes involving more than 1.5 million workers.[41]

If labor relations in the era of World War II could be better understood, then, just possibly, the dramatic erosion of workplace contractualism could be halted, or, failing this, elements of the system could be incorporated into new schemes of labor relations euphemistically described as "managerialism," "industrial democracy," and "quality of worklife" groups in such a way that labor would retain some vestigial rights.

Unquestionably, during the 1990s labor historians have begun a much closer examination of the system of workplace contractualism and grievance arbitration as it emerged in the era of World War II. This is not the place to summarize at length the state of the complex and evolving literature on the subject, but some findings are worth highlighting.[42] In a recent essay, David Brody insisted that "what happens on the shopfloor is not a secondary affair in the lives of working people" while arguing that "signs of workplace contractualism can be found before the CIO, before the Wagner Act, before the first contracts."[43] Both he and Nelson Lichtenstein, however, emphasize that it is wrong to view the outcome of workplace contractualism in the 1930s and 1940s as preordained, as many recent scholars of American labor law have tended to do. Brody stresses that the "workplace rule of law" varied greatly from industry to industry, but, at the same time, he views "workplace contractualism as determined by the contemporary mass-production and legal political regimes." Lichtenstein, however, sees the system as somewhat more "fluid and contingent." In the case of the United Automobile Workers, he believes that by the late 1940s the union began to control and limit grievance procedures specified in the contract, resulting in a "kind of dehydration of the dispute-resolution machinery," although this attempt to institutionalize shop floor struggles was not received favorably by the membership of many locals.[44]

There are elements of difference and ambiguity in the work of Brody, Lichtenstein, and others about the degree to which workplace contract-ualism and grievance arbitration procedures were foreordained by developments during the 1930s and 1940s and the extent to which militancy at the shop floor level was contained later. Many studies stress the somewhat narrow parameters of shop floor militancy over workplace issues in the 1950s and 1960s while noting the persistence of wildcatting in these decades. Brody and Lichtenstein agree, however, that, by contrast with Britain, where "the shop stewards carved out a bargaining realm quite independent of the union structure,"[45] American workers were not able to achieve anything comparable. The complex and unresolved nature of the debate about the degree to which American workers exercised a modicum of power at the workplace in the postwar era is highlighted in an article by Jonathan Zeitlin and Steven Tolliday in which they argue that the weight of research on the British automobile industry indicates that under the shop stewards system, autoworkers in Britain had nothing like the power that Brody and Lichtenstein believe. Moreover, they argue, "'the workplace rule of law' [in the United States] was not in itself so severe a constraint on shopfloor struggles as many historians have claimed." Indeed, they maintain that "the American system of collective bargaining placed greater constraints on man-agement prerogatives in the automobile and other mass production industries than generally supposed."[46]

The vitality of the debate about workplace contractualism and industrial democracy in the era of World War II has contributed to something of a renaissance of institutional labor history. There is much to be said for "Bringing the Unions Back In,"[47] especially in an era when approximately 30 percent of the work force was unionized. Furthermore, institutional labor history as it is now often written is more adept at utilizing both the approaches and findings of the new social history than the old labor history. Thus, in his 1990 assessment of the literature on the CIO, Zieger notes that "although the themes of ethnicity, gender, race, and community reflective of the new social history do inform the recent literature, unions remain at the center."

In the same article, however, Zieger observed that "scholars of the CIO period have not matched their interest in the internal dynamics of the industrial relations machinery and in its shopfloor implications with an equal concern for the political context in which it developed."[48] Several years later, Zieger's observations still ring true. Although the outlines of the accommodation and compromise that the labor movement made nationally have been persuasively sketched by Lichtenstein, in particular, we need more local studies that examine how workers' political consciousness evolved in the period from the late 1930s through the early 1950s. Was the political accommodation as universal and predetermined as Lichtenstein suggests? What role did labor play in state and local politics immediately after World War II? Episodes such as the venture into politics by the labor movement in Oakland, California, suggest that labor may not have been as politically supine as some labor historians have assumed.[49] Overlooked, also, has been the political legislative activity of the labor movement in the 1940s. In California, for example, Philip Taft demonstrated long ago that the state's labor movement remained active, and, in many respects, quite effective, as a political lobbying group at the state level, beating back three right-to-work initiatives and pressing for a variety of social democratic reforms.[50] At the national level, Alan Derickson has traced the attempts of the labor movement to try and obtain national health insurance during the era of World War II.[51] That ultimately this effort failed makes it no less significant.

One of Derickson's most interesting findings was that it was the AFL that pushed hardest for national health insurance. This points to another limitation of the labor history of the period for the late 1930s to the early 1950s: it has focused too exclusively on the CIO. Although, as Brody has noted, the CIO and its leaders have been somewhat deromanticized and more critically assessed than they were in the late 1960s and early 1970s,[52] the preoccupation with the CIO remains. This is in spite of the fact that the AFL emerged from World War II with twice the membership of the CIO. As early as 1979, Christopher Tomlins drew historians' attention to his argument that they had seriously neglected or misunderstood the expansion and character of the AFL's growth during the late 1930s. He concluded that "in concentrating on the newsworthy events of those years and on conflicts between the leadership of the two federations, historians have failed to account for some of the important aspects of the growth of labor organizations in the 1930s." This surely applies even more forcefully with respect to the 1940s, and future work will have to go far beyond studying the rapid growth of the AFL per se.[53]

Although the AFL has received relatively little attention during the era of World War II, large gaps remain in our knowledge of the CIO. As Steve Rosswurm has noted, "Most labor historians of the CIO period concentrate on the industrial proletariat (which they implicitly define as male) — and even here primarily the largest and most organized shops — to the exclusion of the majority of working people in the country."[54] Meanwhile, Zieger observed in his 1990 review article that, aside from the Communist issue and Operation Dixie, historians have been much less interested in the second decade of the CIO's history. In revisiting the literature on the CIO in his second review article, Zieger found encouraging signs that despite the continuing focus on "institutional perspectives," which he defines as the "central legal administrative institutional developments that characterized the New Deal—World War II dispensation in industrial and labor relations," more historians were breaking out of this mold and using approaches and examining issues more commonly associated with the "new" labor history such as race, gender, ethnicity, and working-class culture and, in some cases, the extent to which all or some of these elements intersected. Zieger also noted that these less institutional approaches, where often a community or the rank and file were the focus of the study, indicate "the importance of locale in shaping the industrial relations experience."[55]

If we are to arrive at a better understanding of labor in the era of World War II, we will need a great many more community and regional studies of the AFL and CIO, especially in the immediate postwar period. As has been the case with earlier periods of American labor history, local studies have often proved the best vehicle for examining the issues of race, gender, ethnicity, and every facet of working-class culture. Studies of an institutional and, often, national dimension invariably slight or ignore such issues. Also, both institutional and more new social history-oriented approaches will have to take into account the impact of the huge demographic, economic, and social changes that accompanied the 1940s and their effects on the working class. The importance of these changes has been stressed by Nelson Lichtenstein, Mike Davis, and Marilynn S. Johnson, but relatively few works have examined their implications for American social and labor history.

No region of the country experienced such a dramatic transformation during World War II as the American West. It was, in the words of Richard White, "as if someone had tilted the country: people, money, and soldiers all spilled west."[56] In the period from 1940 to 1947, the Pacific Coast states experienced a 38.9 percent increase in population, while the metropolitan counties of the Northeast lost 1 million people and the nation's population grew by 8.7 percent.[57] More than 8 million people moved into the trans-Mississippi West during the 1940s, and probably fewer than 1 million returned East.[58] In California, the changes were most dramatic and enduring. Almost half of the western migrants went to the Golden State, boosting its population from 6.9 million in 1940 to 10.6 million in 1950.[59]

Massive expenditures by the federal government during World War II and afterward were the main causal factor. During the war, $40 billion was invested in factories, military bases, and other capital improvements, and total expenditures amounted to $70 billion. Overall, the federal government provided 90 percent of investment capital in the West between 1941 and 1945. California alone secured 10 percent of all federal monies expended during the war, with these expenditures accounting for 45 percent of the state's personal income during the war years. Los Angeles, the seventh largest manufacturing center in the nation in 1939, was by 1944 second only to Detroit.[60]

Although the industrialization of the interior West was less dramatic and enduring in many areas, California was forever transformed by what Marilynn S. Johnson calls the "Second Gold Rush." In significant part because of World War II, the economy of California was reshaped from a raw material–producing economy, where agriculture, mining, and lumbering were predominant, to one where the value added by manufacturing enterprises accounted for two-thirds of the entire value of basic production.[61] Pent-up consumer demand, the erection of a military industrial infrastructure during the war,[62] combined, relatedly, with a massive influx of private capital during the late 1940s, significantly in excess of what had been invested by the federal government during the war,[63] ensured this transformation. By the late 1940s, one-eighth of all new business started in the United States began in Los Angeles, and by 1959, California received 24 percent of all prime military contracts.[64]

To an extent, the recomposition of the California working class began before World War II. Several hundred thousand Mexicans entered

California between 1910 and 1940, while over half a million Okies, and an even greater number of migrants from other areas within the United States, moved to the Golden State. However, the war, and the economic growth that followed it, greatly accelerated the remaking of the California working class, with 621,786 Okies entering the state in the 1940s and the African-American population of the state increasing from 124,000 to 462,000.[65]

The significance of the recomposition of the California working class during the 1940s cannot be conveyed by numbers alone. It was the predominantly urban and industrial character of this migration that distinguished it, to a large degree, from the migration of previous decades. Within the space of a few years, hundreds of thousands of white and minority migrants found themselves thrown into the same city (mostly Los Angeles or the San Francisco Bay Area) and in the same massive shipyard or aircraft factories. Inevitably, as some of the chapters in this volume attest to, sharp racial, cultural, and gender conflicts resulted, many of which would persist beyond the post–World War II era.[66] In spite of these tensions, the California labor movement experienced dramatic growth. Between 1931 and 1938, the membership of the California State Federation of Labor increased from just over 100,000 members to 291,000. When, in 1950, the state undertook its first union census, it found that there were 1.354 million union members making up 43 percent of the nonagricultural work force.[67]

The chapters in this book present a balance in their attention to the institutional issues recently raised by labor historians and the broader issues raised by social historians, with special attention paid to the social and labor history of California during World War II.

In the opening chapter, Robert Zieger examines the CIO's three presidents' views on what the relationship between the labor movement and the state should be. He argues that John L. Lewis, Philip Murray, and Walter Reuther had differing conceptions. Although Lewis was aware that state intervention played a crucial role in the launching of the CIO, by 1940, he was concerned about the effects "that enmeshment in the state apparatus were having on the essential character of the industrial union movement." As the federal government assumed almost dictatorial powers over labor relations during the war, Lewis moved farther and farther to the view that the labor movement should have an essentially voluntaristic relationship to the state if it were to maintain a semblance of its autonomy, freedom, and power.

His successor, Philip Murray, on the other hand, shared Sidney Hillman's view that the increasingly interventionist role of the federal government could work only to the benefit of labor. With few exceptions, from the Wagner Act to Truman's mediation in several postwar steel strikes, Murray welcomed the growing involvement of the federal government in the management of industrial relations. At the same time, Murray was quite critical of some labor legislation and federal government policies both during the war and afterward. However, Murray strongly supported anti-Soviet American foreign policy and never fundamentally questioned what he perceived to be a healthy collaborative modus vivendi between labor and government. In Zieger's view, Walter Reuther's ideas were somewhat similar. The difference was that Reuther "fought incessantly for entree into the state apparatus," believing that in cooperation with the federal government lay the best hope for establishing a postwar domestic and international social democratic order.

Since the early 1980s, the new labor law history has made a particularly important contribution to our understanding of American labor relations after the passage of the Wagner Act. In Wythe Holt's view, the new labor law history "rejects the autonomous disconnectedness of law from social control, and attempts to elucidate the social history of labor law."[68] There have been disagreements, however, among the new legal labor historians about the period and manner in which American labor law helped to define postwar labor relations. Some have argued that the outcome was preordained by the Wagner Act itself and that by the late 1930s the character of postwar labor relations had been determined. However, James Atleson argues in his contribution to this volume that the decisions made by the War Labor Board were far more important in defining the parameters of postwar collective bargaining. A group of "industrial pluralists" sought to harmonize relations between labor and capital during the war, and they played a key role on the National War Labor Board. The cumulative legacy of the War Labor Board's decisions were many and included the establishment of arbitration procedures and, even more importantly, a rather broad definition of the scope of managerial prerogatives that were to be outside the realm of collective bargaining. Supreme Court decisions, extending almost 40 years later, reflected in essence the terms of the workplace rule of law that had been hammered out during the war years.

Alan Derickson's chapter examines the little-explored realm of collective bargaining within the orbit of the "private welfare state" through a case study of the United Steelworkers of America (USW) and the issue of health care. He stresses that the steelworkers strongly supported a system of national health insurance from the late 1930s through most of the 1940s. However, when, by 1946, the political prospects for the passage of national health insurance legislation were dimming, the USW fought to extend the scope of the private health plans that had been negotiated with the steel employers. Derickson traces the origins of such plans and the issues that divided labor and management regarding their expansion from the late 1940s to the early 1960s. Disputes occurred over the management and scope of private health insurance plans. By the early 1960s, the USW had obtained a system of fairly comprehensive health benefits for its members. However, the management and supervision of the plans remained largely in the hands of the steel companies.

With the chapter by Marilynn S. Johnson, the second part of the volume commences, focusing on struggles in the workplace. Johnson's chapter grows out of research undertaken for her book *The Second Gold Rush: Oakland and the East Bay in World War II* and examines the world of shipyard workers in San Francisco's East Bay during World War II. The new labor history has stressed the importance of racial, ethnic, and other tensions among workers. Johnson carefully analyzes the role that these factors played in dividing labor in addition to differences resulting from skill, gender, age, and geographic background.

The work force in West Coast defense industries grew phenomenally during the war and so, accordingly, did the potential for expanded unionization and empowerment. In the Kaiser shipyards, new, almost assembly line, shipbuilding techniques significantly reduced the differences in skill. At the same time, however, a pattern of occupational segregation arose in the shipyards. Minorities, women and unskilled white males, many of them new to the Bay Area, were assigned to unskilled tasks with only limited opportunity for upward mobility. The International Brotherhood of Boilermakers, Iron Shipbuilders and Helpers of America, which represented almost 70 percent of shipyard workers and which grew from 28,000 in 1938 to 352,000 by the end of 1943, did not welcome the newcomers. Women very rarely held union offices, and black workers continued to be assigned to auxiliary locals. Although African-American workers challenged this exclusionary policy, they and other new shipyard workers turned to benevolent employers such as Kaiser and to the federal government for social initiation and services. As a result, Johnson argues, newcomers were often more loyal to their employer than to their union.

Most West Coast workers, like others, during the 1940s retained vivid memories of the post–World War I era experiences of the American labor movement. Organized labor not only lost whatever wartime gains it had made but also was thrown on the defensive by aggressive employers in conjunction with a hostile judiciary and federal government. An open shop environment soon prevailed. The chapter by Richard P. Boyden traces the efforts by Bay Area machinists to retain the concessions and prerogatives they had won during the 1930s. During the war, the machinists were not prepared to, in Boyden's words, "relinquish bedrock conditions." By 1944, the militant machinists were faced with U.S. Navy control of their industry, which entailed the loss of union representation and collective bargaining rights while individuals were subject to dismissal, blacklisting, and the draft if they attempted to uphold traditional rights and procedures. When the machinists threatened an overtime ban, the Regional War Labor Board, determined to assert its authority, gave the navy full control over the machinists in Lodge 68. Viewing the machinists' position as an interference with the war effort, the Communist leadership of the International Longshoremen and Warehousemen's Union (ILWU) supported the action. However, when the ILWU, and other unions saw the draconian measures the navy used in an effort to crush the union, they reversed their position. Notwithstanding the navy's antiunion tactics, the machinists maintained their organization and workplace prerogatives. The militancy of Lodge 68 continued into the postwar era, but so did the rift with the ILWU, with very detrimental consequences for the machinists' union.

The chapter by Nancy L. Quam-Wickham explores yet another aspect of workers' struggles during World War II. She analyzes the ILWU wartime experience in a context in which the union simultaneously tried to cooperate with the war effort and preserve the gains that had been made during the previous decade. Her focus is on the friction between a left-led union and some of its rank and file over the crucial issue of control of the hiring hall. The hiring hall and other job control issues had been settled largely in favor of the ILWU during the 1930s, but the exigencies of war threatened that status quo. Although the employers sought to use the problem of labor shortages to nibble away at union control of hiring practices, within the ILWU itself, a nonracist hiring policy was successfully manipulated by rank and filers to prevent the employment or promotion of African- and Mexican-Americans. The leadership, devoted to the war effort and respectful of the principle of autonomy within the union, refrained from interfering with the exclusionary practices of some of its locals. The control of the hiring halls was preserved but at the cost of racism contaminating a union that had previously been remarkably free of its corrosive effects.

The chapters in the third section of this book move from a focus on the workplace to an emphasis on the workers and their communities. The changing demographics of the work force are examined in detail in this section. The authors, often through a reliance on interviews with some of the workers and residents themselves, explore directly the important variables of race, gender, and ethnicity in the expanding working-class population of the war years. In particular, these chapters close a gap in the historiography through their focus on African-American women migrants whose experiences have been neglected in histories of the black migration to the West Coast and in studies of wartime defense work. Clearly building on a theme of the new labor history, these authors demonstrate that it is impossible to understand workers and their experiences without treating them in the context of their lives, cultures, and communities.

Shirley Ann Moore situates her chapter in Richmond, California, and examines not only the role of locale in shaping working people but also how they shaped it. She traces the explosive growth of this sleepy prewar location in the San Francisco Bay Area that attracted thousands of African-Americans in quest of shipyard employment. The migrants' impact on Richmond as well as on its long-time black residents is examined, and the chapter focuses on the experiences of selected African-American female migrants. Women — often young and married — were the majority of the southern-born African-Americans who streamed into town. Many were enterprising women who, not uncommonly, were responsible for the family migration. Some of them were able to take advantage of the opportunities in the emerging North Richmond black economy, where they became entrepreneurs operating their own blues clubs and restaurants. They also joined the National Association for the Advancement of Colored People (NAACP) and took on a wide range of responsibilities, thereby becoming autonomous leaders of the community. The war years for such women was an era of achievement and a high point in their lives.

Gretchen Lemke-Santangelo presents another aspect of the history of the African-American migration to the East Bay. Her chapter, based on dozens of oral history interviews, deals with the multifaceted roles African-American women played in stabilizing their families and neighbors in their new locale. Having grown to maturity in southern, two-parent, working-class families rooted in caring communities, these women sought to recreate in the East Bay the cultural traditions and institutions on which their lives had been built. Accordingly, they took on enormous responsibilities: they were not only homemakers and working women but also community builders, simultaneously struggling against discrimination. These women, believing in the "ethic of care" that was so central to their lives, joined, built, and strengthened their churches and auxiliary services, sustained each other, offered assistance to children and the poor, and developed informal social services. Often employed in defense industries, they, nevertheless, found time also to work in the NAACP or other organizations, never viewing themselves solely as workers but as committed participants in their communities.

The chapter by Delores Nason McBroome further explores the wartime developments in the Richmond African-American community and also touches on the adjacent towns of Oakland and Berkeley. The author focuses on the issue of adequate housing for African-Americans, whose numbers grew sixfold during World War II. McBroome demonstrates that even before the war, long-time African-American residents were driven to organize against a pattern of housing segregation, challenging private landlords as well as the local representatives of the Federal Housing Authority. Arguing that historians have tended to minimize or ignore prewar housing campaigns, the author explores NAACP and labor-led efforts to open both private and public housing to African-American residents. In the war years, with blacks flocking into the area in quest of shipyard and other defense industry work, the further strains on the constricted housing market led to mass campaigns by older residents as well as newcomers to obtain integrated and better housing opportunities. However, discrimination in housing persisted through and after the war, and it took almost 20 years for California's Rumford Fair Housing Act finally to address that issue.

The final chapter in this volume is by David Oberweiser, Jr., and deals with civil rights activities undertaken by the CIO in southern California during World War II, especially as they affected Mexican-American workers. The author shows that the CIO tried to stamp out the lower wage scale paid to Mexican-American workers, promoted open employment policies in the emerging defense industries, and opposed discrimination in the larger community. Building on prewar activities, it prodded both the Fair Employment Practices Committee and the U.S. Employment Service to be more vigilant against the discriminatory hiring practices of many employers, including North American Aviation. It also spearheaded efforts to defend young Mexican-Americans unjustly arrested during the anti-"zoot suit" wave of hysteria that swept California midway through the war, and opposed housing discrimination. Simultaneously, CIO civil rights activists found it necessary to move against some of their own membership who opposed policies of racial equality. Eventually, the CIO succeeded in implementing a campaign of racial unity on behalf of the war effort.

This collection of almost one dozen chapters does not pretend to offer a last word on the topic of labor and World War II. In such a rich and dynamic field, it seeks to promote the discussion further.

NOTES

1. Editors' introduction to "American Labor in the 1940s," *Radical America* 9 (July–August 1975): 4.

2. Among the most valuable works that deal with some of the major aspects of the social history of this period are William O'Neill, *A Democracy at War: America's Fight at Home and Abroad in World War II* (New York: Free Press, 1993); James N. Gregory, *American Exodus: The Dust Bowl Migration and Okie Culture* (New York: Oxford University Press, 1989); James Grossman, *Land of Hope: Chicago, Black Southerners and the Great Migration* (Chicago: University of Chicago Press, 1989); Carole Marks, *Farewell We're Good and Gone: The Great Black Migration* (Bloomington: University of Indiana Press, 1989); Joe Trotter, *Black Milwaukee: The Making of an Industrial Proletariat, 1915–1945* (Urbana: University of Illinois Press, 1985); D'Ann Campbell, *Women at War with America: Private Lives in a Patriotic Era* (Cambridge, Mass.: Harvard University Press, 1984); Miriam Frank, Marilyn Ziebarth, and Connie Field, *The Life and Times of Rosie the Riveter: The Story of Three Million Working Women During World War II* (Emeryville, Calif.: Clarity Educational Productions, 1982); Karen Anderson, *Wartime Women, Sex Roles, Family Relations, and the Status of Women During World War II* (Westport, Conn.: Greenwood, 1981); Susan M. Hartman, *The Home Front and Beyond: American Women in the 1940s* (Boston: Twayne Publishers, 1982); Amy Kesselman, *Fleeting Opportunities: Women Shipyard Workers in Portland and Vancouver During World War II* (Albany: State University of New York Press, 1990).

3. Marilynn S. Johnson, *The Second Gold Rush: Oakland and the East Bay in World War II* (Berkeley: University of California Press, 1993), p. 2.

4. Mike Davis, *Prisoners of the American Dream* (London: Verso, 1986), p. 75.

5. Important recent work on African Americans and the labor movement during World War II include Robert Korstad and Nelson Lichtenstein, "Opportunities Lost and Found: Labor, Radicals, and the Early Civil Rights Movement," *Journal of American History* 75 (December 1988): 786–811; Michael K. Honey, *Southern Labor and Black Civil Rights: Organizing Memphis Workers* (Urbana: University of Illinois Press, 1993); Bruce Nelson, "Organized Labor and the Struggle for Black Equality in Mobile During World War II," *Journal of American History* 80 (December 1993): 952–88; and a special issue of *International Labor and Working-Class History* (Volume 44, Fall 1993) with a symposium on "Race and the CIO: The Possibilities for Racial Egalitarianism During the 1930s and 1940s."

6. These statistics are taken from several general surveys of labor in this period, including Davis, *Prisoners of the American Dream*; Robert H. Zieger, *American Workers, American Unions, 1920–1985* (Baltimore, Md.: Johns Hopkins University Press, 1986); and American Social History Project, *Who Built America? Working*

People and the Nation's Economy, Politics, Culture, and Society (New York: Pantheon, 1992), Vol. 2.

7. Gerald Nash, *The Great Depression and World War II: Organizing America, 1933–1945* (New York: St. Martin's Press, 1979), p. 135.

8. Stuart Bruchey, *The Wealth of the Nation* (New York: Harper & Row, 1988), p. 181.

9. American Social History Project, *Who Built America?* Vol. 2, pp. 445–46.

10. Davis, *Prisoners of the American Dream*, p. 55. These statistics include the first generation as well as the second.

11. Richard Polenberg, *One Nation Divisible: Class, Race, and Ethnicity in the United States Since 1938* (New York: Penguin Books, 1980), pp. 55–57.

12. Lizabeth Cohen, *Making a New Deal: Industrial Workers in Chicago, 1919–1939* (Cambridge: Cambridge University Press, 1991), p. 356.

13. American Social History Project, *Who Built America?* Vol. 2, p. 446.

14. See Gary Gerstle, *Working-Class Americanism: The Politics of Labor in a Textile City, 1914–1960* (Cambridge: Cambridge University Press, 1989); Gary Gerstle, "The Politics of Patriotism: Americanization and the Formation of the CIO," *Dissent* 35 (Winter 1986): 84–92; Nelson Lichtenstein, "The Making of the Postwar Working Class: Cultural Pluralism and Social Structure in World War II," *The Historian* 51 (November 1988): 42–43; Davis, *Prisoners of the American Dream*, p. 89.

15. Some of the most important works devoted to labor in the era of World War II, or containing important contributions on the topic, include David Brody, *Workers in Industrial America: Essays on the Twentieth Century Struggle* (New York: Oxford University Press, 1980); James R. Green, *The World of the Worker: Labor in Twentieth Century America* (New York: Hill and Wang, 1980); Nelson Lichtenstein, *Labor's War at Home: The CIO in World War II* (Cambridge: Cambridge University Press, 1982); Howell John Harris, *The Right to Manage: Industrial Relations Policies of American Business in the 1940s* (Madison: University of Wisconsin Press, 1982); Ruth Milkman, *Gender at Work: The Dynamics of Job Segregation by Sex During World War II* (Urbana: University of Illinois Press, 1987); Gerstle, *Working-Class Americanism*; Steve Fraser and Gary Gerstle, eds., *The Rise and Fall of the New Deal Order, 1930–1980* (Princeton, N.J.: Princeton University Press, 1989); Davis, *Prisoners of the American Dream*; Steve Rosswurm, ed., *The CIO's Left-Led Unions* (New Brunswick, N.J.: Rutgers University Press, 1992); Johnson, *The Second Gold Rush*; Nelson Lichtenstein and Howell John Harris, eds., *Industrial Democracy in America: The Ambiguous Promise* (Cambridge: Cambridge University Press, 1993); Nelson Lichtenstein and Stephen Meyer, eds., *On the Line: Essays in the History of Auto Work* (Urbana: University of Illinois Press, 1989); Zieger, *American Workers, American Unions*; Melvyn Dubofsky, *The State and Labor in Modern America* (Chapel Hill: University of North Carolina Press, 1994); Christopher L. Tomlins, *The State and the Unions: Labor Relations Law, and the Organized Labor Movement in America, 1880–1960* (Cambridge: Cambridge University Press, 1985); Joshua Freeman, *In Transit: The Transport Workers Union in New York City, 1933–1966* (New York: Oxford University Press, 1989); Steven Fraser, *Labor Will Rule: Sidney Hillman and the Rise of American Labor* (New York: Free Press, 1991); Ronald Schatz, *The Electrical Workers: A History of Labor at General Electric and Westinghouse, 1923–1960* (Urbana: University of Illinois Press, 1983); William H. Harris, *The Harder We Run: Black Workers Since the Civil War* (New York: Oxford University Press,

22 Introduction

1982); Clete Daniel, *Chicano Workers and the Politics of Fairness: The FEPC in the Southwest, 1941–1945* (Austin: University of Texas Press, 1991); Barbara Griffith, *The Crisis of American Labor: Operation Dixie and the Defeat of the CIO* (Philadelphia, Pa.: Temple University Press, 1988); Alan Clive, *State of War: Michigan in World War II* (Ann Arbor: University of Michigan Press, 1979); Marc Scott Miller, *The Irony of Victory: World War II and Lowell, Massachusetts* (Urbana: University of Illinois Press, 1988); John Barnard, *Walter Reuther and the Rise of the Auto Workers* (Boston: Little, Brown, 1983); Martin Halpern, *UAW Politics in the Cold War Era* (Albany: State University of New York Press, 1988); Nancy F. Gabin, *Feminism in the Labor Movement: Women and the United Autoworkers, 1935–1975* (Ithaca, N.Y.: Cornell University Press, 1990; George Lipsitz, *Rainbow at Midnight: Labor and Culture in the 1940s* (Urbana: University of Illinois Press, 1994).

16. James Green, "Working Class Militancy in the Depression," *Radical America* 6 (November–December 1972): 1.

17. All are reprinted in Brody, *Workers in Industrial America*.

18. See, in particular, Melvyn Dubofsky, "Not So 'Turbulent Years': Another Look at the American 1930's," *Amerikastudien/American Studies* 24 (1979): 5–20; Bernard Sternsher, "Great Depression Labor Historiography in the 1970s: Middle Range Questions, Ethnocultures, and Levels of Generalization," *Reviews in American History* 11 (June 1983): 300–19.

19. Irving Bernstein, *The Turbulent Years: A History of the American Worker, 1933–1941* (Boston: Houghton Mifflin, 1969).

20. Art Preis, *Labor's Giant Step: Twenty Years of the CIO* (New York: Pioneer Publishers, 1964).

21. Robert H. Zieger, "Toward a History of the CIO: A Bibliographical Report," *Labor History* 26 (Fall 1985): 486.

22. *Radical America* 9 (July–August 1975).

23. Ibid., p. 3.

24. Nelson Lichtenstein, "Ambiguous Legacy: The Union Security Problem During World War II," *Labor History* 18 (Spring 1977): 214–38; Joshua Freeman, "Delivering the Goods: Industrial Unionism During World War II," *Labor History* 19 (Fall 1978): 570–93; Melvyn Dubofsky and Warren Van Tine, *John L. Lewis: A Biography* (New York: Quadrangle, 1977).

25. David Brody, "The New Deal and World War II," in *The New Deal*, eds. John Braeman, Robert H. Bremner, and David Brody (Columbus: Ohio State University Press, 1975); Brody, *Workers in Industrial America*.

26. Brody, *Workers in Industrial America*, pp. 174–75.

27. Lichtenstein, *Labor's War at Home*, p. 51.

28. Harris, *The Right to Manage*, pp. 3–4.

29. Zieger, "Toward a History of the CIO," pp. 500–501. In the bibliographical essay to his 1982 book, *Labor's War at Home*, Lichtenstein observed that "no adequate social and economic history of the American home front during World War II has yet been written" (p. 306). Six years later, Lichtenstein stated that "the social history of the working class in World War II is only now being written" ("The Making of the Postwar Working Class," p. 42).

30. Lichtenstein, "The Making of the Postwar Working Class," pp. 42–43.

31. Robert H. Zieger, "The CIO: A Bibliographical Update and Archival Guide," *Labor History* 31 (Fall 1990): 413–40.

32.   Fraser and Gerstle, *Rise and Fall of the New Deal Order*.

33.   Steven Fraser, "The 'Labor Question,'" in *The Rise and Fall of the New Deal Order, 1930–1980*, eds. Steve Fraser and Gary Gerstle (Princeton, N.J.: Princeton University Press, 1989), p. 62.

34.   Alan Brinkley, "The New Deal and the Idea of the State," in *The Rise and Fall of the New Deal Order, 1930–1980*, eds. Steven Fraser and Gary Gerstle (Princeton, N.J.: Princeton University Press, 1989); and Nelson Lichtenstein, "From Corporatism to Collective Bargaining: Organized Labor and the Eclipse of Social Democracy in the Postwar Era," in *The Rise and Fall of the New Deal Order, 1930–1980*, eds. Steve Fraser and Gary Gerstle (Princeton, N.J.: Princeton University Press, 1989).

35.   Editors' introduction to "American Labor in the 1940s," *Radical America* 9 (July–August): 4.

36.   The 1980s witnessed a stream of books by industrial relations scholars intent on explaining the ever-diminishing power of the American labor movement. As David Brody observed in his article "Labor History, Industrial Relations, and the Crisis of American Labor," *Industrial and Labor Relations Review* 43 (October 1989): 7–18, these industrial relations specialists tended to approach the issue from an historical perspective. Among the important works on the decline of American labor since World War II are Michael Goldfield, *The Decline of Organized Labor in the United States* (Chicago: University of Chicago Press, 1987); Kim Moody, *An Injury to All: The Decline of American Unionism* (London: Verso, 1988); David M. Gordon, Richard Edwards, and Michael Reich, *Segmented Work, Divided Workers: The Historical Transformation of Labor in the United States* (Cambridge: Cambridge University Press, 1982); Richard B. Freeman and James L. Medoff, *What Do Unions Do?* (New York: Basic Books, 1984); Thomas Kochan, Robert McKersie, and Harry Katz, *The Transformation of American Industrial Relations* (New York: Basic Books, 1986); Barry Bluestone and Irving Bluestone, *Negotiating the Future: A Labor Perspective on American Business* (New York: Basic Books, 1992). See also Winter 1992 special issue of *Dissent* devoted to "Labor's Future in the United States."

37.   Eileen Boris and Nelson Lichtenstein, eds., *Major Problems in the History of American Workers* (Lexington, Mass.: D. C. Heath, 1991), p. 496.

38.   Bluestone and Bluestone, *Negotiating the Future*, Chap. 3.

39.   See, for example, Tomlins, *The State and the Unions*; Katherine Van Wezel Stone, "The Postwar Paradigm in American Labor Law," *Yale Law Journal* 90 (June 1981): 1509–80; James A. Gross, *The Making of the National Labor Relations Board: 1933–1937* (Albany: State University of New York Press, 1974); James A. Gross, *The Reshaping of the National Labor Relations Board: National Labor Policy in Transition, 1937–1947* (Albany: State University of New York Press, 1981). For a good overview on the new labor law history, see Wythe Holt, "The New American Labor Law History," *Labor History* 30 (Spring 1989): 275–93.

40.   Lichtenstein, "From Corporatism to Collective Bargaining"; see also his essay "Labor in the Truman Era: Origins of the 'Private Welfare State,'" in *The Truman Presidency*, ed. Michael J. Lacey (Cambridge: Cambridge University Press, 1989).

41.   Bluestone, *Negotiating the Future*, p. 41.

42.   One of the most recent and important books on the subject is Lichtenstein and Harris, *Industrial Democracy in America*.

43.   David Brody, "Workplace Contractualism in Comparative Perspective," in *Industrial Democracy in America: The Ambiguous Promise*, eds. Nelson Lichtenstein and Howell John Harris (Cambridge: Cambridge University Press, 1993).

44.   Nelson Lichtenstein, "Great Expectations: The Promise of Industrial Jurisprudence and Its Demise, 1930–1960," in *Industrial Democracy in America: The Ambiguous Promise*, eds. Nelson Lichtenstein and Howell John Harris (Cambridge: Cambridge University Press, 1993).

45.   Brody, *Workers in Industrial America*, p. 206.

46.   Jonathan Zeitlin and Steven Tolliday, "Shop Floor Bargaining, Contract Unionism, and Job Control: An Anglo-American Comparison," in *On the Line: Essays in the History of Auto Work*, eds. Nelson Lichtenstein and Stephen Meyer (Urbana: University of Illinois Press, 1989).

47.   In an article entitled "Bringing the Unions Back In (Or Why We Need a New Old Labor History)," *Labor History* 32 (Winter 1991): 91–103, Howard Kimeldorf alleges that the new labor history has tended to belittle the role of unions and workers' relationship to them.

48.   Zieger, "The CIO: A Bibliographical Update," pp. 415–16.

49.   On political activity by labor in the wake of the Oakland General Strike and in Richmond, see Johnson, *The Second Gold Rush*, Chap. 7. Also useful on political activity by labor in Oakland are Philip J. Wolman, "The Oakland General Strike of 1946," *Southern California Quarterly* 57 (Summer 1975): 147–78; Jim Rose, "Collaboration with a Dual Union: Oakland AFL Political Practice, 1943–1947" (unpublished paper in possession of Daniel A. Cornford).

50.   Philip Taft, *Labor Politics American Style: The California State Federation of Labor* (Cambridge, Mass.: Harvard University Press, 1968). Useful books on labor's postwar political activities include Alan Draper, *A Rope of Sand: The AFL-CIO Committee on Political Education, 1955–1967* (New York: Praeger, 1989); Gilbert J. Gall, *The Politics of Right to Work: The Labor Federations as Special Interests, 1943–1979* (Westport, Conn.: Greenwood, 1988).

51.   See Alan Derickson's chapter in this volume and his "Health Security for All? Social Unionism and Universal Health Insurance, 1935–1958," *Journal of American History* 80 (March 1994): 1333–56.

52.   David Brody, "The CIO after Fifty Years: A Historical Reckoning," *Dissent* (Fall 1985): 457–72.

53.   Christopher L. Tomlins, "AFL Unions in the 1930s: Their Performance in Historical Perspective," *Journal of American History* 65 (March 1979): 1021–42.

54.   Rosswurm, *The CIO's Left-Led Unions*, p. xv.

55.   Zieger, "The CIO: A Bibliographical Update."

56.   Richard White, *"It's Your Misfortune and None of My Own": A New History of the American West* (Norman: University of Oklahoma Press, 1991), p. 496. On the enormous impact of World War II on the West, see also Gerald D. Nash, *The American West Transformed: The Impact of the Second World War* (Lincoln: University of Nebraska Press, 1985); Gerald D. Nash, *World War II and the West: Reshaping the Economy* (Lincoln: University of Nebraska Press, 1990).

57.   Nash, *American West Transformed*, p. 56.

58.   Ibid., p. 38.

59.   Ibid.

60.   White, *"It's Your Misfortune and None of My Own,"* pp. 496–508.

61. *The California Blue Book, 1946* (Sacramento: California State Printing Office, 1946), p. 435. For a recent assessment of the impact of World War II on California, see "Special Issue: Fortress California at War: San Francisco, Los Angeles, Oakland, and San Diego, 1941–1945," *Pacific Historical Review* 63 (August 1994): 277–420.

62. See, in particular, Roger W. Lotchin, *Fortress California, 1910–1961: From Warfare to Welfare* (New York: Oxford University Press, 1992), although Lotchin argues that the militarization of the California economy was, to a significant extent, put in place before World War II.

63. *California Blue Book, 1950* (Sacramento: California State Printing Office, 1950), p. 784.

64. White, *"It's Your Misfortune and None of My Own,"* p. 515.

65. Particularly good on the twentieth-century "Okie" migration to California is the earlier cited Gregory, *American Exodus.* For a numerical breakdown of Okie migration by decade, see p. 6.

66. Johnson's *The Second Gold Rush* documents this well and sets a new standard for integrating labor, social, and urban history in a regional setting during the World War II period.

67. Statistics from Taft, *Labor Politics American Style*, p. 134; David F. Selvin, *Sky Full of Storm: A Brief History of California Labor* (San Francisco: California Historical Society, 1975), p. 73. Most useful on trends in the post–World War II economy and union movement in California, Oregon, and Washington is a special issue of *Monthly Labor Review* devoted to "Labor and Labor Relations on the West Coast," *Monthly Labor Review* 82 (May 1959). For a case study on federal interest in discrimination by West Coast unions, see William H. Harris, "Federal Intervention in Union Discrimination: FEPC and West Coast Shipyards During World War II," *Labor History* 22 (Summer 1981): 325–47.

68. Holt, "The New American Labor Law History," p. 281.

I

LABOR IN THE
NATIONAL ARENA

1

CIO Leaders and the State, 1935–55

Robert H. Zieger

The differing perspectives of John L. Lewis, Philip Murray, and Walter P. Reuther with regard to the federal government in its role as military mobilizer, diplomatic agent, and world actor in the period of World War II and its aftermath reveal much about the underlying character of industrial unionism and the tensions that afflicted it. Beyond doubt, the Congress of Industrial Organizations (CIO) prospered in its relationship to the federal government. Its three presidents, however, had different conceptions of the connection between the industrial union federation and the state.[1]

Entanglement with government was a central factor in the 20-year history of the CIO. It was under the wartime state and its cold war continuation that the CIO reached its peak membership, its greatest institutional stability, and, at least until the Communist issue came to a head in 1948–49, its most unified internal life. Contemporary critics argued that the CIO paid a heavy price in limitations on its autonomy and the subsumption of its interests to those of the state, claims that historians have echoed. Of the three leaders of the CIO, however, only the first, John L. Lewis, expressed concern about the effects that enmeshment in the state apparatus were having on the essential character of the industrial union movement. His successor, Philip Murray, largely confined his misgivings about state action to detailed complaints about the treatment unions received in the emerging national security machinery. The last of the CIO's leaders, Walter Reuther, embraced partnership with the state as emblematic of organized labor's coming of age.[2]

Of the three men, Lewis most forcefully expressed voluntaristic concerns about the role of the state. The labor movement, from this viewpoint, was and should always remain autonomous and independent. True, Lewis had used the state to rebuild the United Mine Workers (UMW) and launch the CIO, but after the UMW had gained security and the CIO project was underway, Lewis grew increasingly critical of the Roosevelt administration.

State-promoted defense mobilization brought sweeping warnings from him about the dangers that militarized government posed for the labor movement. In his view military growth meant surveillance, repression, hierarchy, and regimentation. World War I, it is true, had led to great gains for the UMW, but the intervention of the militarized state after the war gave the new UMW president an acrid dose of state-conducted surveillance and coercion. "Labor," Lewis told a Labor Day audience in 1940, "wants the right to work and live — not the privilege of dying by gunshot or poison gas to sustain the mental errors of current statesmen."[3]

Lewis and his aides saw in government's military build-up the sinister hand of a corporate-military conspiracy and, beyond that, the evil machinations of Franklin Roosevelt. Aides' warnings that the administration was relying on war production to end the depression and was promoting U.S. intervention in the European war at the behest of eastern seaboard Anglophiles fell on receptive ears. Lewis's closest advisor, attorney Lee Pressman, asserted that "the Conscription Act [passed in October 1940] can be used to compel forced labor and thereby destroy labor organization."[4]

Lewis's shocking endorsement of Republican presidential candidate Wendell Willkie on October 25, 1940, stressed the perils to the nation that war-obsessed government would bring. FDR's reelection "would be a national evil of the first magnitude." He sought dictatorship; he had a "personal craving for power"; he had ambitions to be a "superman."[5]

At the same time, of course, Lewis sought to wring advantages from the opportunities that stepped-up military production brought. Indeed, it was in his response to the organizing prospects of the defense production period that Lewis most sharply clashed with those in the CIO who did not share his views. Lewis feared that the CIO would not exploit the opportunity that expanded production offered to complete the organization of the industrial core. A militarized state, he warned, was emerging, dominated by corporate executives, generals, and admirals, with a tamed labor movement frozen out. Slipping away was the possibility of a powerful, autonomous labor movement.

For others in the CIO, however, notably Sidney Hillman and, increasingly, Philip Murray, other considerations took priority. Hitler was no ordinary bogey man. The fight against fascism was a workers' fight. The president merited support in his efforts to bolster the Western powers. The machinery that the government was establishing to direct the military boom deserved labor's endorsement. Moreover, CIO collaboration with a government that was, after all, headed in the right direction anyway would reap enormous benefits for labor.

In the tense months before Pearl Harbor, Lewis and Hillman squared off. Lewis objected to the process by which Hillman gained appointment as labor advisor to the new National Defense Advisory Council in May 1940 and his subsequent selection as codirector of the Office of Production Management. What right did President Roosevelt have to choose labor's representatives without consultation with workers' elected leaders? Lewis believed that FDR was attempting to shape the basic character of the labor movement. Thus, both Roosevelt and Hillman wanted a resolution of the AFL-CIO split, Lewis charged, on virtually any terms. In Lewis's view, at least, every time Hillman, wearing his government hat, favored an American Federation of Labor (AFL) union in a dispute falling within the Office of Production Management's purview, he was, in effect, promoting Roosevelt's agenda with regard not only to defense production but also to the character and composition of the labor movement itself.

The Lewis-Hillman conflict escalated. Lewis urged the denial of defense contracts to violators of federal labor laws and disdained Hillman's ultimately unsuccessful efforts to attain this goal through bureaucratic arrangements within the defense mobilization apparatus. In the spring of 1941, he attacked Hillman savagely when the government dispatched troops to end the North American Aviation strike. In pointed references to his fellow CIO founder, he told a gathering of unionists that, unlike absent associates, "I hold my first allegiance to labor." Only through returning to first principles, by resisting "the use of the United States Army to break strikes with their bayonets in the back of American workingmen," could the CIO endure as a legitimate labor organization.[6]

The UMW's break with the CIO in 1941–42 revolved around its relations with the government. In effect, Lewis charged, the CIO had become little more than a labor front of the Roosevelt administration. In view of their willingness to knuckle under to governmental dictation under the guise of patriotic necessity, he snarled in 1942, the CIO leadership was a bunch of "lap dogs and kept dogs and . . . yellow dogs." They were "miserable mediocrities."[7]

Beyond the barbed rhetoric was a real, if not always fully articulated, critique of the path organized labor was taking in the age of the national security state. Lewis voiced a legitimate alternative conception of the role of labor in modern society. Lewis warned presciently of the dangers to an independent labor movement of enlistment in the state's apparatus of mobilization. During World War II, he and the miners rejected curtailment of the right to strike and the absorption of collective bargaining into the state bureaucracy, although these views did not prevent Lewis from using the government to achieve significant contract gains for the miners. After the war, he repeatedly defied the government and felt the heavy hand of its retribution.[8]

These experiences convinced Lewis that the labor movement under the national security state was in danger of becoming but a cog in "a vast centralized government" and of becoming a slave to "regulation by federal edict." In a 1945 magazine article, he asserted dramatically that "There Is No Labor Movement." Both the AFL and the CIO depended on government for union security and for assistance in recruiting new members. Both enjoyed cozy relationships with the Democratic party. Under the excuse of wartime exigency, he believed, the organizations affiliated with the AFL and the CIO were little more than "political company unions."[9]

By then, of course, Lewis was long off the CIO reservation. His successor, Philip Murray, had a more conflicted response to the wartime state. As a veteran Mine Worker, the new CIO president remained fearful of government and cherished union autonomy. Throughout his CIO presidency, he opposed governmental presumptions that he believed threatened to compromise or destroy the independence of the labor movement.

At the same time, however, Murray led the steel workers' union, an organization that had relied heavily on government every step of the way in its halting progress from a skeletal organizing committee in 1936 to an industrial giant in the early 1950s. The success of the Steel Workers Organizing Committee in the mid-1930s would have been unthinkable without the La Follette Committee and the National Labor Relations Board. The defense boom and the renewed efforts of the National Labor Relations Board played crucial roles in the delayed conquest of Bethlehem and Republic Steel in 1941 and 1942. War Labor Board

Maintenance of Membership stipulations undergirded the steelworkers' massive growth.

The state continued as a major actor in the United Steel Workers postwar efforts to build comprehensive contracts with the steel companies. In 1946, in 1949, and again in 1952, the Truman administration, often invoking national defense interests, was a major, and prounion, party to the settlements of the three strikes. Although Lewis's miners defied the government in 1943, 1946, and 1947, Murray's steelworkers, always in competition with the UMW for collective bargaining leadership, aligned themselves ever more directly with the Democratic party and the state that had by 1952 become a permanent and all-pervasive feature of American life.[10]

Murray's intense patriotism facilitated his identification of labor's goals with the state. "I love this country, its people, and its institutions," he wrote late in life. "I came as an immigrant, made good as an American. Everything I possess, everything I have achieved, I owe to the United States." His naturalization at age 21 "was just about the proudest moment of my life."[11]

During World War II these feelings were both tested and confirmed. In the pressure cooker of wartime labor relations, Murray conducted a remarkable debate with himself. Wartime labor relations, of course, took place within the boundaries established by the No Strike Pledge of December 17, 1941; the National War Labor Board (NWLB), created by executive order on January 12, 1942; and the complexities of the administration's economic mobilization and stabilization programs. Despite broad CIO endorsement of FDR's policies, the actual workings of the elaborate wartime machinery that was to mobilize and stabilize the American economy spurred intense debate. The Little Steel Formula, which the NWLB promulgated in July 1942, sharply restricted wage increases. Employers exploited the No Strike Pledge, and unresolved disputes clogged the NWLB agenda. Labor leaders found themselves acting as disciplinarians rather than as workers' advocates. In 1943, the challenge to CIO collaboration with the Roosevelt administration mounted, first as Lewis's coal miners breached the No Strike Pledge and faced down the NWLB and then as Congress rushed through the Smith-Connally Act. Toward the end of the war, the threat of a labor draft added to the CIO dilemma.

Murray's response to this tangle of issues was not so much ambivalent as bifurcated. Philip Murray the veteran organizer, Mine Worker, and fighter for the rights of labor lashed out repeatedly at the limitations, injustices, and dangers of government policies and their implementation.

Meanwhile, Philip Murray the labor statesman, the patriot, and the champion of government-sponsored cooperation between labor and capital reaffirmed the CIO's dependence on and basic sympathy with the wartime security state.

Murray the traditionalist had many opportunities to rediscover his view of the state as a potentially deadly adversary. Congress, he told his board in March 1943, was full of "evil-minded citizens . . . hell-bent upon the complete destruction of the labor movement." A year later, as antilabor legislation wound its way through Congress, he warned that the CIO faced "a life and death struggle . . . for the purpose of maintaining our right to live as unions." It was often in debate with CIO leaders close to the Communist party that Murray most clearly reaffirmed his traditional perspective.[12] Thus, at times, Murray's bitterness about the treatment of the CIO at the hands of government agents came close to questioning the limits of the No Stroke Pledge, to the dismay of his pro-Soviet colleagues. Promoting uninterrupted production was one thing, but "I am not going to supinely lay down on the flat of my back and let these people step on my face. . . . I say fight, and I mean fight," he proclaimed after learning of one particularly egregious governmental action damaging to the industrial union federation. Communists and their allies, horrified at any criticism of the pledge, counselled restraint. Thus, Fur and Leather Workers' head Ben Gold warned that if the CIO did anything rash, "the A. F. of L. and our old friend John L. Lewis will finally say to themselves, 'We succeeded in provoking that fellow Phil Murray, got him off that throne, got that C. I. O. into motion now, stripped of that moral strength. . . . Now we have got him on the same basis [as we are], now we can hit'" the CIO.[13]

Early in 1944, Murray clashed again with his pro-Soviet colleagues over the issue of national service legislation. At the CIO's January 1944 board meeting, Murray and Longshoremen's president Harry Bridges squared off. The previous November, the CIO convention had denounced national service legislation, but two months later, President Roosevelt had publicly called for a labor draft, ostensibly as part of a broader program of equality of sacrifice. Moreover, some CIO officials, notably Bridges as the CIO's California director, had endorsed the president's proposals.

Murray seethed with rage, both at the substantive issue and at the wrongheadedness of these CIO leaders. National service in any guise meant regimentation, the destruction of collective bargaining, and the end of the labor movement as an independent force. With proposals of this type, whatever the sugarcoating in the form of progressive taxation, price control, and the like, surely even Bridges could see that fascism is "actually jumping at us." Bridges replied by suggesting that a Rooseveltian national service program would be progressively administered and would actually enhance labor's membership totals and its public image. However, the CIO president brushed aside Bridges' arguments. The militarization of labor was an absolute evil. "All you have to do is commit yourself to the principle and then die from its effect," he insisted. Surely national service would destroy the labor movement and compromise basic democratic principles.[14]

Yet, despite these bristling defenses of laborite autonomy, Murray the statesman prevailed. In July 1943, two weeks after Congress had passed the repressive Smith-Connally Act, angry CIO dissidents urged that the CIO repudiate the No Strike Pledge. On this issue, Murray stood with the CIO's Communists and their allies: not even egregious congressional action justified any semblance of disaffection with the war effort. Indeed, Murray declared that immediately after Congress had overridden FDR's veto on June 25, his first act had been to write to the president expressing gratitude for the veto and reaffirming the CIO's adherence to the pledge. Had he not done so, he feared, "many strikes might very well have ensued, . . . rebellion might have broken out . . . in many of the war industries." Murray vowed that before he would countenance modification, much less recision, of the pledge, he would resign as CIO president.[15]

If antilabor legislation would not impel reconsideration of the No Strike Pledge, neither would the injustices suffered by labor at the hands of the NWLB and the other wartime agencies. Throughout 1943 and 1944, Murray fumed over the labor board's unfair treatment. In November 1944, for example, he admitted that for the past year, "We are virtually shackled. . . . We are in a state of bondage." Stabilization officials invoked skewed statistical "evidence" to prove that workers were prospering. They suggested that the troublemaking union leaders were responsible for the mounting turmoil in the production plants. Meanwhile, these same officials pressured him to suppress the strikes that broke out. To be sure, FDR might express sympathy with workers in tête-à-têtes with labor leaders, but, invariably, he backed his reactionary stabilization czars. From the government's viewpoint, Murray complained, the chief role of organized labor was "to police these damnable and most obnoxious directives." "I have felt," he confessed late in 1944, "a sense of futility and complete frustration, a condition of helplessness" in attempting to right these wrongs.[16]

Yet, five months later, Murray blasted board members who had introduced a resolution of noncooperation with the NWLB. With all its faults, the board had been crucial to CIO success. "Maintenance of membership provisions of the thousands of collective bargaining contracts approved by the War Labor Board," he reminded the dissidents, had been decisive in the CIO's growth "from a paltry million and a half up to the present proud . . . five million." Also, if positive inducements were not enough, Murray reminded NWLB critics of what lay just beyond the circle of friendly administration officials and board functionaries. "The wolves are just around the corner," he warned, "and they have got a ravenous appetite and they are ready to eat you up."[17]

Quite apart from, yet permeating, all these calculations was the overwhelming fact of the war. It was one thing to criticize the injustices of administration and congressional policies that disadvantaged workers and forced labor leaders to act as strikebreakers and quite another to do anything that might seem to jeopardize the Allied cause. Murray's chief aide, David McDonald, reported to the 1944 CIO convention on his experiences in France, where he served as a labor observer in the aftermath of the D-Day invasion. The scope of the war effort, with its vast artificial harbors, its hordes of tanks and armored vehicles, and its unspeakable human suffering, staggered him. With his colleagues, he tried to talk to two men just back from the front lines. "Their eyes blazed," he reported. "They were filthy dirty. . . . They had been clawing into the ground." They seemed not to hear the labor officials' questions, muttering only "'We killed them bastards — we killed them bastards,' with all the hatred they could muster." "If the purpose of that trip was to stoke up the home-front war effort," McDonald later recalled, "it certainly worked with me."[18]

After the war, Murray drew even closer to the government in both domestic and international matters. Despite an early period of antagonism toward President Truman, the CIO chief soon came to rely on the federal government's intervention in the settlements of the steel strikes of 1946, 1949, and 1952. After 1946, he never questioned the anti-Soviet basis of U.S. foreign policy, and he ardently supported American action in Korea.

Murray did retain elements of traditional laborite resistance to government's claims. He initially refused to sign the anti-Communist affidavit introduced in the Taft-Hartley Act. He tested legislative restrictions on laborite political endorsements to the extent of breaking the law to test the law in court.[19] However, he retained a faith that the president was an effective defender of basic American values. As long as a friendly Democrat occupied the White House, a strong labor movement was not incompatible with — in fact, was dependent upon — collaborative association with the government.[20] His sudden death on November 9, five days after the election of Dwight Eisenhower and a Republican-controlled Congress, saved Murray from the need to reassess these basic articles of his faith.

The new CIO president, Walter Reuther, had a different agenda than either of his predecessors. The United Automobile Workers' president had little of the coalminers' and steelworkers' visceral distrust of government. In the battles to organize General Motors and Ford, it was company thugs and local constabularies who administered the beatings, federal and state authorities who provided a modicum of justice. Reuther was at once more political than either Lewis or Murray and less in thrall to FDR, as either a villain or a hero. Coming late to the New Deal coalition, he searched constantly during the 1940s for some alternative to the compromised and flawed Democratic party. At the same time, however, he never doubted that the state, through democratic pressure, would be a primary vehicle through which workers' interests, social justice, and victory in the international workers' movement would be achieved. He fought incessantly for entree into the state apparatus.

His vigorous anticommunism, foreign and domestic, complemented his belief in labor's ability to work with and through the American state for the achievement of a better world. Thus, for the Walter Reuther of 1939–41, the question was not whether America should rearm, aid the Allies, and stand against Hitler. True, he debated the Communists, enamored with the Nazi-Soviet Pact, in these terms, but the need for America to stand with the West was really not open to serious question. For him, the real issue was how could labor claim its rightful role as a partner with business and government in defense production. His 500 planes a day proposals of 1941 were the first in a long line of detailed blueprints for asserting the claims of partnership while advancing the national interest. In speeches and memos filled with inventories of idle machine tools, listings of unused factory space, and manpower assessments, he continually linked military defense, the underlying claims for which he never questioned, with full employment, expansion of production, and technological efficiency.[21]

Reuther never doubted the American mission in the world. Stinging in his constant criticism of the failures of American society with regard to income distribution, social welfare, racial justice, political inequity, and dozens of other concerns, he, nonetheless, assumed a coincidence between his version of universal human rights and social justice on the one hand and American enterprise on the other. To him, the Marshall Plan was nothing short of an "Operation Survival" for freedom (1948): "We . . . must accept the major share [of responsibility] for giving leadership to the building up of the material and productive strength of the free world and mobilizing the spiritual force of free people everywhere" (1951); "We are fighting with our backs to the wall" (1953).[22]

Labor was not a junior partner; quite the contrary. As Reuther frequently pointed out, it was the democratic socialist and labor movements that had warned of the dangers of fascism, had led in the opposition to it, and had been its earliest victims. It was democratic trade unionists who, in 1939 and 1940, when profit-hungry big business and the Stalin-dominated American Communist party were outdoing each other in isolationist rhetoric and vilification of FDR, stood behind the president and urged the full engagement of the United States' productive capacity in defense of freedom. In the postwar world, it was business leaders who brought the accountant's mentality to the massive problem of European recovery while the CIO promoted broad and generous expansion of America's productive energies to answer the needs of desperate people.

Reuther was certainly aware of and disapproving of underhanded and cynical governmental actions in the fight against communism. He regarded official American policies, whether under Democratic or Republican administrations, as too fixated on anticommunism to the exclusion of other concerns. "The chief weakness of American foreign policy is the predilection of our State Department for dealing with anybody who will promise to hate communism," he charged in 1948.[23] He and his brother Victor, who in 1951 headed up the CIO's European operations, regarded the cloak-and-dagger activities of AFL foreign operatives lavishly funded by the Central Intelligence Agency with revulsion. He peppered the State Department and foreign aid administration officials with criticisms and suggestions, continually urging a more vigorous role for labor representation. Governmental and laborite leadership, he declared, were crucial, because timid business leaders "have no faith in America."[24] In contrast, he declared in 1953, the "CIO is the most articulate, the most potent and I think the most reliable force freedom has in America."[25]

Reuther believed in the ultimate triumph of labor. In the late 1930s, he had left the Socialist party largely because he believed that labor had to work with liberal elements within the existing political system. However, in the long run, organized workers represented the next phase of the expansion of democratic values and institutions that would extend increasingly to the economic system. It was the job of the industrial union movement to overcome postwar setbacks and obstacles to give this vision concrete form. Codetermination in industry, powerful instruments of political action, and a growing voice in the councils of government and industry would do this. In his rapid postwar rise and his eventual accession in 1952 to the CIO presidency, Reuther embodied this social democratic faith.

This sense of labor's future lay at the heart of his vigorous anticommunism. It was not only, or even mainly, that Communists were his rivals in the United Automobile Workers. The struggle of the 1930s and the 1940s, although most directly against fascism, was, at root, a struggle for the future of the workers' movement. The future belonged to the Left. Thus, the character of the Left was all-important. The imperative to defeat communism was so important because Stalin and his minions had corrupted the very wellsprings of the Left. The struggle of social democracy was the struggle for the future.

In that connection, collaboration with the state was legitimate and even welcome. If saving democratic unionism in western Europe meant taking $50,000 of Central Intelligence Agency money to distribute there, so be it. If defeating the Communists in the CIO called for signing the Taft-Hartley affidavit (all the while deploring its violation of civil liberties), it was a small price to pay for winning electrical and farm equipment workers to democratic unionism. If the defeat of communism meant euphemism and evasion in discussing the overthrow of popular governments in Guatemala and British Guiana, surely renewed laborite commitment would slowly but surely democratize American foreign policy and build democratic alternatives in the third world.[26]

The American state in peace and war critically influenced the course the CIO followed from its inception in 1935 to its merger with the AFL in 1955. The industrial union federation's three leaders dealt with this fact in diverse ways. Reuther shared little of Murray's tortured ambivalence about the state and none of Lewis's vitriolic hostility. The troubled course of the labor movement over the past four decades suggests the limitations of all three approaches. Lewis's invocation of militant voluntarism was as unrealistic as it was inconsistent. Reuther's optimism about labor partnership in significant national enterprises was misplaced. Perhaps in Philip Murray's tortured ambivalence — if not in his ultimate resolution of it — lies the most helpful guide to contemporary laborites.

NOTES

1.   Basic biographical citations for the three men discussed in this chapter are Melvyn Dubofsky and Warren Van Tine, *John L. Lewis: A Biography* (New York: Quadrangle, 1977); Robert H. Zieger, *John L. Lewis: Labor Leader* (Boston: Twayne, 1988); Ronald Schatz, "Philip Murray and the Subordination of the Industrial Unions to the United States Government," in *Labor Leaders in America*, eds. Melvyn Dubofsky and Warren Van Tine (Urbana: University of Illinois Press, 1987), pp. 234–57; John Barnard, *Walter Reuther and the Rise of the Autoworkers* (Boston: Little, Brown, 1983); Nelson Lichtenstein, "Walter Reuther and the Rise of Labor-Liberalism," in *Labor Leaders in America*, eds. Melvyn Dubofsky and Warren Van Tine (Urbana: University of Illinois Press, 1987), pp. 280–302; Frank Cormier and William J. Eaton, *Reuther* (Englewood Cliffs, N.J.: Prentice-Hall, 1970).

2.   The literature on the CIO's role in World War II and its relationship to the state during the war and into the cold war period is suggestive rather than authoritative. The best works are Steven Fraser, *Labor Will Rule: Sidney Hillman and the Rise of American Labor* (New York: Free Press, 1991), pp. 406–575; David Brody, "The New Deal and World War II," in *The New Deal:* Vol. 1: *The National Level*, eds. John Braeman, Robert H. Bremner, and David Brody (Columbus: Ohio State University Press, 1975), pp. 267–309; Anthony Carew, *Labour under the Marshall Plan: The Politics of Productivity and the Marketing of Management Science* (Detroit, Mich.: Wayne State University Press, 1987); Ronald L. Filippelli, *American Labor and Postwar Italy, 1943–1953* (Stanford, Calif.: Stanford University Press, 1989); Paul A. C. Koistinen, "Mobilizing the World War II Economy: Labor and the Industrial-Military Alliance," *Pacific Historical Review* 42 (November 1973): 443–78; Nelson Lichtenstein, *Labor's War at Home: The CIO in World War II* (Cambridge: Cambridge University Press, 1982); Nelson Lichtenstein, "The Making of the Postwar Working Class: Cultural Pluralism and Social Structure in World War II," *The Historian* 51 (November 1988): 42–63; Howard Schonberger, "American Labor's Cold War in Occupied Japan," *Diplomatic History* 3 (Summer 1979): 249–72; Joel Seidman, *American Labor from Defense to Reconversion* (Chicago: University of Chicago Press, 1953); Peter Weiler, "The United States, International Labor, and the Cold War: The Breakup of the World Federation of Trade Unions," *Diplomatic History* 5 (1981): 1–22; Timothy Alan Willard, "Labor and the National War Labor Board, 1942–1945: An Experiment in Corporatist Wage Stabilization" (Ph.D. dissertation, University of Toledo, 1984); Federico Romero, *The United States and the European Trade Union Movement, 1944–1951*, trans. Harvey Fergusson, II (Chapel Hill: University of North Carolina Press, 1992); Denis MacShane, *International Labour and the Origins of the Cold War* (Oxford: Clarendon Press, 1992).

Apart from Lewis himself, who became increasingly strident in his critique of both the state and the labor movement after the UMW departure from the CIO in 1942, the most trenchant contemporary criticisms of the choices the CIO and other elements of the labor movement made in their relationship with the wartime and postwar state are found in Art Preis, *Labor's Giant Step: Twenty Years of the CIO*, 2d ed. (New York: Pathfinder, 1972).

3.   *New York Times*, September 3, 1940.

4.   Pressman to Lewis, May 22, 1940, UMW warehouse files, CIO: 1940–42 (Legislative/Legal); Pressman to Lewis, January 1, 1941, UMW warehouse files, CIO:

1940–42 (Legislative/Legal).

5. *New York Times*, October 26, 1940.

6. Lewis remarks, CIO legislative conference, July 7, 1941, James B. Carey Papers, Archives of Labor and Urban Affairs, Wayne State University (hereafter ALUAWSU).

7. United Mine Workers, *Proceedings of the United Mine Workers Convention* (1942), pp. 190–91.

8. For the wartime experience of the UMW, see Dubofsky and Van Tine, *Lewis*, pp. 389–455; Zieger, *Lewis*, pp. 132–49; Lichtenstein, *Labor's War at Home*, pp. 158–70.

9. John L. Lewis, "There Is No Labor Movement," *Collier's*, May 5, 1945, p. 63; Dubofsky and Van Tine, *Lewis*, pp. 330–34, 339–70, 456–57, 474–75; Zieger, *Lewis*, pp. 124–31.

10. See Schatz, "Philip Murray and the Subordination of the Industrial Unions to the United States Government"; Frederick H. Harbison and Robert C. Spencer, "The Politics of Collective Bargaining: The Postwar Record in Steel," *American Political Science Review* 48 (September 1954): 705–20; Edward Robert Livernash, *Collective Bargaining in the Basic Steel Industry: A Study of the Public Interest and the Role of Government* (Westport, Conn.: Greenwood, 1976), pp. 231–307.

11. Philip Murray, "If We Pull Together," *American Magazine*, June 1948, pp. 21, 134.

12. CIO Executive Board Minutes, ALUAWSU (hereafter CIOEB), March 23, 1942; CIOEB, February 1942. Citations to the extensive literature on Communists and the CIO are found in Robert H. Zieger, "Toward the History of the CIO: A Bibliographical Report," *Labor History* 26 (Fall 1985): 492–500; Robert H. Zieger, "The CIO: A Bibliographical Update and Archival Guide," *Labor History* 31 (Fall 1990): 421–22.

13. CIOEB, October 29, 1943.

14. CIOEB, January 27, 1944; Lichtenstein, *Labor's War at Home*, pp. 182–85.

15. CIOEB, July 7, 1943.

16. CIOEB, June 18, 1944; November 19, 1944.

17. CIOEB, March 10–11, 1945.

18. McDonald remarks, *Final Proceedings, 1944, Seventh Constitutional Convention of the Congress of Industrial Organizations*, Chicago, November 20–24, 1944, pp. 278–86, not published; David McDonald, *Union Man* (New York: Dutton, 1969), p. 168.

19. I have seen no evidence that Murray personally collaborated with congressional antiradical investigating committees or with administrative agencies conducting surveillance or harassment of leftists. On the other hand, prominent Steelworkers staff members, notable United States Steel Workers of America headquarters functionary Meyer Bernstein and General Counsel Arthur Goldberg, regularly kept government officials abreast of anti-Communist efforts in the CIO. Moreover, the proceedings of the "trials" that the CIO conducted in the ouster of 11 allegedly pro-Soviet unions in 1950 were published with CIO cooperation by the government. See Sigmund Diamond, "Labor History vs. Labor Historiography: The FBI, James B. Carey, and the Association of Catholic Trade Unionists," in *Religion, Ideology, and Nationalism in Europe in America: Essays Presented in Honor of Yehoshua Arieli* (Jerusalem: The Historical Society of Israel and the Zalman Shazar

Center for Jewish History, 1986), pp. 316–19; Ellen W. Schrecker, "McCarthyism and the Labor Movement: The Role of the State," in *The CIO's Left-Led Unions*, ed. Steven Rosswurm (New Brunswick, N.J.: Rutgers University Press, 1992), pp. 139–57; and U.S. Congress, Senate, *Communist Domination of Certain Unions*, 82nd Cong., 1st Sess., 1951, Doc. 89.

20.   See, for example, Philip Murray, "He Was Indispensable," *New Republic*, April 15, 1946, pp. 534–36.

21.   See, for example, Walter Reuther, "Our Social Setup Lags Behind Our Technological Progress," *Labor and Nation*, January–February 1947, pp. 9–10, copy in Walter P. Reuther Papers, ALUAWSU, Box 565, Folder 10; Walter P. Reuther, "Survival or Democratic Survival?" in *Homes for People; Jobs for Prosperity; Planes for Peace* (CIO, Department of Education and Research pamphlet, 1949), copy in Reuther Papers, Box 565, Folder 15.

22.   U.S. Congress, Senate, Committee on Foreign Relations, "European Recovery Program," 80th Cong., 2nd Sess., 1948, Part 3, p. 1387; U.S. Congress, Senate, Committee on Banking and Currency, "Defense Production Act Amendments of 1951," 82nd Cong., 1st Sess., 1951, Part 3, p. 2131; CIOEB, August 20, 1953.

23.   Walter P. Reuther, "How to Beat the Communists," *Collier's*, February 28, 1948, p. 44.

24.   CIOEB, November 22, 1950; Reuther testimony, U.S. Congress, Senate, "Defense Production Act Amendments of 1951," p. 2172.

25.   CIOEB, August 20, 1953.

26.   Versions of the exposé of the Reuther brothers serving as conduits for Central Intelligence Agency money on one occasion in the early 1950s include Barnard, *Walter Reuther and the Rise of the Auto Workers*, p. 128; Cormier and Eaton, *Reuther*, pp. 358–60; Victor Reuther, *The Brothers Reuther and the Story of the UAW: A Memoir* (Boston: Houghton Mifflin, 1976), pp. 424–26. On Reuther's strategic use of the Taft-Hartley affidavit, see Martin Halpern, *UAW Politics in the Cold War Era* (Albany: State University of New York Press, 1988), pp. 239–40. On third world interventionism see CIO, *1954 Proceedings of the Sixteenth Constitutional Convention of the Congress of Industrial Organizations* (n.p., 1954), pp. 639–40.

2

The Law of Collective Bargaining and Wartime Labor Regulations

James B. Atleson

This chapter focuses upon two areas of National War Labor Board (NWLB) jurisprudence during World War II and their current parallels. The first area concerns the administration and enforcement of collective agreements via arbitration, and the second deals with the range of subjects falling within the scope of mandatory bargaining. Prior to the Taft-Hartley Act of 1947, there was little federal law defining collective bargaining or the means by which agreements could be enforced.[1] The Wagner Act of 1935 required employers to bargain in good faith, and the Supreme Court had made collective agreements predominant over individual contracts of employment.[2]

The Wagner Act, however, did not focus upon dispute resolution and, certainly, not upon arbitration, except for its general encouragement of collective bargaining. The administration and enforcement of collective agreements was necessarily left to the vagaries of state law.

State courts, however, had initially encountered difficulty envisioning collective bargaining agreements as enforceable contracts or unions as

A longer version of this chapter appeared in Nelson Lichtenstein and Howell John Harris, editors, *Industrial Democracy in America: The Ambiguous Promise* (Cambridge: Cambridge University Press, 1993). Reprinted with permission.

proper vindicators of employment rights. Although some courts began to enforce agreements against employers in the 1920s and 1930s, belatedly paralleling the traditional willingness to enjoin breaches of contract by unions or to enjoin strikes, promises to arbitrate were not enforceable in most states.[3] Since the enactment of the Taft-Hartley Act of 1947, however, one of the most creative and vital areas of federal labor policy has concerned the contractual relationship of employers and unions, and the views of the judiciary have been profoundly affected by the writings of academics and industrial relations practitioners and scholars.

Section 301 of the Taft-Hartley statute permits unions and employers, and employees as well, to bring actions in federal court to enforce collective agreements. To find the statute constitutional, the Supreme Court was moved to hold that federal courts were empowered to create substantive law, that is, judicially created policies that would define the nature of "mature" collective bargaining agreements, their methods of enforcement, and the remedies for breach.[4]

While the NWLB encouraged the use of arbitration, it also adopted a restrictive view of the scope of mandatory bargaining, that is, the subjects upon which employers were legally compelled to bargain. Although the postwar National Labor Relations Board (NLRB) would adopt a less limited view of such bargaining, the notion that a vague zone of managerial exclusivity existed stems from several key NWLB decisions.

A loose-knit group of postwar scholars and practitioners, often referred to as "industrial pluralists," are largely responsible for the current body of rules regulating collective bargaining, as well as the supportive vision of industrial relations.[5] This group developed a set of assumptions about the necessary legal structure of collective bargaining, its regulation, and the appropriate forms of dispute resolution, which are reflected in the Supreme Court decisions of the late 1950s and 1960s. In this period the federal judiciary for the first time defined the legal structure of collective bargaining, creating a system dominated by the promotion of arbitral settlement of contract disputes and the discouragement of collective action.[6]

Industrial pluralist thought had much in common with consensus theories in other disciplines in the 1940s and 1950s, combining a search for peaceful dispute resolution mechanisms with a reluctance to discuss existing imbalances in power or issues of class. The pluralists desired to humanize and regularize the workplace, transforming "the anarchy of the marketplace, which exploited workers, into the harmony of a 'modern' cooperative capitalism, which protected workers."[7] The industrial pluralists focused upon the creation of legal rules and administrative processes to resolve workplace conflicts. The predominant device, however, was to be consensual arbitration, a private mechanism that could supplant worker self-help, judicial intervention, or administrative regulation.

Many of the pluralists were in government positions during World War II, a period in which it was critical to find efficient systems to resolve labor disputes and serve as alternatives to strikes. Labor lawyers and economists supplied the demand for wartime specialists. The first public members of agencies such as the NWLB were men skilled in mediation and arbitration. As characterized by Howell Harris:

They were liberal pluralists, committed to the development of a labor relations system in which the triple objectives of efficiency, order, and representative democracy could be reconciled. They believed in the Wagner Act's legislative philosophy, and in strong, responsible unions as agents for its implementation. They preferred to see industrial disputes settled in decentralized, voluntarist negotiations between the parties rather than on terms imposed by the state from the center, or unilaterally determined by employers.[8]

One of the NWLB's most important and enduring contributions was the development of a group of experienced arbitrators who profoundly affected postwar labor law and practice. As Edwin Witte noted in 1952, the "great majority of the labor arbitrators of the present day gained their first direct experience in service on the staff of the War Labor Board or on its disputes panels."[9] With much justification, a speaker at an early meeting of the National Academy of Arbitrators greeted his audience as "The War Labor Board Alumni Association."[10]

The academy's first president, Ralph T. Seward, for instance, had been executive secretary of the National Defense Mediation Board and a public member of its successor, the NWLB. In 1944 he became the impartial umpire for General Motors and the United Automobile Workers (UAW). William Simkin, one of the association's vice-presidents, had been chairman of the Shipbuilding Commission and associate member of the NWLB. The association's original board of governors was also filled with veterans of wartime Washington. Although not active in the formation of the National Academy of Arbitrators, George W. Taylor often spoke at early meetings and helped draft the code of ethics eventually accepted by the academy as well as the American Arbitration Association and the Federal Mediation and Conciliation Service.[11]

This group's government experience during the war stressed productivity and the critical need for labor peace, profoundly shaping their views on arbitration and collective bargaining. In addition, this group would become influential postwar writers and practitioners of labor law and labor relations as well as arbitrators, and they are the crucial link explaining why the current law of collective bargaining mirrors the web of rules created by the NWLB.

THE NATIONAL WAR LABOR BOARD

American entry into the war made necessary a major expansion of the federal role in labor-management relations. Six days after Pearl Harbor, President Roosevelt issued a call for a conference of representatives of labor and management. In issuing the proclamation convening the conference, the president declared that he desired speed, a complete agreement that all wartime disputes would be settled peacefully, and a no-strike pledge.[12] The conference responded by recommending the creation of a war labor board having jurisdiction over all issues, although no agreement was reached on the politically charged union security issue.[13]

The NWLB was formally created on January 12, 1942, in a tersely worded Executive Order 9017.[14] The board was to be composed of 12 members, of which 4 each would represent, respectively, labor, management, and the public.[15] If a dispute threatened to interrupt work related to war production, the Department of Labor could certify the case to the NWLB if it could not be resolved by its own conciliation service.[16] Once the board assumed jurisdiction, its powers were all-encompassing. The board was empowered to reach a final settlement of any labor dispute that might interrupt work "which contributes to the effective prosecution of the war." Unlike the NLRB, the NWLB's responsibility extended to the actual settlement of disputes by "mediation, voluntary arbitration, or arbitration." Under the 1943 War Labor Disputes Act, for instance, the NWLB had the power "to decide the dispute and provide by order the wages and hours and all other terms and conditions (customarily included in collective bargaining agreements) governing the relations between the parties" and "provide for terms and conditions to govern relations between the parties which are to be fair and equitable between an employer and an employee under all the circumstances of the case."[17]

Thus, the NWLB largely determined the wartime terms of employment in American industry. In its first three years, the NWLB decided 14,000 dispute cases, affecting a majority of the organized workers in the country. Not only was a firm foundation created for the Congress of Industrial Organizations, but also wartime regulation had permanent consequences for mass production unionism. Nelson Lichtenstein has noted, "It was the specific social and political context of World War II that created the institutional framework for the kind of collective bargaining that evolved in the decade or so after the war."[18] The NWLB helped in setting industry-wide wage patterns, legitimized fringe benefits bargaining, encouraged arbitration as a method of resolving contractual disputes, and influenced the internal structure and role of new unions, primarily through the grant of union security clauses.

World War II required unprecedented efforts to maintain and stimulate production. The NWLB believed that "maximum production during the war is a duty; the duty is not discharged when production is impaired by lowered morale or strikes caused by the failure to settle grievances. The duty to achieve and maintain production implies, therefore, the establishment of grievance procedures and the prompt settlement of grievances according to that procedure."[19] Labor arbitration, backed by federal support, required stable unions, both to effectuate such procedures and also to contain rank-and-file militance. World War II, therefore, provided a rational basis for stressing bureaucratic dispute resolution, the restriction of midterm strikes, and union control over rank-and-file action. More broadly, the war itself affected the way Americans viewed labor, and the images remained after the war. When the emergency ended, the "needs of the peacetime economy" replaced the requirements of war, and federal policy continued to be based upon increased and continuous production and the stability of labor relations as well as unions.

The underlying themes of contemporary law were not, of course, exclusively created in wartime, for many of the underlying values in American labor law long predate federal statutes.[20] The war, however, helped to create, encourage, or cement visions of the proper labor-management system and the appropriate role of the state. The NWLB helped advance a definition of industrial democracy exclusively in process terms as particular outcomes or some substantive notions of fairness were to be irrelevant. Postwar labor law has proceeded in a similar fashion.[21] In addition, the Supreme Court in the postwar period has, like the NWLB, repeatedly demonstrated its opposition to collective action or self-help in the resolution of contractual labor disputes.[22] This concern is especially reflected in cases where "private" and "peaceful" avenues of resolution, such as arbitration, exist. The result is a set of rules that protect the "integrity" of arbitration, permitting this institution to carry out federal policy and making the intentions of parties less important than the language of contractualism might initially suggest.

"TO MAKE COLLECTIVE BARGAINING WORK"

Although grievance procedures and arbitration clauses were included in some prewar collective bargaining agreements[23] and may well have flourished even without the strong encouragement of the NWLB, "it was left to the War Labor Board to convince American industry and labor that here was an indispensable tool to 'make collective bargaining work.'"[24] As the NWLB Termination report stated in 1943: "The basis for the national war labor policy in America today is still the voluntary agreement between the responsible leaders of labor and industry that there be no strikes or lockouts for the duration of the war. All labor disputes, including grievances, therefore, must be settled by peaceful means."[25] The NWLB stressed the indispensable value of this dispute-resolution process, refined its structure and scope, forced the system on unwilling employers, and provided rules for legal enforcement that would eventually be adopted by the Supreme Court almost 20 years later.

From the beginning, the board set up arbitration panels to decide specific cases, generally appointing the arbitrator.[26] Early decisions also encouraged the parties to voluntarily agree to arbitration clauses for future disputes.[27] Unions that had voluntarily surrendered the right to strike had an especially critical need to find a means to hold employers to their promises, and after 1943, the board often imposed arbitration clauses,[28] despite employer objections. The board's public members noted that "grievance procedures without eventual arbitration is a one-sided affair." The absence of arbitration systems "does not assure the employees of any settlement except on the company's terms and in that respect it invites labor trouble."[29]

Within a year of the board's creation, the basic contours and rules of arbitration were established. Thus, decisions in 1943 reflected the board's support for a formalized, multistep grievance process that could ultimately end in adjudication by a neutral arbitrator, a pattern that has long since become commonplace.[30] The Supreme Court in the 1960s would adopt the basic design set by the NWLB, albeit without attribution. The NWLB's structure of rules, although explainable by wartime exigencies, would also be consistent with the themes of industrial pluralism in the postwar period. More broadly, these themes were congruent with contractualist notions long present in American legal thought. Thus, for instance, the jurisdiction of the arbitrator would be restricted to the settlement of questions concerning the interpretation or application of the terms of collective bargaining agreements.[31] Arbitration fit a voluntarist, contractual model of industrial relations in which disputes could be settled without apparent government involvement.[32]

The contractualist vision extended beyond the scope of arbitration. If the parties had an arbitration agreement, for instance, the NWLB would order arbitration despite an employer objection that the grievance lacked merit.[33] Moreover, after an award was rendered, the board held that "every reasonable presumption is made in favor of such an award" and that awards would be upheld if there was no proof "of fraud, misconduct, or other equally valid objection."[34] Thus, the refusal to comply with an award was treated as a refusal to comply with an order of the NWLB.[35] Moreover, the NWLB affirmed arbitration awards despite an employer's contention that compliance would not be "in the interests of full production." As the board noted in one decision, "labor and industry generally throughout the country have come to regard arbitration as the wisest, fairest, and speediest method of settling industrial disputes, especially during wartime."[36] This broad protection of arbitration awards would also be reflected in the Supreme Court's postwar jurisprudence. In addition, the determinations of the NWLB would not be affected by any arbitration laws that might exist in various states.[37] Subsequently, the Supreme Court would also determine that collective bargaining law was exclusively federal, thus, preempting contrary state statutes and rules.

Despite the board's protection of arbitral systems, some revealing limitations were recognized, perhaps because of managerial concern that arbitrators would have "the final decision on all matters which the union may want to treat as grievances."[38] A revealing ruling in 1942 made clear that arbitration would not involve matters of "managerial prerogative."[39] As the following section reveals, the board believed in the existence of a zone of managerial exclusivity over certain decisions.

Managerial authority was also recognized in areas clearly within arbitral jurisdiction. The board had no difficulty in holding that disciplinary matters were subject to arbitration, especially given the high incidence of clauses in collective bargaining agreements preventing discipline or discharge without "just cause." The board, nevertheless, strongly supported management's authority to take prompt action, including suspending or removing an employee from a job pending investigation or a hearing, subject to the right of the employee or the union to grieve. As NWLB public members Jessie Freiden and Francis Ulman confidently stated in 1945, "Arrangements have never been directed whereby the union's approval must be secured before discipline can be meted out." Thus, the now common notion that the employer acts and the employee or union can only grieve is not so much designed to avoid the possibility that employees will otherwise engage in self-help or because it is a necessary requirement of the grievance process, as would be argued after the war. Instead, it is based upon the board's assumption that such a concept was an incident of managerial prerogative protecting hierarchy and aiding continued production.[40]

These views were forcefully expounded by Yale Law School's Harry Shulman, who also served as an associate public member of the NWLB. Shulman, who became umpire for the Ford Motor Company/UAW in 1943, recognized the role of law in protecting unions, but he stressed that the law left the conditions of work to the "autonomous determination" of employers and unions.[41] Like all the pluralists, Shulman recognized that employment was a conflictual relationship, a view that must have been repeatedly highlighted by the contentious labor relations at Ford, but he believed conflict should be restricted because of the imperatives of production and that disputes would "be adjusted by the application of reason guided by the light of the contract, rather than by force or power."[42] Strikes, an "integral part of the system of collective bargaining," were referred to as a "cessation of production" rather than as a refusal to work. Although Shulman believed that litigation was unsuited to the enforcement of agreements, he stressed that it did not "follow that the alternative is jungle warfare," because arbitration "is an integral part of the system of self government. And the system is designed to aid management in its quest for efficiency, to assist union leadership in its participation in the enterprise, and to secure justice for the employees. It is a means of making collective bargaining work and thus preserving private enterprise in a free government."[43]

Grievance procedures to Shulman not only were an "orderly, effective and democratic way of adjusting such disputes" but also represented the substitution of "civilized collective bargaining for jungle warfare."[44] The repeated reference to "jungle warfare" is instructive, because the notion apparently includes the concerted withdrawal of labor, the basic right underlying the National Labor Relations Act (NLRA). Note that Shulman's argument is not premised upon an explicit union promise to avoid strikes. Instead, the very existence of an arbitration procedure was deemed to foreclose strikes over matters that fell within the ambit of such clauses.

Shulman was the most influential arbitrator during the war and in the immediate postwar period, but many of his most-cited decisions were reached in wartime. Thus, his statement that "while management and labor are in adverse bargaining positions, they are joint participants in the productive effort" flows smoothly from wartime needs, as does his comment that "maintenance of efficient production is of vital importance . . . to the community as a whole."[45]

In perhaps his most well-known award, Shulman in 1944 stressed that employees were required to follow the grievance procedure instead of resorting to self-help. Such behavior was "essential in order to avoid disruption of relations between the parties and anarchy in the operation of the plant." In one of his most famous phrases, he argued that an "industrial plant is not a debating society."[46] This sentiment, reflected in thousands of postwar arbitration awards, makes it clear that contract rights of unions will be treated differently than the assertion of such rights by employers, because "to refuse obedience because of a claimed contract violation would be to substitute individual action for collective bargaining and to replace the grievance procedure with extra-contractual methods." Self-help, therefore, was "extra-contractual" when a grievance procedure was in existence. "When a controversy arises, production cannot wait for exhaustion of the grievance procedure. While that procedure is pursued, production must go on." A challenge to a managerial order interferes with the "authority to direct work," which, Shulman believed, is vested in supervision "because the responsibility for production is also vested there, and responsibility must be accompanied by authority."[47]

The argument that arbitration tames the often unruly rank and file has been used to criticize the institution and by the postwar judiciary to strengthen it. Few authorized strikes occurred during the war, but employee militance is revealed by the large number of wildcat strikes that did occur. It is not at all clear that arbitration procedures avoid wildcat strikes, because arbitral resolution is not necessarily quick and the process does not always involve the workers actually affected. Indeed, the existence of arbitration and the NWLB seemed almost irrelevant to most wildcat strikers, except to the extent that frustration with NWLB delays and policies can be deemed to have been the partial cause of some wartime stoppages. Regulators might have believed in such a connection, however, and experience in the apparel industry earlier in the century suggested that rank-and-file militance can be moderated, at least with time, and replaced by a more bureaucratized system of dispute resolution.

By war's end, the basic structures of today's common arbitral system were in place. Typically, contracts called for a multistep grievance process that had the effect of transferring authority from shop floor leaders to the union hierarchy. Rights were no longer to be based upon tradition or custom but upon the contract and arbitral case law, a process thought to parallel the "rule of law" in society. Discharge or discipline could be only for "just cause," but supervisory orders had to be obeyed, that is, the grievance system would substitute for self-help. Such a process requires patience over militancy, a substitution of third-party resolution in place of the exercise of shop floor power.[48]

Collective bargaining and the arbitration process also were thought to require a different kind of union leader. Golden and Ruttenberg noted in 1942 that "most militant local union leaders, who rise to the surface in the organizing stage of unions, fall by the side when the union moves into the state of constructive relations with management."[49] "Constructive" labor relations, therefore, require responsible unions led by "cooperative" leaders.[50]

In addition to the supposed need to alter the kind of leaders needed, bargaining and arbitration tend to alter the issues to be decided. A grievance process transforms disputes, which could be based upon concerns for personal integrity or moral and political issues, into narrower, more legalistic questions.[51] Indeed, over time, disputes become contractual or, else, they are improper. As rights become more clearly based solely upon the contract, disputes over other matters are treated as irrelevant, unimportant, or, at least, unjustifiable.

The move from a system of workplace confrontation to higher-level bargaining or arbitration, therefore, may alter the *substance* of bargaining, that is, the nature of the issues. Workplace conflict tended to deal with speed of production, discipline, or actions of foremen.[52] "Mature" collective bargaining, on the other hand, often deals with other issues. Thus, a change in focus of concern, in the definition of what is important, occurred, rather than simply a change in the location of and participants in dispute resolution. Although unions of the 1940s often declared their intention to invade hitherto sacred management preserves and although employers clearly believed that such threats were real,[53] the labor movement primarily sought involvement in major capital decisions, not the types of workplace issues that often seem of greater immediacy to workers. Nevertheless, the combination of legal restrictions on the scope of bargaining and the protection of arbitration tended to deprive workers of influence on both capital decisions and workplace conflicts.

MANAGERIAL PREROGATIVES: THE
LIMITS OF COLLECTIVE BARGAINING

At the end of the war, American employers expressed great fear concerning the union challenge to managerial control of the workplace. Executives focused this concern less on strikes than on "the serious and lasting limitations on their freedom of action resulting from the orderly collective bargaining achievements of bureaucratic unionism, assisted by the orders of arbitrators and the NWLB."[54] Managerial fears, however, must have been based primarily upon union bargaining power and workplace pressures, because the wartime "law" certainly was generous in regard to managerial prerogatives.[55]

The first NLRB, created by Executive Order in 1934, had endorsed a broad reading of the duty to bargain, expanding interpretations from its predecessor, the National Labor Board.[56] Despite this history, the NWLB at an early date recognized an area of decision making it designated as "managerial prerogatives." The determination that a matter is solely a management function means, first, that the employer need not bargain about such a matter despite the union's request that it do so, nor would the NWLB restrict managerial authority in these areas. Second, and often most important, an employer can initiate action in these areas without first bargaining with the union and without subsequent arbitral challenge. Although the scope of bargaining should be a vital question under the NLRA, little litigation under that statute had occurred on these questions between the determination that the NLRA was constitutional in 1937 and the outbreak of war.[57] Thus, the NWLB's assumptions would become deeply embedded in NLRA jurisprudence after the war.[58]

In 1946 Ludwig Teller, prolific writer of relatively conservative labor law articles and treatises, was pleased to report that "the decisions of the War Labor Board in labor dispute cases did much to reinstate management confidence in business continuity, and in the right to initiate business decisions."[59] Teller argued that when the war and the NWLB ended, there was "increasing reliance" on the decisions of the NWLB "because of the belief that its decisions are a source of guidance for desirable practices in the field of labor relations." As Teller perceptively noted in 1946, the NWLB's "decisions are the beginnings of a labor jurisprudence." Indeed, it was the NWLB, not the NLRB, that institutionalized the notion that the scope of mandatory bargaining is restricted by certain inherent managerial rights.

The NWLB tended to be keenly protective of managerial rights, and it routinely denied union welfare proposals. The NWLB, it was said, was "hesitant about breaking new ground." The NWLB, however, did grant unions a measure of participation in many matters previously thought to be exclusively managerial. For instance, the board supported automatic wage progression plans, which affected employers' control of labor costs and the work force. In addition, board-ordered job classification plans and other work arrangements gave unions the right to be consulted in both the creation and the administration of such schemes.[61] Neverthe-less, what is noteworthy about the board's rulings is the lack of any felt need to explain the nature or scope, or to even justify the existence, of managerial prerogatives.[62]

The board's clearest statement of its approach is probably to be found in its *Montgomery Ward* decision. Management functions were excluded from arbitration to the extent that they related to "changes in the general business practice, the opening or closing of new units, the choice of personnel, the choice of merchandise to be sold, or other business questions of a like nature not having to do directly and primarily with the day-to-day life of the employees and their relations with their super-visors."[63] The scope of bargaining, therefore, was to be narrowed to the "day-to-day" concerns of employees. As under the NLRA, it is the challenge to the employer's control of production and the state's unwillingness to sanction such challenges that seem to underlie these cases.

A good deal of labor's creativity in creating bargaining proposals arose from the fact that possible wage gains were strictly controlled by the board''s "Little Steel" wage formula. Even matters clearly involving working conditions, however, were often avoided by the board. The board would not always explicitly rule that particular issues were improper subjects for bargaining; instead, the NWLB often sent such issues back to the parties for further negotiation, a resolution with foreseeable results given the no-strike pledge. As Aaron Levenstein, a left-wing critic of NWLB, noted, the board's "refusal to decide made it impossible for the unions to bargain on those matters altogether. Since the strike weapon had been put in cold storage, the issue remained an economic no man's land which the Board would not enter and which labor could not invade because it had no persuasive power. In this region of disputed issues, the employers' only obligation was to negotiate before saying no."[64] The unions argued that the no-strike pledge obliged the board to rule on all issues. The "no-strike, no lockout agreement," they argued in vain, was conditioned on the submission of "all disputes" to the board. The board's position was essentially that its jurisdiction was narrower than the no-strike promise. Effectively, then, the no-strike obligation was unlimited, but the right to bargain was not.[65]

In one case, the UAW demanded that General Motors create an employee security fund equal to the one it had already put aside for postwar business contingencies. The fund would purchase war bonds, and, after the war, it would supplement unemployment insurance for workers who could not be provided with a 40-hour workweek. The board agreed with General Motors that the union's demand was essentially a "profit-sharing plan and is beyond the powers of the War Labor Board to adjudicate."[66] The public members of the board believed they should prevent the introduction of "sociological innovations" during the war. The powerful wartime interest in labor peace could have led to a broad, inclusive reading of the scope of bargaining, especially given the unions' no-strike pledge. Yet, the interest in cooption, or in the institutionalization of dispute resolution, was apparently weaker than the NWLB's preference for unrestricted managerial freedom over certain matters.

In the NWLB's first decision in which the issue was raised (*Arcade Malleable Iron Co.*[67]), the board denied an employer's request for a clause that specifically listed various management functions. Without dissent from its labor representatives, however, the board agreed to insert a clause to the effect that "the functions of management are vested exclusively in the Company except as modified by the specific provisions of this agreement." The union was enjoined from interfering "in the rights of the management in the matter of hiring, transfer, or promotion of any employees and in the general management of the plant." The board's only objection was to the employer's proposed "long list" of exclusive management functions.

The basis for the decision became clear in the later *Banner Iron Works* decision: "The rights are inherent in management anyhow."[68] Nevertheless, the board in 1942, often without comment, began to approve management requests to insert clauses into collective bargaining agreements that would protect specific management rights.[69] Inherent rights, apparently, were sometimes deemed worthy of clear expression. These clauses generally gave management, among other things, the exclusive power to hire, promote, fire for just cause, and maintain and schedule production. Moreover, the clauses often explicitly acknowledged the employers' exclusive control over the products to be manufactured as well as the locations of plants.[70]

Under the rubric of "plant operations," the NWLB deferred to many aspects of management decision making. For instance, the board denied a union request to reestablish a six-day workweek instead of a five-day swing-shift week, stating that "this matter is a technical administrative problem, which should be left to management to decide, involving as it does the rearrangement of working schedules by large scale transfers of personnel and changes in the entire system of the company's operations."[71] The NWLB also generally believed that limitations and arbitration of employee transfers would interfere with efficiency.[72]

Indeed, the board's decisions on the scope of managerial prerogatives were far broader than the positions of the postwar NLRB. For instance, the NWLB held that even the distribution of overtime work was within the exclusive prerogative of management. Thus, the board denied a union's request for an equal division of overtime work on the ground that the "ultimate decision as to who is qualified to perform specific overtime work should rest with management."[73] Other matters swept into the broad management prerogatives category were the initiation of technological changes, even if layoffs would result, determination of the size of the work force, and the determination of supervisors.[74]

Also, as noted previously, "management functions" were not to be subject to arbitration.[75] Thus, the board had occasion to expressly exclude from arbitration the transfer and promotion of employees, the adjustment of piece rates, the determination of whether additional employees should be hired for certain operations, the retention of probationary employees, and the determination of work schedules.[76]

The board's willingness to grant a detailed management prerogative clause, after its initial refusal to do so, actually reflects a more liberal approach to collective bargaining. The board initially may have believed that no explication of management rights was required, because they were "inherent" in the relationship. This is a reflection of what could be referred to as the "Genesis" theory of collective bargaining, one often found in judicial decisions and especially in postwar arbitration awards. "In the beginning," the theory goes, there was light, and then there were inherent managerial powers over the direction of the enterprise. Such power obviously included unfettered control to direct production and the work force and to make all decisions involving these matters. Later, there came statutes and collective bargaining, but employers, nevertheless, still possess all powers that have not been expressly restricted by statute or agreement.[77] The inclusion of express managerial rights in collective agreements, however, weakens the argument that certain prerogatives are "inherent" in the relationship.

A more sophisticated argument, and one made by the conservative legal scholar Ludwig Teller, is that collective bargaining was a replacement for rather than a supplement to common law theories of labor relations. Thus, collective bargaining was created to supplant "common law individualism" with "new conceptions suitable to problems and situations which did not exist when the common law molded its intensely individualistic structure." Teller was aware that, having replaced the old order with the new, "organized labor is properly suspicious of efforts to give continued life to the old order through the medium of emphasis upon 'the common law rights of management.'" Moreover, as many observers of industrial relations recognized, there is no objective or rational way to determine what is or what is not a managerial prerogative.[78] A decision concerning which matters should be exclusively in the managerial domain is basically a determination of the area from which labor should be excluded. In addition, as David Montgomery's work has shown, the context of this issue involves those areas in which management/ownership has taken power from employees as well as those areas in which collective employee action and statutes have restricted managerial control.[79]

An explicit managerial prerogatives clause offers a number of other values, both real and symbolic. First, it "has certain value in teaching the contracting union to think in terms of the problems and rights of management."[80] More importantly, such a clause limits the scope of proper union concern, a serious matter in a period in which many unions were both developing *and* experiencing economic power. Indeed, in one case, the board upheld the grant of a management functions clause by a regional board because "the present union is a new union and the inclusion of the clause will serve to educate the union more definitely as to management functions, thus serving to reduce the areas of conflict between union and management without loss of protection of the union under the other terms of the contract and especially of the grievance machinery."[81] In addition, the managerial functions clause creates a source of legitimation when management takes a particular action, a further reflection of the contractualization of labor-management relations.

The NWLB's recognition of a zone of managerial exclusivity would eventually be reflected in Supreme Court decisions that narrowed the scope of bargaining under the NLRA. The Supreme Court held in 1964, for instance, that subcontracting, at least in certain situations, was within the ambit of mandatory bargaining in *Fibreboard Paper Products* v. *NLRB*.[82] The opinion, typical of Warren Court opinions, began with broad statements of policy only to finish by narrowing the ruling to the precise and very limited facts of the case before it.[83] A concurring opinion by Justice Potter Stewart noted that not "every management decision which necessarily terminates an individual's employment is subject to the duty to bargain." Echoing *Montgomery Ward*, Stewart noted that even decisions clearly affecting "conditions of employment" are excluded because of the nature of the managerial action, listing, among others, decisions to invest in labor-saving machinery or decisions to liquidate assets and go out of business. These decisions, Stewart argued, "lie at the core of entrepreneurial control." Stewart's explanation was that "decisions concerning the commitment of investment capital and the basic scope of the enterprise are not in themselves primarily about conditions of employment, though the effect of the decision may be necessary to terminate employment." Thus, excluded from the zone of mandatory bargaining are matters of capital investment and decisions "fundamental to the basic direction of a corporate enterprise."[84] Despite the union's victory in *Fibreboard*, Stewart's cautionary phrases were not significantly at variance with the majority's conclusion that mandatory bargaining in this instance would not "significantly abridge . . . [the employer's] freedom to manage the business."

The court's concern for the freedom to manage subsequently would become the basis for restrictive rulings of the Burger Court. In 1981, for instance, the Supreme Court held that a partial closing of the enterprise was not subject to mandatory bargaining.[85] The issue, said Justice Blackmun, is whether a decision to terminate "should be considered part of petitioner's retained freedom to manage its affairs unrelated to employment." Like the NWLB, Blackmun, thus, assumed that an inherent body of exclusive management functions existed and that "management must be free from the constraints of the bargaining process to the extent essential for the running of a profitable business." Congress, said the court, "had no expectation that the elected union representative would become an equal partner in the running of the business enterprise in which the union's members are employed."[86]

CONCLUSION

Although there are negative aspects of contractualism, there are also clear advantages for unions. Institutionally, grievance procedures, like collective bargaining, centralize power in the hands of union officials, but there are gains for employees as well. Guarantees written into collective agreements cannot be taken away easily, and this becomes the basis for one of the unions' most powerful arguments for representative status. In light of labor's relative weakness, the constant and very real threat of hostile legislation throughout the war, and the erosion of public support due to wartime strikes, these gains are significant.[87]

Nevertheless, despite the gains, the practices and law of arbitration also have negative effects on industrial democracy. First, arbitration focuses upon the written agreement as the exclusive source of employee rights. The agreement, although supplemented by customs and past practices, is the result of economic struggle and, thus, represents the balance or imbalance of economic power. Indeed, the reliance upon contractualism means that contract rights are based upon the very kinds of economic imbalance that the Wagner Act sought to ameliorate. Moreover, the relative power of the parties is itself affected by the interpretations of the NLRA, often not favorable to union interests, especially in periods when unions are perceived to be weak. Second, arbitration removes the conflict, and its resolution, from the workplace and its affected workers. Just as important, arbitration and centralized bargaining alter the kinds of issues that are thought to be important.

Finally, arbitration procedures reflect the hierarchical system of the plant, and the substantive rules indicate, despite the rhetoric, that no participatory democracy is to be created. The key rule of arbitration, that employees must obey work orders and grieve, makes it clear that management may act upon its interpretation of the agreement but that the union may not. Arbitration becomes the device to maintain production and the only avenue to test the union's view of its contractual rights. Inherent in the rule itself is a choice of managerial hegemony and continued production over more participatory industrial self-government.

This is not to argue that legal rules necessarily reflect reality or substantially affect behavior. The argument is only that the very assumptions of, and tensions within, pluralist thought would affect the shape of postwar law and aid in creating restrictive rulings, especially when labor's power is perceived to wane. Pluralist thought, after all, was immeasurably aided by the appearance of relative equality in the postwar period. Alan Fox's perceptive analysis of labor relations in the United Kingdom in the early 1970s is also applicable to the experience of the United States in the 1970s. With few exceptions, Fox argued that labor accepted

As given those major structural features which are crucial for the power, status and rewards of the owners and controllers. It is because this condition is usually fulfilled that owners and controllers are rarely driven to call upon their reserves of power in any overt and public exercise. Only the margins of power are needed to cope with marginal adjustments. This, then, is what accounts for the illusion of a power balance. Labour often has to marshal all its resources to fight on these marginal adjustments; capital can, as it were, fight with one hand behind its back and still achieve in most situations a verdict that it finds tolerable.[88]

The generally superior power of capital has been unleashed in a period when reduced profit margins and international competition induced management to contest labor and working conditions, the one aspect of production over which it historically has had most control.

Arbitration is but a part, albeit perhaps a necessary part, of collective bargaining, and it is no more confining than bargaining itself. Bargaining, after all, is affected by relative economic power, and imbalances will be reflected in the resulting contracts that arbitrators are called upon to interpret. Perhaps the most important legacy of the NWLB is its view that the scope of bargaining is itself limited to only those matters not deemed critical to managerial efficiency and, especially, capital mobility. Such assumptions after the war became part of the underlying basis of the NLRA, tending to seriously restrict defensive efforts when faced with the torrent of plant transfers and closures in the 1970s and 1980s.

Pluralist premises rest upon substantially equal power because only then can collective bargaining be considered "industrial self-government." The current sharp decline in the labor movement, matched by a crisis in pluralist circles, reveals that equal power does not exist and that the bargaining system, both defined and limited by legal decisions, will not likely result in substantial equality. The seeds of the problem stem in part from the NWLB's recognition and protection of inherent managerial or property rights, a concern that even the needs of wartime could not weaken. The recognition of managerial rights would lead the Supreme Court to hold in 1981 that, with the Wagner Act, Congress had no expectation that the elected representative would become an equal partner in the running of the business enterprise in which the union's members are employed.

The pluralists as well as the NWLB deferred to the rights of owners and managers to direct their enterprises, although they qualified the arbitrary exercise of such power by insisting that responsible unions have a voice in the determination of those conditions of employment that did not invade the protective zone of managerial prerogative. The conflict between the protection of management decision making and the encouragement of collective bargaining has never been resolved, either by the pluralists or by the courts.[89]

Collective bargaining in its decentralized American form has left the labor movement particularly dependent upon the success and viability of certain mass production industries. Their decline weakens the institutional strength of unions, but the unions' history provides no way to question current institutional arrangements or to propose transformative ideas. Union structure has tended to match that of the employers with whom they bargain, but locally based bargaining would appear to make little sense in relation to large, multiplant firms with typically centralized labor policy making. Moreover, the modern growth of conglomerates and multinational corporations drastically affects the power relationships of labor and capital. Unions find themselves increasingly dealing with firms that can easily weather economic struggles, conceal information, and transfer, or (more credibly) threaten to transfer, work to other locales or, indeed, other countries. This drastic change in corporate and capital structure mandates a rethinking of our labor laws.

Labor law reform, however, is unlikely as long as unions are perceived to be weak, because the system responds to the strong and the troublesome. Instead, unions are likely to participate more willingly in "nonadversarial" participation schemes, such as quality circles and team arrangements, generally more favored by employees than by union officials. These arrangements, hearkening back to employee representation structures in the early part of the century,[90] likely will become the hallmark of unorganized employers as well. As early as 1982, a survey found that at least a third of Fortune 500 companies, organized and unorganized, have some form of participative management or quality of work life program and that such programs have generally resulted in improved employee morale and increased productivity.[91] Although these arrangements are sometimes created to deter the possibility of union organization, they tend in organized workplaces to deal with matters not covered by collective bargaining. Indeed, participation plans in unionized workplaces generally restrict the jurisdiction of participatory arrangements to matters not covered by the collective agreement. These arrangements, therefore, actually recognize the failure of collective bargaining to deal with the full range of employee interests and to respond to employee concerns for integrity on the job.

NOTES

1. The 1937–41 period was too brief for a significant body of NLRA law to develop. In one significant case, however, the Supreme Court had held that strikes in breach of contract would be unprotected by NLRA Section 7, but the court assumed it

had the power to interpret the agreement. See *NLRB* v. *Sands Mfg. Co.*, 306 U.S. 332 (1939); Karl Klare, "Judicial Deradicalization of the Wagner Act and the Origins of Modern Legal Consciousness, 1937–1941," *Minnesota Law Review* 62 (1978): 303. The union had sought to enforce its interpretation of the agreement, announcing that employees would not work unless this view was upheld. The court interpreted the agreement to favor the employer's contractual position; thus, the workers "were irrevocably committed not to work in accordance with their contract" (306 U.S. 344). Such a "repudiation" by employees of the agreement was deemed a severance of their employment. The decision suggests that the court would be no less hostile to self-help when an arbitration procedure was present.

2.   *J. I. Case Co.* v. *NLRB*, 321 U.S. 332 (1944).

3.   See, generally, James Atleson, "The Circle of *Boys Market*: A Comment on Judicial Inventiveness," *Industrial Relations Law Journal* 7 (1985): 88; Katherine Von Wezel Stone, "The Post-War Paradigm in American Labor Law," *Yale Law Journal* 90 (1981): 1518–21.

4.   Federal courts under Article 2 of the Constitution have authority only to enforce rights under federal statutes and the Constitution. Generally, federal courts cannot be given jurisdiction to enforce rights that do not arise from these sources.

5.   Stone, "The Post-War Paradigm," pp. 1509–80; Staughton Lynd, "Government Without Rights: The Labor Law Vision of Archibald Cox," *Industrial Relations Law Journal* 4 (1981): 483; Howell John Harris, "The Snares of Liberalism? Politicians, Bureaucrats, and the Shaping of Federal Labour Relations Policy in the United States, ca. 1915–1947," in *Shop Floor Bargaining and the State*, eds. Steven Tolliday and Jonathan Zeitlin (Cambridge: Cambridge University Press, 1987).

6.   The Supreme Court in *Textile Workers* v. *Lincoln Mills*, for instance, cites Archibald Cox, "Grievance Arbitration in the Federal Courts," *Harvard Law Review* 67 (1954): 602–4, to support its conclusion that the Norris-LaGuardia Act does not bar specific enforcement of the arbitration clause. In the famous trilogy of arbitration decisions in 1960, Cox is cited in two cases and Harry Shulman is cited in *United Steelworkers* v. *Warrior & Gulf Navigation*, 363 U.S. 574, 578–9, 579 n.6, 581, 583 n.7 (1960). See also *United Steelworkers* v. *American Mfg.*, 363 U.S. 564, 568 n.6 (1960).

7.   Melvyn Dubofsky, "Legal Theory and Workers' Rights: A Historian's Critique," *Industrial Relations Law Journal* 4 (1981): 497. The pluralists' relationship to the government-liberal tradition embodied by Senator Robert Wagner has not been studied. Both groups believed in a government framework for private action, although the Wagner Act focused upon bargaining, not contract administration. See Daniel Sipe, "A Moment of the State: The Enactment of the National Labor Relations Act, 1935" (Ph.D. diss., University of Pennsylvania, 1981); Stanley Vittoz, *New Deal Labor Policy and the American Industrial Economy* (Chapel Hill: University of North Carolina Press, 1987); Theda Skocpol, "Political Response to Capitalist Crises: Neo-Marxist Theories of the State and the Case of the New Deal," *Politics and Society* 10 (1980): 155–201; Peter Irons, *The New Deal Lawyers* (Princeton, N.J.: Princeton University Press, 1982).

8.   Howell Harris, *The Right to Manage: Industrial Relations Policies of American Business in the 1940s* (Madison: University of Wisconsin, 1982), p. 49.

9.   Edwin Witte, quoted in Roger Abrams and Dennis Nolan, "American Labor Arbitration: The Maturing Years," *Florida Law Review* 35 (1983): 577.

10.   Charles Killingsworth, "The Chronicle," *Journal of the National Academy of Arbitrators*, February 1988, p. 5.

11.   Other influential scholars and writers who gained experience in the wartime agency were Benjamin Aaron, David L. Cole, G. Allan Dash, Alex Elson, Nathan E. Finesinger, Jesse Freiden, Alexander H. Frey, Sylvester S. Garrett, Jr., Lloyd Garrison, Lewis M. Gill, James J. Healy, Theodore W. Kheel, Thomas E. Larkin, Eli Rock, Peter Seitz, Ralph T. Seward, Harry Shulman, William E. Simkin, George W. Taylor, and W. Willard Wirtz. In addition, NWLB staff positions were filled with people who would become influential in labor history, economics, and labor relations, such as E. Wright Bakke, Douglas V. Brown, John T. Dunlop, George H. Hildebrand, Louis Jaffe, Vernon H. Jenson, Clark Kerr, Richard Lester, E. Robert Livernash, Lester B. Orfield, Sumner H. Slichter, Edwin H. Witte, and Dale Yoder. These individuals are listed in the National War Labor Board Termination Report, Vol. 1, pp. 2–46; 6 War Labor Reports (hereafter cited as WLR) xxiv; 7 WLR xxvi. This listing omits those who served with other wartime agencies such as the Office of Price Control and the War Production Board.

12.   Fred Witney, *Wartime Experiences of the National Labor Relations Board* (Urbana: University of Illinois, 1949), p. 118.

13.   The president accepted the conference's agreement and short-circuited the issue by interpreting the conference report as meaning that "all disputes," including the closed shop controversy, were within the jurisdiction of the NWLB. Witney, *Wartime Experiences*, pp. 118–19; Joel Seidman, *American Labor from Defense to Reconversion* (Chicago: University of Chicago Press, 1953), pp. 80–81.

14.   See National War Labor Board Termination Report, Vol. 2, p. 49.

15.   William Davis, the former chair of the National Defense Mediation Board, was named chair of the NWLB. The other public members were George W. Taylor, Frank P. Graham, and Wayne L. Morse.

16.   Executive Order 9017, 3 C.F.R. 1075 (1938–43 compilation).

17.   Public Law No. 89, 59 Stat. 163 (1943). The statute was commonly referred to as the Smith-Connally Act.

18.   Nelson Lichtenstein, "Industrial Democracy, Contract Unionism and the National War Labor Board," *Labor Law Journal* 33 (August 1982): 524.

19.   "Instructions to Regional War Labor Boards: Importance of Grievance Machinery," 9 WLR xxiv–xxv (1944) (National War Labor Board Memorandum Release, issued July 24, 1943).

20.   See, generally, James Atleson, *Values and Assumptions in American Labor Law* (Amherst: University of Massachusetts, 1983).

21.   Karl Klare, "Labor Law and Liberal Political Imagination," in *The Politics of Law*, ed. David Kairys (New York: Pantheon, 1982), pp. 60–61.

22.   Ibid., p. 51; Atleson, *Values and Assumptions*, Chap. 3.

23.   Sylvester Garrett, "Resolving the Tension: Arbitration Confronts the External Legal System," *Case Western Reserve Law Review* 39 (1988–89): 557; Nolan and Abrams, "American Labor Arbitration," pp. 575–77.

24.   Paul Fisher, "The National War Labor Board and Post-War Industrial Relations," *Quarterly Journal of Economics*, August 1945, p. 505. See also, Benjamin Aaron, "Catalyst: The National War Labor Board of World War II," *Case Western Reserve Law Review* 39 (1988–89): 519.

25.   National War Labor Board Termination Report, Vol. 1, p. 65. Within weeks of Pearl Harbor, both the American Federation of Labor and the Congress of Industrial Organizations voluntarily surrendered the right to strike for the duration.

26.   See, for example, New York Telephone Co., 1 WLR 259 (1942); Williamette Valley Lumber Operators, 1 WLR 151 (1942); Steel Drop Forge Group, 1 WLR 22 (1942).

27.   Acmeline Mfg. Co., 9 WLR 524 (1943).

28.   Chrysler Corp., 10 WLR 551 (1943); Champlin Refining Co., 3 WLR 155 (1942); Nolan and Abrams, "American Labor Arbitration," pp. 571–73; Lichtenstein, "Industrial Democracy," p. 524.

29.   Niles-Bement-Pond Co., 5 WLR 489 (1943).

30.   See, for example, Eclipse Fuel Engineering Co., 6 WLR 279 (1943).

31.   Chrysler Corp., 3 WLR 447 (1942); 10 WLR 551 (1943).

32.   See, for example, National War Labor Board Termination Report 131; Realty Advisory Board, 2 WLR 183 (1942).

33.   Texoma Natural Gas Co., 10 WLR 438 (1943). The state courts generally had been hostile to arbitral arrangements, apparently because they viewed arbitration as a threat to supplant the courts. See for example, *Gatliff Coal Co.* v. *Cox*, 142 F.2d 876 (6th Cir. 1944); Charles Gregory and Richard Orlikoff, "The Enforcement of Labor Arbitration Agreements," *University of Chicago Law Review* 17 (1950): 233. Many, therefore, refused to enforce such promises. Breaking from the common law view, the NWLB held that parties to an arbitration agreement must live up to their promises to arbitrate, and the board would enforce such awards. See, for example, Smith & Wesson, 10 WLR 148 (1943). See, generally, Jessie Freiden and Francis J. Ulman, "Arbitration and the War Labor Board," *Harvard Law Review* 58 (1945): 315.

34.   See Sullivan Drydock & Repair Co., 6 WLR 467 (1943); Smith & Wesson, 10 WLR 148, 153 (1943); National War Labor Board Termination Report, Vol. 1, pp. 404–5. The board would refuse to review an award even though the arbitration agreement stipulated that either party could appeal to the NWLB. Sullivan Drydock & Repair Co., 6 WLR 467 (1943). See also "Statement of Policy Concerning Review of Arbitration Awards," National War Labor Board Termination Report, Vol. 2, p. 694.

35.   National War Labor Board Termination Report, Vol. 1, pp. 411–12; Vol. 2, pp. 694–95.

36.   Alexander Milburn Co., 5 WLR 529 (1942).

37.   Ibid.

38.   Montgomery Ward & Co., 10 WLR 415, 420 (1943).

39.   See, for example, Atlas Power Co., 5 WLR 371 (1942) (denial of extension of arbitration to cover transfer and promotion disputes where hazardous nature of operations necessitates complete control by company). See also Harris, *The Right to Manage*, pp. 55–56.

40.   See, for instance, Brewster Aeronautical Corp., 12 WLR 40 (1943); Norge Machine Products Division of Borg-Warner Corp., 15 WLR 651 (1944); Briggs Mfg. Co., 5 WLR 340 (1942).

41.   Harry Shulman, "Reason, Contract and Law in Labor Relations," *Harvard Law Review* 68 (1955): 1000. Harry Shulman's 1955 Holmes Lecture, "Reason, Contract and Law in Labor Relations," was printed in both the *Harvard Law Review* and in the *Proceedings of the Ninth Annual Meeting of the National Academy of Arbitrators*. It is probably the most widely quoted article in the area of arbitration and contract dispute settlement.

42.   Ibid., p. 1007.

43.   Ibid., p. 1024.

44. *Opinions of the Umpire, Ford Motor Co. and UAW-CIO, 1943–1946*, Case No. A-116.

45. Ibid., A-561.

46. Ibid., A-116 (also published as Matter of Ford Motor Co., 3 LA 779 [1944]). See also A-29.

47. Ibid., A-116.

48. The board's policies fostering the routinization of workplace disputes combine by late 1943 with a managerial counterattack on union power in the workplace. For a description of the centralization and bureaucratization of disciplinary power at Ford's Rouge plant, see Nelson Lichtenstein, "Life at the Rouge: A Cycle of Workers' Control," in *Life and Labor: Dimensions of American Working Class History*, eds. C. Stephenson and Robert Asher (Albany: State University of New York Press, 1986), pp. 248–51. The NWLB would insist that strikes were improper while disputes were being processed through the contractual grievance system. This notion would find favor long after, both in the Supreme Court and in arbitral decisions barring self-help where grievance systems existed.

49. Clinton Golden and Harold Ruttenberg, *The Dynamics of Industrial Democracy* (New York: Harper and Brothers, 1942), p. 58. In Richard Lester's words, the successors of the founding leaders of a union tend to be not "crusading agitator[s]," but the "skillful political operator and level-headed administrator." Richard Lester, *As Unions Mature* (Princeton, N.J.: Princeton University Press, 1958), p. 26.

50. Although nonmilitant, "constructive" union officials were not the exclusive type of leader, the pattern described does seem to parallel that of some revolutions, in which militant leaders are often forced out, killed, or shipped abroad to be replaced by more managerial, bureaucratic types.

51. Lynn Mather and Barbara Yngvesson, "Language, Audience, and the Transformation of Disputes," *Law & Society Review* 15 (1981): 775.

52. "Reported Work Stoppages in Automobile Plants in Dec. 1944, Jan., Feb. 1945," set out in Martin Glaberman, *Wartime Strikes: The Struggle Against the No-Strike Pledge in the UAW During World War II* (Detroit, Mich.: Bewick Editions, 1980).

53. Harris, *The Right to Manage*. Although unions seem to deemphasize such attempted incursions during the 1945–49 period, there were economic reasons for such behavior. The primary concern of unions during this period was job security and protection against raging inflation concurrent with a vigorous managerial counterattack. See David Brody, *Workers In Industrial America* (New York: Oxford University Press, 1980), pp. 173–214.

54. Harris, *The Right to Manage*, p. 67. For an argument that managers lost considerable power during the war years, see Robert M. C. Littler, "Managers Must Manage," *Harvard Business Review* 24 (1946): 366.

55. Despite the wartime statements by some union officials expressing their interest in further influence in management, statements by unionists supporting the concept of managerial rights could also be found. Thus, Philip Murray and Morris J. Cooke stated in 1940: "To relieve the boss or the management of proper responsibility for making a success of the enterprise is about the last thing any group of employees — organized or unorganized — would consider workable or even desirable. The Unions are on record in numerous instances as recognizing that in the last analysis management has to manage, if any concern is to be a success financially or in any other way." Philip

Murray and Morris Cooke, *Organized Labor and Production* (New York: Harper, 1940), p. 84.

56. Employers had been ordered to bargain over a wide range of matters that had an impact on terms and conditions of employment, including changes in terms occasioned by plant relocation or the introduction of a new line of products. Atleson, *Values and Assumptions*, p. 118.

57. Ibid., pp. 115–22.

58. See, generally, Atleson, *Values and Assumptions*.

59. Ludwig Teller, "The War Labor Board and Management Functions," *New York University Law Quarterly Review* 21 (1946): 365.

60. Constance Williams, "Note on Management Prerogatives," National War Labor Board Termination Report, Vol. 2, p. 623.

61. Timothy Willard, *Labor and the National War Labor Board 1942–1945: An Experiment in Corporatist Wage Stabilization* (Ph.D. diss., University of Toledo, 1984), p. 40.

62. "One of the most remarkable features of the War Labor Board cases dealing with management functions is the failure to define at length the meaning of management function in a union relationship, or even to discuss its essential qualities as a guide to future policies." Teller, "The War Labor Board," p. 365.

63. Montgomery Ward, 10 WLR 415 (1943).

64. See Aaron Levenstein, *Labor Today and Tomorrow* (New York: Knopf, 1946), p. 102.

65. Unions did broaden the scope of bargaining, however, despite the board's lack of support. The United Mine Workers of America developed the concept of a royalty for every ton of coal mined to be used to create a fund for medical service, hospitalization, rehabilitation, and general economic protection. Levenstein, *Labor Today and Tomorrow*, pp. 103–4. Other unions, like the International Ladies Garment Workers Union, required employers to contribute to union health and vacation funds.

66. General Motors Company, 22 WLR 484 (1945).

67. In re Arcade Malleable Iron Co., 1 WLR 153 (1942).

68. 15 WLB 332, 335 (1944).

69. Because of space limitations and my own interests, I have not discussed debates within the board. The emphasis here is on the board's orders and their parallels in current law.

70. Levenstein, *Labor Today and Tomorrow*, p. 109; in re Fulton County Glove Industry, 4 WLR 307 (1942); Teller, "The War Labor Board," p. 322, n.11.

71. Mead Corp., 8 WLR 471, 474 (1943); Towne Robertson Nut Co., 3 WLR 40 (1942).

72. See, for example, Detroit Steel Products Co., 6 WLR 495 (1943).

73. Bethlehem Steel, 11 WLR 190, 196 (1943).

74. Riverside and Dan River Cotton Mills, Inc., 8 WLR 274 (1943); Western Union Telegraph Co., 6 WLR 133 (1943); Petroleum Specialties Co., 24 WLR 597 (1945) (the board refused the union request to remove a supervisor who had been convicted of assaulting employees). Subcontracting work generally was regarded as a managerial prerogative despite a union's claim that the company had used subcontracting in the past to evade contractual provisions and wage rates. Tinius Olsen Testing Machine Co., 11 WLR 301 (1943); Bethlehem Steel, 6 WLR 513 (1943). Yet, in one case, the board approved a clause restricting subcontracting until all employees

were fully employed and the full capacity of plants was utilized. Fulton County Glove Industry, 4 WLR 307 (1942).

75. Teller, "The War Labor Board," p. 329.

76. Ibid., p. 339; see also Bethlehem Steel, 11 WLR 190 (1943). Similarly, the hazardous nature of the work was used to deny arbitral jurisdiction over transfer and promotion grievances, suggesting some lack of faith in both arbitrators and unions. Atlas Powder Co., 5 WLR 371 (1942).

77. See Atleson, *Values and Assumptions*, pp. 122–23.

78. Teller, "The War Labor Board," pp. 348–49; Atleson, *Values and Assumptions*, Chap. 9.

79. D. Montgomery, *Workers Control in America* (Cambridge: Cambridge University Press, 1979).

80. Teller, "The War Labor Board," p. 349.

81. United Aircraft Corp., 18 WLR 9 (1944).

82. 379 U.S. 203 (1964).

83. "We are thus not expanding the scope of mandatory bargaining to hold, as we do now, that the type of contracting involved in this case — the replacement of employees in the existing bargaining unit with those of an independent contractor to do the same work under similar conditions of employment — is a statutory subject of collective bargaining under 8(d)." Ibid., p. 223.

84. 379 U.S. at 223 (J. Stewart concurring).

85. *First National Maintenance Corp.* v. *NLRB*, 452 U.S. 666 (1981).

86. Ibid., p. 676.

87. Strong pressures were applied to unions during both the mobilization period and the war to curb the rank and file and strikes in general. Indeed, proposals for outlawing strikes in defense plants were introduced as early as 1941. Seidman, *American Labor*, pp. 43–46. Chairman Hatton W. Sumners of the House Judiciary Committee suggested that, "If it is necessary to preserve this country, [the Committee] would not hesitate one split second to enact legislation to send them to the electric chair." *New York Times*, March 29, 1941.

Four days later, a bill was introduced to make strikes treasonable, providing for 25 years in prison as a minimum penalty and execution as the maximum sentence. Throughout the war period, unions would fear such legislation, and such fears would explain a good deal of their behavior.

The NWLB strongly criticized strikes as early as mid-1942, and public member Wayne L. Morse, especially upset over union jurisdictional conflicts, warned that the laws against treason would be applied to strikers in such disputes. In the 77th Congress alone, 21 bills were introduced dealing with wartime strikes, 3 of which sought to make strikes in defense plants treasonous and punishable by death. Employer groups, notably the National Association of Manufacturers, charged that strikes were damaging war production even though days lost to strikes were very few. It was the successive miners' strikes of 1943 that made that year so exceptional, strikes that led to the War Labor Disputes Act of 1943 and helped inflame public opinion against strikes. Seidman, *American Labor*, pp. 135–42; David Ziskind, "The Impact of the War on Labor Law," *Law & Contemporary Problems* 9 (1942): 385.

88. Alan Fox, *Beyond Contract: Work, Power and Trust Relations* (London: Faber, 1974), pp. 279–80.

89.   Stone, "The Post-War Paradigm," pp. 1544–58; Atleson, *Values and Assumptions*, Chap. 9.

90.   Thomas Kohler, "Models of Worker Participation: The Uncertain Significance of Section 8(a)(2)," *Boston College Law Review* 27 (1986): 519–27; Sanford M. Jacoby, *Employing Bureaucracy: Managers, Unions, and the Transformation of Work in American Industry, 1900–1945* (New York: Columbia University, 1985), pp. 187–89; Reinhard Bendix, *Work and Authority in Industry* (Berkeley: University of California Press, 1956).

91.   Office of Economic Research, New York Stock Exchange, *People & Productivity: A Challenge to Corporate America*, (November 1982); see Michael J. Piore and Charles F. Sabel, *The Second Industrial Divide* (New York: Basic Books, 1984), pp. 240–50.

3

The United Steelworkers of America and Health Insurance, 1937–62

Alan Derickson

The main terms and consequences of a far-reaching accord between industrial labor and oligopolistic capital following World War II are well-known. In a series of postwar battles with organized labor, corporate management repelled demands for greater industrial democracy by the Congress of Industrial Organizations (CIO) unions. Employers in basic industries successfully reasserted strong, often unilateral, rights to make decisions regarding production standards, technological change, investment strategy, and other important business matters. In return for abandoning their claims to participate in big decisions, unions accepted enhanced compensation as well as the promise of an added measure of employment security for their members. Managers strengthened their prerogatives; workers gained a higher standard of living.[1]

Nelson Lichtenstein and Beth Stevens have insightfully analyzed one particular facet of this settlement, the emergence of a "private welfare state" for employees in the core of the economy. Lichtenstein and Stevens describe the gradual expansion of benefit packages in the 1940s and 1950s to include retirement pensions, life and disability insurance, health protection, and supplemental unemployment compensation. Both scholars accurately identify fringe benefits as one sizable part of labor's consolation prize for exclusion from strategic decision making.[2]

However, the establishment of benefit programs through collective bargaining involved more than a straightforward transaction in which workers ceded claims to a shred of power in return for a measure of security. This case study of the steel industry shows that the health-insurance issue itself became the focus of a lengthy battle over decision-making prerogatives in the postwar years. For more than a decade after the war, the United Steelworkers of America (USW) repeatedly brought pressure for a more democratic approach to the governance of benefit programs. Management consistently opposed these attempts to bring a sort of codetermination to health-care financing.[3] Only in the early 1960s did the union finally resign itself to a small role in protecting its members' access to health services. In the preceding quarter century, however, hospital and medical insurance was the object of recurrent conflict.

Health-care financing came within the orbit of private negotiations only after the defeat of labor's legislative proposals in the 1930s and 1940s. Indeed, the majoritarian aims of the steelworkers' organization in this area crystallized through its participation in a frustrated campaign for protective legislation. Inclusion of a health-insurance section in a preliminary draft of the Social Security bill raised hopes in labor circles. After the deletion of this provision from the Social Security Act of 1935, unionists immediately set out to remedy this deficiency. At its first convention in December 1937, the Steel Workers Organizing Committee (SWOC) fell in line with the recently declared legislative objectives of the CIO. The organizing committee unanimously resolved to try to extend Social Security to both health expenses and loss of income during illness.[4] The SWOC convention made no mention of negotiating private group-insurance plans with employers.

The legislative drive began in earnest at a major conference in Washington in July 1938, sponsored by the Roosevelt administration's Interdepartmental Committee to Coordinate Health and Welfare Activities. The National Health Conference gave organized labor an unprecedented opportunity to take a larger part in shaping national policy on behalf of the uninsured masses.[5] Labor delegates fervently argued for government intervention in health-care financing. Florence Greenberg of the SWOC women's auxiliary attacked the medical establishment, the chief obstacle to progress. Countering the American Medical Association's (AMA) self-satisfied invitation to conference participants to visit its headquarters in Chicago to witness its good works, Greenberg offered to show conferees "a sick Chicago, a Chicago of dirt and filth and tenements." She traced some of the major health problems of her community back to the workplace, making a connection that the AMA and its corporate allies were loathe to admit: "No wonder pneumonia is so common around the steel mills, when the workers who sweat in the heat of the furnaces must rush out into the cold before they can cool off. If life were as important as high production and speed-up, perhaps the pneumonia rate could be reduced." She pointed out that the health status of African-American workers was "especially bad," noting that the prevalence of tuberculosis was six times higher among blacks than whites. Greenberg called for a health-insurance amendment to the Social Security statute. In the same vein, Lee Pressman, general counsel for both SWOC and the CIO, launched a scorching attack on "the upper hierarchy of these medical associations that simply refuses to give adequate health service to the people of this country" and reiterated the demand for a public insurance program. The SWOC, thus, helped to begin to recast the health-care debate in terms of progress toward a social-democratic entitlement to a necessity for survival, rather than in terms of the AMA's hallowed individual freedom of the physician to pursue his or her profession.[6]

This conference encouraged Senator Robert Wagner of New York to introduce the National Health Bill in February 1939. The bill proposed that, as with unemployment insurance, the federal government make grants to the states to establish insurance schemes. Labor supported this measure, despite fears as to the likely inadequacy of such programs in less-unionized states. Labor's misgivings and, more important, those of President Roosevelt doomed the Wagner bill in the face of opposition from health-care providers and business interests, and it died in committee. Undeterred, SWOC's convention of 1940 unanimously reaffirmed its demand for immediate adoption of federal health insurance for all U.S. residents.[7]

Interest in reform revived as postwar planning began. In June 1943, Senators Wagner and James Murray of Montana, along with Representative John Dingell of Michigan, put forward a purely federal, not federal-state, insurance plan. The United Steelworkers took an active part in the coalition of unionists, public-health professionals, social-welfare advocates, and other liberals who pressed for the Wagner-Murray-Dingell (W-M-D) bill. Steelworkers' vice-president Van Bittner chaired the CIO's Committee on Social Security, which helped to formulate the proposal. Secretary-treasurer David McDonald and lobbyist Robert Lamb also served on this committee. Once again, however, fear of the AMA kept Roosevelt at a distance, and the bill stalled.[8]

The campaign for national health insurance gained a key ally when Harry Truman assumed the presidency on Roosevelt's death on April 12, 1945. On November 19, 1945, Truman made a strong endorsement of health security as essential to his proposal for an economic bill of rights. In response, Wagner, Murray, and Dingell introduced a bill devoted solely to health reform, severing the issue from the movement for wholesale changes in the Social Security system. To ensure this plan's responsiveness to citizens' concerns, this version of W-M-D called for the establishment of a National Advisory Medical Policy Council, which would include representatives of the general public. In February 1946, the Committee for the Nation's Health formed to lobby for the national health plan. Philip Murray served as a vice-chairman of this advocacy group. To its many proponents, the long-awaited advance of social insurance seemed imminent in the aftermath of the war.[9]

The forces of reform could not overcome entrenched, increasingly ideological opposition, however. Senate conservatives, led by Robert Taft and Forrest Donnell, used the charge of "socialized medicine" and the immensity of this proposal to throw its proponents on the defensive. Even with presidential support and Democratic control of Congress, the movement of health legislation faltered yet again in the spring of 1946.[10]

World War II had opened unprecedented opportunities to obtain welfare benefits through the employment relationship. When federal authorities moved to control wage increases with the so-called Little Steel formula, employers and unions in industries beset by labor shortages sought innovative ways to enhance compensation.[11] The Steelworkers frequently brought the insurance question into negotiations. At Timken Roller Bearing, the USW won the incorporation of company-paid hospital benefits into the collective bargaining agreement, beginning in March 1944. The vast majority of steelmakers, however, would not go this far. They preferred to expand unilaterally their own welfare pro-grams, without recourse to the collective bargaining process. The National War Labor Board encouraged but refused to compel manage-ment to bargain formally over this subject.[12]

Convening only two weeks after the disastrous elections in which the Republicans took control of both houses of Congress, the CIO adjusted to changed political conditions in November 1946. After perfunctory endorsement of the W-M-D bill, the CIO convention took up a resolution that called for vigorous efforts to negotiate health-insurance and income maintenance benefits. David McDonald joined the discussion to express the Steelworkers' impatience with the legislative failures since 1939. McDonald stated that his organization was "not going to wait for perhaps another ten years before the Social Security laws are amended adequately." The privatization resolution passed without controversy.[13]

More than any other union, the United Mine Workers of America (UMW) showed the Steelworkers the way to privatization. In the spring of 1946, John L. Lewis had finally responded to rank-and-file frustration with the "company doctor" system. Under the program inaugurated in the bituminous industry in 1946, payroll deductions went, not to company doctors, but, rather, to a UMW-controlled fund. The following year, the union went further, winning a jointly governed welfare and retirement program endowed by a royalty on each ton of coal extracted. The miners' fund undertook a thoroughgoing effort to restructure health services across the Appalachian mining region. Unequivocally reorienting its health policy, the UMW withdrew its support for national health insurance.[14]

In response to both the precedent set by their sponsors in the mining union and to its failure in the legislative arena, the USW also sought privatization during the late 1940s. However, unlike the UMW, the USW pursued an ambivalent strategy. Throughout the postwar decade, the steel union maintained its support for protective legislation. The organization assumed that national health insurance would eventually be added to the Social Security Act and continued to work to hasten that development.[15] In 1950, the USW was one of the unions that stepped forward to donate enough money to avert the collapse of the committee for the Nation's Health, the stalwart advocates for insurance legislation. The Steelworkers and their allies kept the committee alive for several more years, despite the bleak prospects for reform.[16]

At the same time, however, the USW increasingly devoted its energies to negotiating private plans. As always, the immediate difficulties confronting workers justified opportunism. Philip Murray unapologetically explained his pragmatic priorities in 1948: "[W]e should energetically apply ourselves to the task of securing under existing circumstances the best kind of agreements obtainable, so that our people may be provided a measure of relief, particularly in the field of social insurance and pensions." In some negotiations, the USW sought to win health insurance where no such benefits existed. In many other cases, however, the union set out to alter the coverage, financing, and administration of preexisting benefit plans.[17]

Products of welfare capitalist solicitude, the first health insurance schemes in steel mills were generally funded by employee payroll deductions and controlled by management-sponsored benefit associations. Indeed, the provision of health insurance benefits fit naturally within a longstanding paternalistic tradition in the industry. A number of steel makers set up sick benefit clubs to administer income-maintenance indemnities around the turn of the century. In the same vein, in 1902, American Steel and Wire Company began to give pensions to retired employees. The establishment of the Carnegie Relief Fund in 1910 consolidated the extensive welfare activities at U.S. Steel, which came to encompass not only retirement pensions and disability insurance but also death benefits and, in some locations, direct delivery of health care at company-built hospitals. By the 1930s, many firms began to offer Blue Cross or other group hospitalization plans. Of 244 iron and steel companies that responded to a survey by the National Industrial Conference Board in 1939, 72 had hospital insurance benefits for their workers. Clearly, the tradition of corporate welfarism in steel survived the Great Depression.[18]

During the war, a growing number of steel makers began to insure hospital and surgical services. By mid-1947, more than half the employees in basic steel already had employment-based hospital insurance; more than one-third had coverage for inpatient surgical procedures. The widespread prevalence of this group insurance helps to explain some of the managerial intransigence in negotiations at this time. Employers believed that their charitable initiatives were being unappreciatively rebuffed and that the union was trying to take credit for solving a problem that they had already taken care of.[19]

Of course, steelworkers and their leaders saw the matter differently. Many distrusted the paternalistic approach. The plan at Bethlehem Steel, according to union consultant Murray Latimer, "had come to be identified in the minds of employees as part of the old company-union apparatus." USW Local 1913 ungratefully observed that firms had "offered, established, or arbitrarily forced various types and plans of hospitalization, life insurance, and disability insurances upon their employees." Resentful of such an imposition, this Pittsburgh local told the USW convention of 1944 that collective bargaining, not managerial fiat, should determine insurance arrangements. Clearly, the issue at stake was not provision of insurance per se but, rather, control over the benefit plan.[20] Indeed, where the USW dealt with firms whose welfare measures left employees paying most or all of the costs of benefits over which they had little or no control, issues of governance and redistribution of the financial burden were bound to arise.

As they had during the war, steel makers resisted demands to bargain over health insurance. Many firms owned extensive coal-mining operations and, thus, were already suffering the UMW's intrusions into benefits management. In addition, at its general meeting in 1946, the American Iron and Steel Institute had received a blunt warning from economist Leo Wolman about the development of labor-management programs. "Joint operation," Wolman advised, "very swiftly deteriorates, degenerates into operation of these welfare funds by the unions." The USW was forced to file unfair labor practice charges with the National Labor Relations Board against W. W. Cross and Company for refusing to discuss welfare issues. In 1949, the Federal judiciary upheld the board's decision that the National Labor Relations Act obliged employers to negotiate in good faith over health and welfare programs.[21]

The union did not wait passively for a judicial mandate. By June 1948, it had signed over 300 bargaining agreements with some provision for health or welfare, covering 137,685 workers. The following month, the international office sent its district directors a model contract provision. This provision called for joint labor-management trust funds to design and run benefit plans, a reflection of the influence of the UMW example and of the approach taken by other industrial unions.[22]

The USW also actively sought to promote an alternative to commercial insurance carriers. Compared to conventional profit-making corporations, the nonprofit community-based Blue Cross and Blue Shield plans looked quite attractive. Even as in May 1948 the union and its allies maneuvered to push the National Health Assembly toward endorsement of the W-M-D bill, USW research director Otis Brubaker met with Blue Cross-Blue Shield chief executive Paul Hawley to seek standardized benefits under agreements for firms operating on a national basis. Brubaker reported to Philip Murray that Hawley had assured him that "Blue Cross would do all possible to force the issue of a uniform national plan as quickly as possible."[23]

Thus prepared, the Steelworkers waged a major battle for insurance and pensions in the basic steel industry in 1949. The USW demanded more extensive health protection, including a national Blue Cross plan. It sought a role in administering benefits. In addition, it demanded that the steel corporations assume all costs of this program. The employers adamantly rejected these proposals. The parties' strong, diametrically opposed positions predisposed against any difference-splitting compromise: labor wanted to help oversee a program paid for entirely by management; management wanted workers to help pay for a plan over which they were to have no influence. On July 12, Murray dismissed out of hand U.S. Steel's offer: "[A]lthough the employees would be forced to contribute to the cost of this insurance, the plan would be administered solely by the Corporation. No self-respecting union could accept such a proposal." Not surprisingly, negotiations broke off at this time, and the union got ready to strike.[24]

Fearing disruption of the national economy, the Truman administration entered the dispute in August 1949. The USW welcomed the appointment of the Steel Industry Board and agreed not to suspend work while the government investigated the issues and recommended a settlement. "We will no longer tolerate the double standard whereby machines are preferred over men," Philip Murray told the board. "Every well-operated company sets aside money for depreciation, repair, and replacement of machinery." Steel management, for its part, dwelt on the insidious effects of noncontributory insurance on the moral character of employees, who might lose all vestiges of self-reliance and self-respect. Howard Holtzmann of Colorado Fuel and Iron considered joint financing "[t]he only way that needed security can be provided, without destroying the fabric of our society." This plea fell on deaf ears. On September 10, 1949, the fact-finding panel suggested that employers pay the full expenses of both pensions and health insurance. The steel makers refused these terms. U.S. Steel president Benjamin Fairless denounced noncontributory insurance as "a revolutionary doctrine of far-reaching and serious consequences to the whole nation." An industry-wide stoppage by 500,000 workers began on October 1.[25]

After lengthy negotiations, the union reached a compromise settlement with Bethlehem Steel Company on October 31, 1949. This agreement set a pattern that the other major firms in this oligopolistic industry soon accepted. (Indeed, here and throughout the subsequent quarter century, the centralization of bargaining did much to facilitate the privatization of health security and related welfare questions.) The contract called for the employer to bear the full expense of pensions but for the financial obligation for health, disability, and life insurance to be split evenly with employees. It left the precise composition of the health benefits and the mechanics of their administration for labor and management to determine jointly; control of the program was no longer solely within the purview of management's prerogatives. Within a few months, the union and the steel industry worked out the first nationwide Blue Cross hospitalization contract. A similar plan for surgical insurance through Blue Shield soon followed.[26]

This settlement had an impact well beyond the steel industry. Other unions naturally followed where such moderate, replicable concessions led. For example, by mid-1950, the UAW had secured from the three leading automakers hospital and surgical programs in which the employee and the employer each paid half of the insurance premium.[27]

Despite the opening they had made in the 1949 round of bargaining, the Steelworkers made little headway toward control over their health programs in the decade that followed. Certainly, some rank-and-file activists were ready to take on more responsibility in managing benefits. Local 1104 proposed in 1950 that "hospitalization boards be set up in each local union . . . [with] costs borne by Blue Cross." Pursuing this interest, the international union convention in 1952 called on local branches to "participate fully in community health activities by pressing for representation on the governing boards of voluntary health insurance plans and of hospitals." To be sure, union representatives did gain seats on the boards of some units of the Blues as a result of this initiative, but only a few. All efforts at the community level faced an uphill battle, given that the 1949 agreement had not established any permanent structure, such as a joint labor-management trust, through which the USW could routinely take part in benefits decision making. Blue Cross and Blue Shield entered into insurance policies with steel management only. Creation of long-term national contracts made the insurers even less responsive to the concerns of rank-and-file workers and their families. Centralized bargaining chilled the potential to handle insurance problems — nonpayment of claims, the eligibility of employees and their dependents, poor quality of care, limitations in coverage — on a local basis.[28]

Plainly, the structure of bargaining necessitated that the USW gain input at the top as well as at the community level. In the 1953 wage reopener, the Steelworkers got employers to accede to a joint study of insurance problems. Based on this study, the union won some substantive improvements the following year, the most important of which was the extension of hospital coverage from 70 to 120 days. In addition, the 1954 agreement called for the establishment at each firm of a joint committee on insurance, half of whose members would be chosen by the USW. The pattern-setting provision at U.S. Steel promised that the committee would receive a quarterly financial report and "such additional information as shall be reasonably required for the purpose of enabling it to be properly informed concerning the operation of the insurance program." This advance brought the union to the threshold of health-benefit governance but did not grant it any affirmative policy-making role during the term of the contract.[29] Nonetheless, merely by gaining the right to examine periodically some financial data, the USW became more involved in the governance of its health plans than did most other industrial unions. In the majority of plans outside the steel industry, workers still commonly incurred payroll deductions that paid a portion of insurance premiums, but neither they nor their representatives received any information on the disposition of these often-substantial contributions.[30]

At this point, the Steelworkers' leadership viewed with some wariness any role larger than oversight. Lurid revelations of union corruption arising from the Senate investigation of jointly trusteed benefit funds gave the USW ample reason to let management alone handle insurance money. Accordingly, the right to knowledge won in 1954 was not immediately used as a lever to pry loose a right to act to influence the limits, quality, and implementation of health protection. The 1956 bargaining agreement made clear that insurance plans were to be "administered by the company or through arrangements provided by it." Moreover, the contract barred the union from using the grievance procedure to settle benefit claims disputes. At this juncture, the union did, however, strengthen its position in a somewhat safer province of policy making by clarifying its right to help select insurance carriers and to veto unacceptable options.[31]

Just when it appeared that the Steelworkers were settling into a relatively marginal role in handling benefit matters, a new set of forces drew the organization back toward assuming fuller responsibility. As the 1950s wore on, the honeymoon with the Blues ended. Disenchantment grew as the middlemen continually raised premium rates while resisting coverage of outpatient and preventive services. With much exasperation, John Tomayko, head of the union's insurance and pension department, warned a national Blue Cross-Blue Shield conference in 1957 of a "tremendous groundswell of resentment" against increasingly expensive programs that remained riddled with loopholes. Tomayko criticized Blue Shield's failure to give labor adequate representation on its boards of directors. The USW benefits specialist threatened that the union was giving "serious study and consideration" to setting up its own health plans.[32]

Invidious comparisons with the experiments of other labor groups also contributed to a desire for reform. The UMW Welfare and Retirement Fund launched several prepaid group medical practice plans, beginning in the early 1950s. These plans, forerunners of today's health maintenance organizations, delivered comprehensive services, including preventive measures like periodic examinations and immunizations, while restraining unnecessary utilization, especially in appropriate surgery and other expensive hospital-based procedures. At group-practice institutions like the Russellton Miners' Clinic, situated in the Pittsburgh metropolitan area, a commitment to democratic governance included substantial representation of mine workers on the board of directors. Moreover, the flourishing Kaiser Permanente Health Plan, patronized by a number of USW locals on the West Coast, offered another variation in cutting-edge reform. Beside such bold structural innovations, the attractiveness of mere insurance through the Blues paled.[33]

Discontent and awareness of viable options led to plans to explore sweeping changes in the delivery, not just the financing, of health services. The Steelworkers convention of 1958 resolved to "examine the possibility of establishing our own hospitals, clinics, diagnostic centers, rest homes, rehabilitation centers, nursing homes, and the development of fully prepaid medical care plans utilizing group practice medicine." Following through on this decision, the union's staff, along with consultant I. S. Falk, conducted a thorough study of existing benefits and the alternatives to them.[34]

In the 1959 basic steel negotiations, the USW demanded that the parties "jointly develop a program for providing suitable facilities and arrangements" where existing medical programs were deemed inadequate. Predictably, management rejected the idea. Health-benefit reform was but one of several issues still in dispute when the union stopped work on July 15, 1959. The matter remained unresolved five months later when Falk declared before the Industrial Relations Research Association that labor "insists on an equal role with management in the planning and design of its health insurance and in the policy control of its administration." Finally, after 42 million worker days of strike activity and much federal mediation, the parties came to an agreement. The strike settlement announced on January 4, 1960, contained no commitment to embark on any experiment in caring for steelworkers' illnesses and injuries. Instead, the contract referred the question to the newly created Human Relations Research Committee.[35]

The human relations group did not serve as midwife to any bold ventures in codetermination of health security for steelworkers. Two years later, the radical notion of delivering health care either through the union or through a collaborative project was quietly dropped, because of the unwavering opposition of management representatives on the committee. Hence, the union's role in benefits administration remained a small one, largely confined to analyzing periodic reports from Blue Cross and Blue Shield on their soaring remuneration of hospitals and doctors.[36] Only in Sault Sainte Marie, Ontario, did the Steelworkers go ahead to found and operate its own prepaid group practice plan. Established in 1963 under the auspices of five USW locals, the Group Health

Center made available comprehensive health services to several thousand union members and their families.[37]

Instead of the sort of control it enjoyed in Sault Sainte Marie, the steel union generally negotiated improved insurance coverage under conventional arrangements during the 1950s and 1960s. USW representatives gradually won coverage of a wider range of services, benefits for workers' dependents, and a curtailment of employee financial contributions. The organization could boast in 1960 that 99 percent of its 1.1 million members had hospitalization benefits and that 98 percent had some surgical coverage. In addition, by the early 1960s, the USW had reached the objective of comprehensive benefits, fully financed by employers, for a substantial share of its members.[38] These advances contrasted sharply with the situation of unorganized workers on the periphery of the economy, who still had minimal protection or none at all.[39] The USW, thus, succeeded to a great extent in delivering health security for its members.

On the other hand, steel management ultimately won the 20-year battle for control over health benefits. To be sure, the virtually unmitigated paternalism of early twentieth-century welfare capitalism did not return. Obviously, organized labor did help to shape health programs in the steel industry in significant ways, but it is also clear that by the mid-1960s, the Steelworkers had been forced into a circumscribed role that largely left to management the construction and supervision of insurance plans. In health affairs, as in many other areas of postwar industrial relations, employers contained union power within quite narrow bounds.

NOTES

1.   Howell John Harris, *The Right to Manage: Industrial Relations Policies of American Business in the 1940s* (Madison: University of Wisconsin Press, 1982); Nelson Lichtenstein, "From Corporatism to Collective Bargaining: Organized Labor and the Eclipse of Social Democracy in the Postwar Era," in *The Rise and Fall of the New Deal Order, 1930—1980*, eds. Steve Fraser and Gary Gerstle (Princeton, N.J.: Princeton University Press, 1989), pp. 122–52; David Brody, *Workers in Industrial America: Essays on the Twentieth Century Struggle* (New York: Oxford University Press, 1980), pp. 173–214; Robert H. Zieger, *American Workers, American Unions, 1920–1985* (Baltimore, Md.: Johns Hopkins University Press, 1986), pp. 147–58. On the Steelworkers' ill-fated ambitious plans for taking a larger role in shaping their industry, see Clinton S. Golden and Harold J. Ruttenberg, *The Dynamics of Industrial Democracy* (New York: Harper & Brothers, 1942). On the narrow role left to the USW by the postwar accord, see John P. Hoerr, *And the Wolf Finally Came: The Decline of the American Steel Industry* (Pittsburgh, Pa.: University of Pittsburgh Press, 1988), pp. 278–88 and passim.

2. Nelson Lichtenstein, "Labor in the Truman Era: Origins of the 'Private Welfare State,'" in *The Truman Presidency*, ed. Michael J. Lacey (Cambridge: Cambridge University Press, 1989), pp. 128–55, esp. 139–40, 151–54; Beth Stevens, "Labor Unions, Employee Benefits, and the Privatization of the American Welfare State," *Journal of Policy History* 2 (1990): 233–60, esp. 244–46; Beth Stevens, "Blurring the Boundaries: How the Federal Government Has Influenced Welfare Benefits in the Private Sector," in *The Politics of Social Policy in the United States*, eds. Margaret Weir, Ann Shola Orloff, and Theda Skocpol (Princeton, N.J.: Princeton University Press, 1988), pp. 123–48, esp. 144, 146.

3. Cf. Raymond Munts, *Bargaining for Health: Labor Unions, Health Insurance, and Medical Care* (Madison: University of Wisconsin Press, 1967), pp. 53–67.

4. Steel Workers Organizing Committee, *First Wage and Policy Convention, 1937* (n.p., n.d.), pp. 108 (quotation), 40–41, 68.

5. U.S., Interdepartmental Committee to Coordinate Health and Welfare Activities, *Proceedings of the National Health Conference* (Washington, D.C.: Government Printing Office, 1938), pp. 14, 159–62; Josephine Roche, "The Worker's Stake in a National Health Program," *American Labor Legislation Review* 28 (September 1938): 125.

6. Interdepartmental Committee, *National Health Conference*, pp. 84 (Greenberg quotations), 106 (Pressman quotation), 84–85, 105–7.

7. Robert F. Wagner, "The National Health Bill," *American Labor Legislation Review* 29 (March 1939): 13–17; J. Joseph Huthmacher, *Senator Robert F. Wagner and the Rise of Urban Liberalism* (New York: Atheneum, 1968), pp. 263–64; U.S., Senate, Committee on Education and Labor, *To Establish a National Health Program: Hearings before the subcommittee of the Committee on Education and Labor on S. 1620*, 76th Cong., 1st Sess. (Washington, D.C.: Government Printing Office, 1939), esp. pp. 205–13; Michael M. Davis, *Medical Care for Tomorrow* (New York: Harper & Brothers, 1955), p. 279; Daniel S. Hirshfield, *The Lost Reform: The Campaign for Compulsory Health Insurance in the United States from 1932 to 1943* (Cambridge, Mass.: Harvard University Press, 1970), pp. 151–53; Steel Workers Organizing Committee, *Proceedings of the Second International Wage and Policy Convention, 1940* (n.p., n.d.), p. 178.

8. Monte M. Poen, *Harry S Truman versus the Medical Lobby: The Genesis of Medicare* (Columbia: University of Missouri Press, 1979), pp. 29–34; Philip Murray to Robert F. Wagner, May 15, 1943, Isidore S. Falk Papers (Manuscripts and Archives Department, Sterling Memorial Library, Yale University, New Haven, Conn.), folder 525; United Steelworkers of America, *Proceedings of the Second Constitutional Convention, 1944*, 2 vols. (n.p., n.d.), Vol. 1, pp. 61–62, 105, 150; Congress of Industrial Organizations, *Final Proceedings of the Sixth Constitutional Convention, 1943* (Washington, D.C.: Congress of Industrial Organizations, n.d.), pp. 85–86, 180–81; David J. McDonald, "Discussion of a National Social Security Program," January 14, 1944, David J. McDonald Papers (United Steelworkers of America Archives, Historical Collections and Labor Archives, Pennsylvania State University, University Park [hereafter cited as USW Archives]), box 1, folder 23; "Social Security Conference," February 5, 1944, Wilbur J. Cohen Papers (Archives Division, State Historical Society of Wisconsin, Madison), box 53, folder 4; Van A. Bittner to Robert F. Wagner, April 26, 1945, Wilbur J. Cohen Papers, box 27, folder 1.

9.   Harry S Truman, "A National Health Program: Message from the President," November 19, 1945, reprinted in *Social Security Bulletin* 8 (December 1945): 7–12; U.S., Senate, Committee on Education and Labor, *National Health Program: Hearings before the subcommittee of the Committee on Education and Labor on S. 1606*, 79th Cong., 2d Sess. (Washington, D.C.: Government Printing Office, 1946), p. 21; Katherine P. Ellickson to I. S. Falk, March 11, 1946, RG 47: Records of the Social Security Administration (National Archives, Washington, D.C.), Division of Research and Statistics, General Correspondence, 1946–50, box 30, folder 22; Michael M. Davis, "Report of the President," May 9, 1947, Michael M. Davis Papers (New York Academy of Medicine, New York), drawer J-2; Poen, *Truman versus Medical Lobby*, pp. 51–53, 83–84.

10.   U.S. Senate, *National Health Program*, passim, esp. pp. 47–52, 474–84, 1520–50; United Steelworkers of America, *Proceedings of the Third Constitutional Convention, 1946* (n.p., n.d.), pp. 52–53, 98, 188–90.

11.   Florence Peterson, Everett Kassalow, and Jean Nelson, "Health-Benefit Programs Established through Collective Bargaining," *Monthly Labor Review* 61 (August 1945): 191–209; Lacy M. Kramer, "Collective-Bargaining Developments in Health and Welfare Plans," *Monthly Labor Review* 64 (February 1947): 191–93.

12.   Timken Roller Bearing Company and United Steelworkers of America, *1946 Agreement* (n.p., n.d.), p. 34; United Steelworkers of America, *National War Labor Board Case No. 111-6230-D 14-1, In re United Steelworkers and United States Steel Corp et al: Brief Submitted by the United Steelworkers of America* (Washington, D.C.: n.p., 1944), pp. 1–3, 113, 118; *Steel Labor*, December 1944, p. 3; U.S. Senate, Committee on Labor and Public Welfare, *Welfare and Pension Plans Investigation: Final Report*, 84th Cong., 2d Sess. (Washington, D.C.: Government Printing Office, 1956), p. 89.

13.   Congress of Industrial Organizations, *Final Proceedings of the Eighth Constitutional Convention, 1946* (Washington, D.C.: Congress of Industrial Organizations, n.d.), pp. 186 (McDonald quotation), 181–88.

14.   U.S., Coal Mines Administration, *A Medical Survey of the Bituminous-Coal Industry* (Washington, D.C.: Government Printing Office, 1947), pp. 65–193, 224–27; Alan Derickson, "Part of the Yellow Dog? U.S. Coal Miners' Opposition to the Company Doctor System, 1936–1946," *International Journal of Health Services* 19 (1989): 709–20; United Mine Workers of America and U.S. Coal Mines Administrator, *National Bituminous Wage Agreement, Effective May 29, 1946* (Washington, D.C.: United Mine Workers of America, 1946), pp. 2–3; United Mine Workers of America and Operators, *National Bituminous Coal Wage Agreement of 1947* (Washington, D.C.: United Mine Workers of America, 1947), pp. 3–5; Janet E. Ploss, "A History of the Medical Care Program of the United Mine Workers of America Welfare and Retirement Fund" (Master's thesis, Johns Hopkins University, 1981); Edward Berkowitz and Kim McQuaid, *Creating the Welfare State: The Political Economy of Twentieth-Century Reform*, 2d ed. (New York: Praeger, 1988), p. 167.

15.   United Steelworkers of America, *Proceedings of the Fourth Constitutional Convention, 1948* (n.p., n.d.), pp. 157, 167; *Steel Labor*, May 1950, p. 11; United Steelworkers of America, *Proceedings of the Fifth Constitutional Convention, 1950*, (n.p., n.d.), pp. 212–13; United Steelworkers of America, *Proceedings of the Sixth Constitutional Convention, 1952* (n.p., n.d.), pp. 229–32; United Steelworkers of America, *Proceedings of the Seventh Constitutional Convention, 1954* (n.p., n.d.),

pp. 142, 148; United Steelworkers of America, *Proceedings of the Eighth Constitutional Convention, 1956* (n.p., n.d.), p. 265. For a longer discussion of the ongoing tension within labor between privatization and legislation during this period, see Alan Derickson, "Health Security for All?: Social Unionism and Universal Health Insurance, 1935–1958," *Journal of American History* 80 (March 1994): 1333–56.

16.   Executive Committee, Committee for the National Health, "Minutes," June 15, 1950, Davis Papers, drawer J-2; Congress of Industrial Organizations, *Proceedings of the Sixteenth Constitutional Convention, 1954* (Washington, D.C.: Congress of Industrial Organizations, n.d.), p. 295.

17.   *Steel Labor*, June 1948, p. 4. (Murray quotation); International Executive Board, United Steelworkers of America, "Proceedings," December 17, 1946, pp. 25, 30, United Steelworkers of America International Executive Board Records, USW Archives, box 42, folder 13; Evan K. Rowe and Abraham Weiss, "Benefit Plans under Collective Bargaining," *Monthly Labor Review* 67 (September 1948): 233.

18.   David Brody, *Steelworkers in America: The Nonunion Era* (New York: Harper Torchbooks, 1969), pp. 89–93, 167–69; Stuart D. Brandes, *American Welfare Capitalism, 1880–1940* (Chicago: University of Chicago Press, 1976), pp. 28–29, 93, 100, 114; National Industrial Conference Board, *Personnel Activities in American Business* (New York: The Board, 1940), p. 24; Lawrence S. Root, *Fringe Benefits: Social Insurance in the Steel Industry* (Beverly Hills, Calif.: Sage, 1982), pp. 44–45; *Conference Board Management Record*, January 1940, p. 9.

19.   Joint Fact Finding Committee on Insurance, "Report," March 1, 1948, pp. 1, 5, 48, 59, McDonald Papers, box 134, folder 14; U.S. Senate, Committee on Labor and Public Welfare, Subcommittee on Welfare and Pension Funds, *Welfare and Pension Plans Investigation: Final Report*, 84th Cong., 2d Sess. (Washington, D.C.: Government Printing Office, 1956), p. 88; U.S. Steel Industry Board, *Company Testimony before Presidential Factfinding Board, Steel Industry Case, August 1949*, 5 vols. (New York: American Iron and Steel Institute, 1950), Vol. 1, pp. 128–33; Vol. 3, pp. 1474–75.

20.   Murray Latimer, "Instructions Relating to Social Insurance Fact Finding," p. 8, November 14, 1949, McDonald Papers, box 68, folder 17; United Steelworkers of America, *Proceedings, 1944*, Vol. 2, p. 70 (Local 1913 quotation); United Steelworkers of America, *Proceedings, 1946*, pp. 197–99, 201–3.

21.   Leo Wolman, "The Conditions of Labor Peace," *Yearbook of the American Iron and Steel Institute, 1946* (New York: The Institute, 1946), pp. 42 (quotation), 41–42; *Conference Board Management Record*, March 1947, p. 57; Rowe and Weiss, "Benefit Plans," p. 234; A. Norman Somers and Louis Schwartz, "Pension and Welfare Plans: Gratuities or Compensation?" *Industrial and Labor Relations Review* 4 (October 1950): 77–88.

22.   Research Department, United Steelworkers of America, "Health, Welfare, Insurance and Pension Plans under Collective Bargaining," June 3, 1948, USW Archives, box 65, folder 10; United Steelworkers of America, *Insurance Plan Documents, July 7, 1948* (Pittsburgh, Pa.: United Steelworkers of America, 1948); Rowe and Weiss, "Benefit Plans," p. 233; Nathaniel M. Minkoff, "Trade-Union Welfare Programs," *Monthly Labor Review* 64 (February 1947): 206–11.

23.   Otis Brubaker to Philip Murray, May 19, 1948, USW Archives, box 65, folder 8; Brubaker to Murray, May 21, 1948, USW Archives, box 65, folder 8; *New York Times*, June 1, 1948, p. 26.

24. Philip Murray, "Report," July 12, 1949, USW Archives, box 36, folder 3; John A. Stephens to Murray, July 6, 1949, USW Archives, box 36, folder 3; United Steelworkers of America, "1949 Wage Policy," May 5, 1949, USW Archives, box 36, folder 2; *Steel Labor*, May 1949, pp. 3–4; U.S. Steel Industry Board, *Report to the President of the United States on the Labor Dispute in the Basic Steel Industry* (Washington, D.C.: Government Printing Office, 1949), pp. 56–60.

25. Philip Murray, *The Steelworkers' Case for Wages, Pensions, and Social Insurance as Presented to President Truman's Steel Industry Board* (Pittsburgh, Pa.: United Steelworkers of America, 1949), pp. 20 (quotation), 18–23; Steel Industry Board, *Company Testimony*, Vol. 1, p. 561 (Holtzmann quotation), pp. 559–69, 805, Vol. 3, pp. 1476–80, Vol. 4, pp. 2014–20; A. H. Raskin, "U.S. Steel Rejects Findings of President's Fact Board as 'Revolutionary Doctrine,'" *New York Times*, September 15, 1949, pp. 1 (Fairless quotation), 23; *Steel Labor*, September 1949, pp. 1–2; Frederick H. Harbison and Robert C. Spencer, "The Politics of Collective Bargaining: The Postwar Record in Steel," *American Political Science Review* 48 (September 1954): 709; Steel Industry Board, *Report*, pp. 63, 65–69.

26. *Steel Labor*, December 1949, p. 2; *Steel Labor*, February 1950, pp. 1–2; Latimer, "Instructions," pp. 1–8, 123–24, 139–43; Benjamin F. Fairless, "Statement," November 11, 1949, USW Archives, box 5, folder 19; Carnegie-Illinois Steel Corporation and United Steelworkers of America, *Insurance and Pension Agreement* (Pittsburgh, Pa.: n.p., 1949); Manuel Eber and Thomas H. Paine, "Health and Welfare Plans in the Basic Steel Industry," *Monthly Labor Review* 73 (October 1951): 447–51; George Seltzer, "Pattern Bargaining and the United Steelworkers," *Journal of Political Economy* 59 (August 1951): 319–31, esp. 321; Robert Tilove, *Collective Bargaining in the Steel Industry* (Philadelphia: University of Pennsylvania Press, 1948), pp. 2–3.

27. David J. McDonald, *Union Man* (New York: E. P. Dutton, 1969), p. 209; Evan K. Rowe, "Health and Welfare Plans in the Automobile Industry," *Monthly Labor Review* 73 (September 1951): 277–82; Evan K. Rowe, "Employee-Benefit Plans under Collective Bargaining, Mid-1950," *Monthly Labor Review* 72 (February 1951): 156–62, esp. 156.

28. Paul Schremp and Frank J. Horvath, "Resolution on Contract Changes," August 7, 1950, USW Archives, box 36, folder 1; United Steelworkers of America, *Proceedings, 1952*, pp. 230 (quotation), 232; *Steel Labor*, May 1953, p. 5. For a case in which local unions built and governed their own hospitals, see Alan Derickson, *Workers' Health, Workers' Democracy: The Western Miners' Struggle, 1891–1925* (Ithaca, N.Y.: Cornell University Press, 1988), pp. 86–154.

29. United Steelworkers of America and U.S. Steel, *Pension and Insurance Agreements* (Pittsburgh, Pa.: n.p., 1954), p. 15; United Steelworkers of America, *Proceedings, 1954*, pp. 186–88; U.S. Department of Labor, E. Robert Livernash, *Collective Bargaining in the Basic Steel Industry: A Study of the Public Interest and the Role of Government* (Washington, D.C.: Government Printing Office, 1961), pp. 98, 285, 287.

30. U.S. Senate, *Welfare and Pension Investigation*, pp. 3, 14, 91, 94, 101–3, 126, 135–36; Sylvia A. Law, *Blue Cross: What Went Wrong?* (New Haven, Conn.: Yale University Press, 1974), pp. 29–30, 178.

31. United Steelworkers of America and U.S. Steel, *Insurance Agreement* (Pittsburgh, Pa.: n.p., 1956), pp. 8 (quotation), 11; *Steel Labor*, June 1955, p. 12; U.S. Senate, *Welfare and Pension Investigation*, pp. 91–96.

32. *Steel Labor*, May 1957, p. 15 (Tomayko quotations); *Steel Labor*, November 1958, p. 3. United Steelworkers of America, *Proceedings of the Ninth Constitutional Convention, 1958* (n.p., n.d.), pp. 425, 433–34. For the same frustrations among unionists in New York City, see Gerald Markowitz and David Rosner, "Seeking Common Ground: A History of Labor and Blue Cross," *Journal of Health Politics, Policy and Law* 16 (Winter 1991): 707–13.

33. Leslie A. Falk, "Group Health Plans in Coal Mining Communities," *Journal of Health and Human Behavior* 4 (Spring 1963): 4–13; *Steel Labor*, November 1958, p. 3; Daniel Fine, interview with author, February 18, 1992, New Kensington, Pennsylvania (tape in author's possession); Rickey Hendricks, *A Model for National Health Care: The History of Kaiser Permanente* (New Brunswick, N.J.: Rutgers University Press, 1993), pp. 68, 94, 148.

34. United Steelworkers of America, *Proceedings, 1958*, pp. 425 (quotation), 434; Allen N. Koplin to I. S. Falk, October 22, 1958, Falk Papers, box 103, folder 1197; Daniel G. Wray to Falk, February 19, 1959, Falk Papers, box 107, folder 1264; United Steelworkers of America, Insurance, Pension and Unemployment Benefits Department, *Special Study on the Medical Care Program for Steelworkers and Their Families: A Report* (n.p.: United Steelworkers of America, 1960); I. S. Falk and Joseph J. Senturia, "The Steelworkers Survey Their Health Services: A Preliminary Report," *American Journal of Public Health* 51 (January 1961): 11–17.

35. United Steelworkers of America, International Wage Policy Committee, "Proceedings," Vol. 44, pp. 149 (quotation), 148ff, May 1, 1959, USW Archives; I. S. Falk, "A Formulation of Labor's Views," *Proceedings of the Twelfth Annual Meeting of the Industrial Relations Research Association, 1959* (Madison, Wis.: The Association, 1960), pp. 65 (quotation), 56–69; United Steelworkers of America, Benefits Department, *Special Study*, passim, esp. pp. 8–9; Department of Labor, *Bargaining in Basic Steel*, pp. 300–7; U.S. Steel Corporation and United Steelworkers of America, *Insurance Agreement* (Pittsburgh, Pa.: n.p., 1960), pp. 7–8.

36. I. S. Falk to Arthur J. Altmeyer, November 14, 1960, Falk Papers, box 103, folder 1188; Medical Care Subcommittee, Human Relations Research Committee, "Insurance and Medical Care Problems," p. 24, January 22, 1962, USW Archives, box 66, folder 22; David J. McDonald, "Human Relations Committee," June 12, 1962, USW Archives, box 66, folder 22.

37. *Steel Labor*, November 1963, p. 20; *Steel Labor*, January 1967, p. 4; I. S. Falk, "Medical Care: Its Social and Organizational Aspects," *New England Journal of Medicine* 270 (January 2, 1964): 25.

38. United Steelworkers of America and U.S. Steel, *Insurance Agreement, 1960*; U.S. Bureau of Labor Statistics, *Wage Chronology: United States Steel Corporation and United Steelworkers of America (AFL-CIO), March 1937–1974*, Bulletin 1814 (Washington, D.C.: Government Printing Office, 1974), pp. 47–57; United Steelworkers of America, Benefits Department, *Special Study*, pp. 18–29.

39. Walter W. Kolodrubetz, "Two Decades of Employee-Benefit Plans, 1950–70: A Review," *Social Security Bulletin* 35 (April 1972): 10; Hugh Mosley, "Corporate Social Benefits and the Underdevelopment of the American Welfare State," *Contemporary Crisis* 5 (1981): 146–48.

II

STRUGGLES AT THE WORKPLACE

4

Wartime Shipyards: The Transformation of Labor in San Francisco's East Bay

Marilynn S. Johnson

"The Second Gold Rush Hits the West," announced the *San Francisco Chronicle* in the spring of 1943.[1] Like so many Californians, the author of this rather sensational headline was struck by the parallels between the wartime defense boom and the gold rush of the 1840s. In many ways, the comparison was an apt one; not since the gold rush of 1849 had the economy and population of the Bay Area grown so dramatically, nor would any single event so transform the population composition, labor force, and urban geography of the region. Indeed in California, World War II was to the twentieth century what the gold rush had been to the nineteenth.

Although historians have spilt much ink over the events of the 1840s, the region's "second gold rush" remains relatively unexplored. This chapter attempts to redress this deficiency by examining labor migration and the transformation of work and labor relations in wartime shipyards located in the East Bay region of the San Francisco Bay Area. As one of the nation's largest shipbuilding centers, the East Bay hosted 12 major shipyard operations, including the mammoth Kaiser complex in Richmond; Moore Dry Dock in Oakland; and General Engineering, Pacific Bridge, Bethlehem Steel, and Pacific Coast Engineering in Alameda. At the height of the wartime emergency shipbuilding program, these yards employed over 150,000 workers and manufactured more cargo ships than any other West Coast port.

With their massive labor demands, East Bay shipyards offered new work opportunities for both local residents and in-migrant workers. The influx of new, largely unskilled workers led to a major reorganization and deskilling of the work process and to bitter conflicts between old and new workers within shipyard unions. The study of such labor conflicts provides a window into the larger newcomer-oldtimer schism that soon pervaded all aspects of urban life in the East Bay.

The study of East Bay shipyards also can offer broader perspectives on the experience of labor during the war years. As Nelson Lichtenstein and Ruth Milkman have shown, the deskilling and reorganization of labor was a widespread practice during World War II, affecting nearly all defense industries to some degree.[2] Nowhere was this reorganization more evident, however, than in shipbuilding. In the East Bay, shipbuilding magnate Henry Kaiser led the nation in new industrial practices, transforming skilled trades into assembly-line production. East Bay shipyards, then, offer a case study of wartime industrial trends and some of the ways in which unions responded to these changes.

Prior to World War II, shipbuilding had been a highly skilled trade, with over 80 percent of jobs in the skilled and semiskilled categories. On the West Coast, American Federation of Labor (AFL) trade unions such as the International Brotherhood of Boilermakers, Iron Shipbuilders, and Helpers represented most of the industry's skilled work force. This relationship was strengthened during the war under the Shipyard Stabilization Agreement of 1941. Under the governance of the National War Labor Board, shipyard employers offered AFL metal trades unions a closed shop and guaranteed wages and benefits in return for a no-strike pledge.[3]

The shipbuilding boom had begun in the late 1930s but accelerated dramatically with the start of the U.S. Maritime Commission's emergency construction program in 1941. In the East Bay, older shipyards like Moore Dry Dock expanded their operations, while brand new yards like Kaiser sprang up along the undeveloped Richmond shoreline. To staff these operations, defense contractors worked with the federal government in recruiting hundreds of thousands of new workers, including women, teenagers, the elderly, and the handicapped.

Most importantly, however, Kaiser and other shipyard employers scoured the country for potential labor, importing workers and their families from every state. The vast majority came from the South and Midwest, particularly from the south central states of Texas, Oklahoma,

Arkansas, and Louisiana. The wartime migrants were both black and white and were joined by thousands of depression-era Okie migrants who left agricultural work in the Central Valley to take up more lucrative jobs in coastal defense centers.[4]

As thousands of unskilled workers streamed into East Bay yards, industrial managers faced the problem of integrating these newcomers into the workplace. To speed up production and facilitate the introduction of unskilled labor, shipyard managers reorganized the work process itself, breaking down older craft lines and diluting skills accordingly. The emergency shipyards, especially, experimented with new materials and techniques in specially designed wartime plants. The Maritime Commission proudly compared the new process with the automobile assembly line, and, indeed, the two systems had much in common.

Beginning in May 1942, coinciding with increased recruitment of women, black, and out-of-state workers, Kaiser instituted a new system of prefabrication in the Richmond yards. Under this system, whole sections of the ship's superstructure — boilers, double bottoms, forepeaks, after peaks, and deckhouses — were preassembled in the new prefabrication plant located between Yards Three and Four. This system allowed more work to be carried out away from the ships with less welding, riveting, and crane lifts required during hull erection. Richmond was only one of many shipyards that adopted these techniques. Prefabrication was also implemented in the Kaiser yards in Portland, Oregon, and Vancouver, Washington; the Bechtel yards in Marin County, California; Calship in southern California; and several other war-born shipyards.[5]

For the worker, prefabrication meant increased specialization and deskilling of basic trades. In the boilermaker trade alone, subassembly techniques fostered over 17 different job classifications. The occupation of shipfitter, for example, was broken down into categories of layoutman, loftsman, and duplicator. Welders were confined to specific kinds of welding, and electricians were assigned specific wiring jobs, such as control panels or cabin lighting. With such narrow job classifications, advancement from one grade to another was quite rapid, normally under 60 days. Under the right conditions, an unskilled newcomer could advance from trainee to journeyman status within a few months — a fraction of the normal time required. As Henry Kaiser put it, "production is not labor anymore, but a process."[6]

In order to facilitate this system, Kaiser introduced a variety of new organizational techniques and practices. The proliferation of new job classifications was codified in an elaborate insignia system in which each worker bore a trade symbol on their hard hat. The list of insignias filled up several pages of the employee handbook, a printed booklet for new workers explaining basic shipyard procedures and regulations. In addition, the use of security badges, timekeepers, tool checkers, pay windows, and (for the first time) income tax withholding practices made for a highly bureaucratized work climate.

Even the physical environment reflected the large-scale urban-industrial organization of wartime shipyards. Kaiser, for instance, designed the Richmond yards with a city-like grid system of numbered and lettered streets. As one worker explained, "It was a city without houses, but the traffic was heavy. Cranes, trucks, trains noised by." Another newcomer, a recent migrant from a small Iowa town, recalled her initial bewilderment at the immensity and seeming confusion of the yards. "It was such a huge place, something I had never been in," she said. "People from all walks of life, all coming and going and working, and the noise. The whole atmosphere was overwhelming to me." For many newcomers unfamiliar with an urban-industrial work climate, the shipyards could be a disorienting and alienating experience.[7]

The new system had other important implications for workers and their occupational mobility within the yards. The replacement of riveting with welding and the proliferation of jobs in downhand welding (considered the easiest position) facilitated quick placement of new workers. Employers channeled women especially into this trade, seeing them as better suited for this lighter work. At peak employment in the Richmond yards, approximately 40 percent of all welders were women. Female employees were also used extensively in "prefab," an indoor shop offering supposedly lighter, sheltered work. As Ruth Milkman has pointed out, women entered new jobs in wartime industries, but a modified version of occupational segregation remained in place.[8]

Similar occupational stereotypes emerged to justify the placement of other newcomer groups. Seeing them as well-suited to arduous labor, shipyard employers concentrated black workers in the hull trades — hard, outdoor work on a year-round basis. By contrast, Chinese-American workers were often placed in electrical work, a lighter, detail-oriented trade considered more suitable for them. Although such cultural stereotypes were deeply ingrained, they were not immutable. As Ruth Milkman has shown, the "idiom" of occupational segregation changed during the war to suit the needs of particular industries. As labor demands dictated, employers channeled women and minority workers into welding, burning, shipfitting, and a number of other semiskilled trades.[9]

Although the expansion of skilled and semiskilled categories offered higher status and pay for some newcomers, further occupational mobility was rarely possible. Foreman, leaderman, and other supervisory positions were dominated by old-timers and other white male workers. There were virtually no female supervisors in East Bay shipyards, and women found their occupational mobility blocked on many fronts. Employers were very reluctant to promote women into positions overseeing men, and the double burden of home and work responsibilities made such promotions even less likely. Married women, especially, had a higher rate of absenteeism than men or single women. Because of rationing and other wartime conditions, home responsibilities became more time-consuming than usual, and such pressures adversely affected women's job performance.[10]

Furthermore, women in nontraditional jobs found that many male coworkers resented their presence, seeing them as temporary interlopers in a male domain. Katherine Archibald, a sociologist and employee at Moore shipyards, commented on the constant barrage of sex jokes and innuendoes directed at women, the end result of which was "to deny the possibility of the establishment of businesslike relationships between men and women on the job and to discredit them as effective workers." Several accounts from East Bay shipyards refer to the activities of professional prostitutes working in warehouses and ship compartments, a claim which Archibald discounted as pernicious rumor.[11] Whether such accusations were true or not, the tendency to view women as sexual distractions served to discredit them as serious workers or potential supervisors.

African-Americans and other minority workers also encountered great difficulty breaking into supervisory ranks. The few minority supervisors in East Bay yards generally oversaw racially segregated work crews, functioning as straw bosses and "pushers" of their coworkers. At Moore Dry Dock, employers experimented with all-Chinese electrical crews and all-black laborer and rigger gangs.[12] Management justified such practices in terms of productivity, as it believed racial intermixing to be highly volatile and disruptive.

The integration of blacks, women, and other newcomers was indeed a sensitive issue among white workers, as Katherine Archibald observed. Although blacks and whites worked side by side, racial tensions were all-pervasive. "The slightest touch," said Archibald, "revealed the impermanence of the surface calm and the depth of the hatred beneath." The hostility, she added, was most evident among white Southerners and was often couched in gender terms invoking the threat of miscegenation.

"The Okies," she felt, "were especially disturbed and found it hard to accept the casual contact between Negro men and white women to which Northern custom had long been indifferent. . . . Tales of lynching with a background of sexual ravishment were much in demand." As a result, she said, friendly relations between black men and white women on the job were virtually impossible. White shipyard workers also expressed a constant fear of racial violence following the Detroit race riots in the summer of 1943. "Any incident of interracial conflict would give rise to talk of rioting," Archibald said, and Southerners had "especially dire predictions."[13]

Ultimately, though, Archibald believed that native western workers were equally antagonistic toward blacks and were keenly aware of the threat to their job security. "Except for the greater emotionality of the Southerner, and his more frequent talk of lynchings, riots, and reprisals," she explained, "the attitudes of the two groups were hard to distinguish."[14] Southerners, then, manifested a more virulent style of racism brought with them from the South but did not create the institutionalized racial system that characterized the shipyards and other defense work.

In an effort to ameliorate social tensions and other obstacles to productivity, Kaiser implemented a number of work incentive programs based on patriotic appeals. Management conducted regular efficiency and safety contests among Richmond workers and challenged other shipyards to production races in the building of Liberty ships. In November 1942, Richmond set the all-time record with the launching of the *Robert E. Peary*, built in 4 days, 15 hours, and 26 minutes. Although the *Peary* was a mere demonstration project designed to garner publicity and boost morale, the average construction time for Liberty ships was, in fact, reduced to 17 days.

One of the methods for speeding production was the broadcasting of up-tempo popular music over the shipyard public address system. Although some workers enjoyed the music, others became irritated and took active measures of resistance. One 50-year-old employee, Roy Christison, was arrested by the Federal Bureau of Investigation in 1943 for cutting the cable to the loudspeaker every other day for two months. According to a local newspaper, many employees supported Christison's protest.[15] Kaiser also instituted a program to stem labor turnover in which he offered membership in the "Anchormen," a kind of honor society for long-term employees. Workers received bronze pins for six months' service, silver pins after one year, and gold after 18 months. Out of the estimated 200,000 workers who came to Richmond during the war, though, only 23,000 achieved gold medal status.[16] For all the hype, Kaiser's incentive programs did not prove especially effective.

Despite the push for increased speed and efficiency, production bottlenecks continued to occur under the prefabrication system. A shortage of cranes or the absence or delay of one part or section could undermine the entire assembly process. Workers often complained of having to "sit around" waiting for parts to arrive or of not doing a full day's work. Workers voiced similar complaints at Moore shipyards. "Many another was vaguely troubled at the ease with which he earned his wages," said Katherine Archibald, "and it was a standard joke among the men that they should walk backward to the pay window." The worst situation occurred at Pacific Bridge shipyards in Alameda, where one survey revealed that workers were idle for at least three hours per day.[17] Indeed, production bottlenecks were common among all wartime cost-plus contractors, who had easier access to labor than to parts and supplies.

Production bottlenecks were further aggravated by the widespread practice of labor hoarding by major shipbuilders. Following the labor freeze measures of 1943, employers used some of their profit margin to hire excess workers to compensate for anticipated high turnover. The result was "enforced idleness" and periodic mass layoffs at Kaiser and other shipyards. In the first four months of 1943, a peak production period with full-scale labor recruitment in progress, Kaiser dismissed thousands of workers on two separate occasions because of production imbalances.[18] Such practices prompted criticism of the preassembly system by the Congress of Industrial Organizations (CIO), the Oakland City Council, and other community groups.

The strongest opposition to prefabrication and other cost-plus practices came from the ranks of old-timers and their unions, who feared the effects of deskilling on their trades. Such men, according to the Kaiser company history, tended to leave the Richmond yards for older, more traditionally organized shipyards. "One after another, their beliefs and traditions outraged, they left the ranks to give their valuable services where they would not be trampled upon by the new-fangled notions of upstarts."[19] Eventually, though, the introduction of new unskilled workers and preassembly techniques affected all Bay Area shipyards.

The International Brotherhood of Boilermakers, Iron Shipbuilders and Helpers, the union that represented the majority of West Coast shipyard workers, was the most vocal opponent of prefabrication. Although the union manifested the traditional exclusivity and conservatism of craft unions affiliated with the AFL it also addressed legitimate concerns about the deskiling of the shipbuilding trades.

Throughout the war years, the Boilermakers opposed the new assembly process as an effort by management to erode the position of journeyman mechanic by breaking it down into a set of semiskilled trainee classifications. The result was "a motley collection of one-process worker Johnny-come-latelies." The Boilermakers continued to favor the "interchangeability" system in which journeyman mechanics performed a wide variety of skills in different phases of production. Under pressure from the Maritime Commission and the National War Labor Board, however, the Boilermakers reluctantly accepted prefabrication as a temporary wartime arrangement.[20]

To protect their craft prerogatives, the Boilermakers instituted a special wartime union organization based on centralized control and increased hierarchy. Under the impact of mass migration, the membership of shipyard unions mushroomed to many times their original size. The Boilermakers' union grew by several hundred thousand nationwide during the war, expanding from 28,609 in 1938 to 352,000 in November 1943. West Coast shipbuilding affiliates showed the greatest gains, with several local memberships of over 35,000 — including Richmond's newly created Local 513. According to union officials, Local 513 conducted up to three initiations per day of 200 to 300 workers each during 1942–43. With 36,511 members in 1943, the Richmond local was larger than the entire national membership of the Boilermakers' union five years earlier. During the war years, Local 513 became the third largest Boilermakers' local in the country after those in Los Angeles and Portland, Oregon. Other East Bay Boilermakers' affiliates, including Local 9 (Shipfitters), Local 681 (Burners and Welders), and Local 39 (Boilermakers), also grew by tens of thousands during this period.[21]

Very few of these new workers had any prior experience with unions and tended to be somewhat distrustful of them initially. According to Katherine Archibald, most workers had little contact with unions beyond paying their initiation fee and consequently became distrustful of union leaders, whom they suspected of bilking the membership.[22] Unfortunately, the Boilermakers did very little to dispel this attitude and, in fact, exacerbated the situation in an attempt to protect the interests of their old-time membership.

The economic threat posed by newcomers in the shipyards fostered a sense of resentment among old-time workers. They felt that newcomers had not participated in the struggle to build the union and were essentially "freeloaders" on the system. They particularly resented the easy terms under which new workers could advance to journeyman status. An article in the *Oakland Tribune* titled "From Bond Salesman to Leaderman Shipfitter in Four Easy Steps" provoked angry outcries from one skilled old-timer, who complained that "we got hard-earned conditions and wages, and now the overnight mechanics step in and collect the cream."[23] Union leaders also claimed that newcomers were inept and accident-prone, putting old-timers at risk on the job.

In addition to legitimate labor concerns, racial, sexual, and cultural biases also influenced the Boilermakers' response to the newcomers. The Boilermaker leadership denounced newcomers as drunks and "misfits" who were lazy and irresponsible. "The 'bottom of the barrel' was being scraped," said the Boilermakers about Richmond workers, "and the human scale found thereon resented the necessity of having to go to work." The Boilermakers also publicly ridiculed the backwardness of rural Midwestern migrants, the aggressiveness of "hotheaded Southern Negroes," and the frailness of women workers.[24]

As antinewcomer bigotry clouded legitimate labor issues, shipyard unions attempted to protect their craft control by creating an elaborate hierarchy of auxiliary unions for migrants, blacks, and other newcomers. In order to "protect the interests of the Brotherhood," the Boilermakers provided for direct international control of local affiliates — particularly for the new war-born locals. International governing boards not only barred unwanted newcomers from full membership but also served to keep leftist "subversives" from challenging the entrenched leadership.[25] The Boilermakers passed this provision at their 1937 national convention in anticipation of the defense build-up; there was no possibility of appeal for another seven years, because all national conventions were postponed until 1944 because of the war.

When Richmond Local 513 was chartered in August 1942, the international took immediate control through a governing board consisting of prominent union officers. According to the international, "the vast majority of people seeking clearance to work in Richmond were complete strangers to this area, knew little or nothing about Unions or Union procedure, and unfortunately didn't want to learn. . . . Nothing but internal strife would have prevailed had this great mass of new members, uninitiated in the trade union movement, exercised control."[26] At a time when these members most needed education and experience with unionism, the international suspended all elections, meetings, and regular publications for the duration of the war. By 1944, the international directly governed at least ten locals nationwide, including Locals

72 (Portland) and 401 (Vancouver), both emergency shipyard locals with thousands of new members.[27]

Women and black workers were excluded from union affairs to an even greater extent. With a widespread consensus that women's sojourn in the shipyards would be temporary, the Boilermakers' executive council ruled to admit women to membership in September 1942 in accordance with federal government and employer demands. With their brief tenure, however, women did not qualify for office holding or other official duties and were often enrolled in the newer international-controlled locals anyway. Black workers fared even worse. Anticipating the coming shipbuilding expansion, the Boilermakers provided for the establishment of auxiliary locals for blacks in 1937. The auxiliaries first appeared in the South, but during the war years, they also sprang up in Midwestern and West Coast cities experiencing large-scale in-migration. By 1944 there were 44 auxiliary lodges nationwide, with 13,678 men and 2,532 women.[28]

In the East Bay, there were three active auxiliaries: A-26 (Oakland), A-36 (Richmond), and A-33 (San Francisco-based Shipfitters). The auxiliaries were controlled by their white "parent" locals and had no vote or representation at national conventions, no grievance mechanisms, no business representatives, and reduced insurance benefits.[29] Moreover, their existence was dependent on the whim of the international, which could dissolve the auxiliaries at any time.

Initially, East Bay shipyards either did not hire black workers or referred them to A-26, the first black auxiliary formed in Oakland in February 1942. As black migration accelerated, discriminatory hiring practices at Kaiser and other yards came to light. In late 1942–43, Richmond's Local 513 required black applicants to have proof of one year's residency in Contra Costa County — a requirement the union had dropped for whites at the beginning of the war. The measure effectively barred all black migrants and most old-time black residents who lived in adjoining Alameda County. In addition, the War Manpower Commission received complaints from over 100 blacks (mainly women) who were turned away by Local 513 after completing welding courses under government auspices.[30]

In an attempt to fight such practices, a group called the East Bay Shipyard Workers' Committee Against Discrimination was formed under the leadership of Ray Thompson, a black shipfitter at Moore Dry Dock. Born in San Francisco and educated at Tuskegee Institute in Alabama, Thompson worked out of his south Berkeley community, coordinating efforts to improve black housing and employment and to educate black newcomers about unions. According to Thompson, the group had over 5,000 members at its peak.

Thompson's efforts were part of a rising tide of black labor activism in West Coast shipbuilding centers. Several similar organizations formed on the West Coast during the war, including the San Francisco Committee against Segregation and Discrimination, the Shipyard Negro Organization for Victory in Portland, and the Shipyard Workers' Committee for Equal Participation in Los Angeles. The politics and tactics of the groups, however, varied. Thompson's group in the East Bay, for instance, grew out of the local Communist party network, while its San Francisco counterpart was closely affiliated with the National Association for the Advancement of Colored People.[31]

The tactics of each group varied accordingly. The East Bay Shipyard Workers' Committee initially attempted to challenge racist union policy from within the segregated auxiliary system. This strategy was designed to avoid direct confrontation with the Boilermakers International but also probably was influenced by prowar Communist party members on the committee. When the Boilermakers chartered two new East Bay auxiliaries in early 1943 (A-36 and A-33), the Shipyard Workers' Committee urged blacks to participate in auxiliary elections and to vote for progressive leaders who would spearhead the fight for equal membership. Soon after, however, the strategy backfired when the International, fearing a "subversive" takeover, suspended pending elections for A-33.[32] The experience was repeated in several auxiliaries around the country; such locals either had no officers or had them appointed by supervising white locals (as did A-36 in Richmond). Not surprisingly, black leaders became increasingly dissatisfied with the "boring from within" approach.

Across the Bay, the San Francisco Committee, led by Joseph P. James, pursued a more confrontational approach. As Charles Wollenberg has shown in his book, *Marinship at War*, the San Francisco group took up the cause of disgruntled black boilermakers at the Marinship yards near Sausalito. Refusing on principle to join the segregated auxiliaries, hundreds of black shipyard workers turned to the committee for legal representation when Marinship fired them for nonmembership in 1943. In February 1944, a Marin County judge ruled in favor of the fired workers, prohibiting membership in segregated auxiliaries as a condition of employment.

Encouraged by the decision, black workers in East Bay yards adopted the same strategy. When Moore Dry Dock fired 230 black workers who refused to join the local auxiliary, the East Bay Shipyard Workers'

Committee filed suit against Moore Dry Dock and Locals 9 and 39 in
Oakland and against Kaiser and Local 513 in a similar case in Richmond.
Although the East Bay cases were stalled or defeated, the Boilermakers
appealed the Marinship case, tying it up in the state Supreme Court until
January 1945. The state court upheld the decision, ruling that a restricted
union was incompatible with a closed shop agreement. Because the war
was nearly over, though, the ruling had little impact; most black shipyard
workers were soon laid off and their union memberships terminated.[33]

During the same period, the federal Fair Employment Practices
Commission (FEPC) also conducted hearings concerning the legality of
auxiliaries in Los Angeles, Portland, and San Francisco. The FEPC
likewise condemned the practice, but the Boilermakers simply ignored
the toothless agency, claiming it had no jurisdiction over internal union
affairs. Renouncing their own role in fueling racial animosity, the
Boilermakers asserted that the FEPC "will have to bear full responsibility for racial outbreaks that will shock the nation — if not the world."
As for black activists in their locals, the Boilermakers dismissed them as
"professional agitators and negro uplifters who find it more profitable to
dress well and live off the contributions exacted from the negroes by
appeals to their prejudice than it is for them to build ships and thus make
a real contribution to the war effort."[34] The racism and intransigence of
the international, however, would provoke strong rank-and-file opposition, particularly on the West Coast.

When the Boilermakers finally convened in Kansas City in 1944, the
national meeting was riven with dissent. For nearly three days, West
Coast delegates filibustered over the issue of international governing
boards and the right to local elections. A couple of these locals even
elected rival officers and attempted to seat them. East Bay locals alone
submitted some 20 resolutions to the constitution, indicating strenuous
rank-and-file activism on the local level despite repressive control by the
International.

Welders and Burners Local 681, which had, at one point, lost the right
to meetings, elections, and publications, was most vociferous in
defending the rights of local affiliates. The suspension or delay of
elections and meetings, they said, "has created an anti-union sentiment
among the new members." Oakland Local 39 backed a similar measure
specifically regarding the international-controlled Richmond local.
Local 681 also supported an antidiscrimination resolution prohibiting
segregated auxiliaries and advocating open membership regardless of
race, sex, creed, or national origin. The resolution was supported by
petitions with over 6,000 signatures from East Bay shipyard workers,

both black and white.[35] As with the court cases and FEPC rulings, however, the International managed to shelve most of these proposals until after the war. As massive layoffs forced most newcomers out of the shipyards, the issue of newcomer rights became moot.

As the shipyard work force dwindled, Kaiser worked with the Boilermakers' union to reinstitute the prewar, craft-based system of interchangeability in mid-1944. Using the occasion of a jurisdictional dispute, management and labor agreed to discontinue the prefabrication system.[36] Although Kaiser terminated all work in Richmond by 1946, the reconversion to skilled craft work effectively excluded the more specialized newcomers from even short-term postwar employment. This episode illustrates how management and organized labor cooperated in expanding and contracting the wartime labor force while denying newcomers any legitimate role in industrial governance. Migrants and other newcomers, thus, remained second-class workers, easily dispensable at war's end.

It is important to note, however, that not all unionswere as inhospitable to newcomers as the Boilermakers. Some of the smaller shipyard craft unions actively encouraged the participation of new members. Oakland Steamfitter's Local 530 even elected a woman to their executive board during these years.[37] Most importantly, the more liberal CIO unions like the Machinists, the Electrical Workers, and the Longshoremen and Warehousemen often championed the rights of newcomers in the East Bay. Unfortunately, however, the CIO's influence in the West Coast shipbuilding industry, where the largest number of new industrial workers were concentrated, was negligible. Most of the CIO's activities on behalf of new workers occurred outside the workplace through ad hoc committees to improve housing, transportation, health care, race relations, and other community issues affected by the war.

For thousands of new defense workers, then, their only exposure to the labor movement came at the hands of a fiercely conservative, exclusionary organization. This experience had serious implications for these workers and their attitudes toward labor and management. In the absence of meaningful outreach by organized labor, migrants and other new workers came to rely on employers and the federal government for social initiation and services.

East Bay shipyards, like other large defense industries, provided a wide array of corporate welfare services for their wartime employees. Workers at Kaiser's Richmond yards could take advantage of on-the-job training, counseling, child care, lunchtime entertainment programs, sports teams, company newspapers, and scores of other services. Most

noteworthy was the Permanente Health Plan, a prepaid health plan for
Kaiser workers launched in 1942. Kaiser, Moore, and other East Bay
shipyard employers also saw to it that their employees received priority
placement in nearby government war housing projects. With this
impressive array of publicly funded services at their disposal, shipyard
managers appeared as benevolent employers who looked after the needs
of their workers.[38]

Under these conditions, many newcomers turned their loyalties toward
employers while remaining alienated from the labor movement. The
undemocratic treatment of migrants, women, and black workers served
to heighten their distrust of unions and encouraged loyalty toward management. As a reporter from *The Nation* described it, newcomer workers
at the Kaiser shipyards were "quite possessive about the yards and just as
paternalistic toward Kaiser as he [was] toward them, regarding him with
a fond and fatherly incredulity."[39] Leftists warned their unions of these
tendencies throughout the war, but to little avail. In the East Bay and
elsewhere, organized labor's failure to educate and organize this mass of
new workers represents one of the great missed opportunities of World
War II.

The schism between old-timers and newcomers in East Bay shipyards
also carried over into the community at large. After work, most newcomers found themselves living in "migrant ghettoes" — temporary war
housing projects served by separate project schools, clinics, stores, and
churches. Although unions and shipyards soon disposed of these
workers, East Bay cities were burdened with thousands of unemployed,
ill-housed newcomers after the war. What to do with these displaced
migrants became the great dilemma of the postwar era, one that led to
bitter class — and especially racial — antagonisms, the legacies of
which still plague the East Bay today.

NOTES

1.   Milton Silverman, "The Second Gold Rush Hits the West," series of articles
in the *San Francisco Chronicle*, April 25–May 20, 1943. Important works of the impact
of World War II on the American West include: Gerald D. Nash, *The American West
Transformed: The Impact of the Second World War* (Lincoln: University of Nebraska
Press, 1985); Gerald D. Nash, *World War II and the West: Reshaping the Economy*
(Lincoln: University of Nebraska Press, 1990); Marilynn S. Johnson, *The Second Gold
Rush: Oakland and the East Bay in World War II* (Berkeley: University of California
Press, 1993). For a symposium on the impact of World War II on California see
"Special Issue: Fortress California at War: San Francisco, Los Angeles, Oakland, and
San Diego, 1941–1945," *Pacific Historical Review* 63 (August 1994): 277–420.

2. See Nelson Lichtenstein, *Labor's War at Home: The CIO in World War II* (New York: Cambridge University Press, 1982); Ruth Milkman, *Gender at Work: The Dynamics of Job Segregation by Sex during World War II* (Urbana: University of Illinois Press, 1987).

3. Frederick C. Lane, *Ships for Victory: A History of Shipbuilding under the U.S. Maritime Commission in World War II* (Baltimore, Md.: Johns Hopkins University Press, 1951), pp. 268–78, 288–90, 296–97; Sheila Tropp Lichtman, "Women at Work, 1941–1945: Wartime Employment in the San Francisco Bay Area" (Ph.D. diss., University of California, Davis, 1981), p. 118.

4. U.S., Department of Commerce, Bureau of the Census, *Wartime Changes in Population and Family Characteristics, San Francisco Bay Congested Production Area, April 1944*, Series CA-2, No. 3, July 15, 1944, pp. 1–2; James N. Gregory, *American Exodus: The Dust Bowl Migration and Okie Culture in California* (New York: Oxford University Press, 1989).

5. Alyce Mano Kramer, "The Story of the Richmond Shipyards," (typewritten draft) Henry Kaiser Papers, Bancroft Library, Berkeley, California, carton 330, pp. 22, 26–28.

6. International Brotherhood of Boilermakers, Iron Shipbuilders and Helpers of America, *Arsenal of Democracy* (Berkeley, Calif.: Tam, Gibbs Co., n.d.), p. 66; Office of Defense Health and Welfare Services, "Composite Report on Richmond Area," June 2, 1942, p. 1, located in Community Reports File, Region XII, Office of Community War Services, Record Group 215, National Archives, Washington, D.C.; Lichtman, "Women at Work," p. 119.

7. William Sokol, "Richmond During World War II: Kaiser Comes to Town" (unpublished paper, University of California, Berkeley, 1971), p. 36; Joseph Fabry, *Swing Shift* (San Francisco, Calif.: Strawberry Hill Press, 1982), p. 16; Margaret Louise Cathey, "A Wartime Journey: From Ottumwa, Iowa to the Richmond Shipyards, 1942," an oral history conducted by Judith K. Dunning, Regional Oral History Office, Bancroft Library, University of California, Berkeley, 1990, p. 7.

8. Lane, *Ships for Victory*, pp. 239, 258; Lichtman, "Women at Work," p. 119; Milkman, *Gender at Work*, p. 9.

9. Katherine Archibald, *Wartime Shipyard: A Study in Social Disunity* (Berkeley: University of California Press, 1947), p. 104; Wilson Record, "Willie Stokes at the Golden Gate," *The Crisis* 56 (June 1949): 176; *Oakland Tribune*, February 1, 1943; Milkman, *Gender at Work*, pp. 60–64.

10. Lichtman, "Women at Work," p. 171. For other accounts of working women during the war, see Karen Anderson, *Wartime Women: Sex Roles, Family Relationships, and the Status of Women During World War II* (Westport, Conn.: Greenwood Press, 1981); Amy Kesselman, *Fleeting Opportunities: Women Shipyard Workers in Portland and Vancouver During World War II and Reconversion* (Albany: State University of New York Press, 1990); Milkman, *Gender at Work*.

11. Archibald, *Wartime Shipyard*, p. 19; Kesselman, *Fleeting Opportunities*, p. 61.

12. Archibald, *Wartime Shipyard*, pp. 84, 104; *Oakland Tribune*, February 1, 1943.

13. Archibald, *Wartime Shipyard*, pp. 61, 70–75.

14. Ibid., p. 94.

15. *Richmond Record-Herald*, September 18, 1943.

16. Kramer, "The Story of the Richmond Shipyards," p. 64.

17. Archibald, *Wartime Shipyard*, p. 195; *Daily People's World*, June 5, 1943.

18. *Daily People's World*, January 5, April 10, 1943.

19. Kramer, "The Story of the Richmond Shipyards," p. 28.

20. Boilermakers, *Arsenal of Democracy*, p. 68; Lane, *Ships for Victory*, p. 241.

21. International Brotherhood of Boilermakers, Iron Shipbuilders and Helpers of America, *Report and Proceedings of the Seventeenth Consolidated Convention* (Kansas City, Mo.: n.p., January 31, 1944), pp. 72, 114–22; Boilermakers, *Arsenal of Democracy*, p. 43.

22. Archibald, *Wartime Shipyard*, pp. 131, 134.

23. *Oakland Tribune*, August 27, 1942.

24. Boilermakers, *Arsenal of Democracy*, pp. 23, 44–45, 59.

25. Boilermakers, *Proceedings*, p. 64.

26. Boilermakers, *Arsenal of Democracy*, pp. 33, 83.

27. Ibid., p. 83; Boilermakers, *Proceedings*, pp. 123, 145, 170. In Portland, disgruntled members of Local 72 filed at least 15 court cases in an effort to have duly elected officers seated. The International, however, rejected any interference on the part of the state into internal union affairs.

28. Boilermakers, *Proceedings*, p. 56.

29. Charles Wollenberg, "James vs. Marinship," *California History* 60 (Fall 1981) 267.

30. *Daily People's World*, February 4, May 7, 1943.

31. *Daily People's World*, May 13, 1943; William H. Harris, "Federal Intervention in Union Discrimination: The FEPC and West Coast Shipyards During World War II," *Labor History* 22 (Summer 1981): 331; Ray Thompson, interview by Jesse J. Warr, III, October 11, November 6, 1978, transcript, Oral History Project: Afro-Americans in San Francisco Prior to World War II, Friends of the San Francisco Public Library and San Francisco African-American Historical and Cultural Society, pp. 52, 60; Charles Wollenberg, *Marinship at War* (Berkeley, Calif.: Western Heritage Press, 1990), p. 75.

32. *Daily People's World*, May 5, 8, 13, 1943.

33. Wollenberg, "James vs. Marinship," pp. 267, 272; *Daily People's World*, April 3, May 10, 1944.

34. Boilermakers, *Proceedings*, pp. 58, 61.

35. Wollenberg, "James vs. Marinship," p. 272; Boilermakers, *Proceedings*, p. 317.

36. Boilermakers, *Arsenal of Democracy*, pp. 68–75.

37. Archibald, *Wartime Shipyard*, p. 38.

38. For more information on corporate welfare services, see Kaiser Industries, *The Kaiser Story* (Oakland, Calif.: Kaiser Industries, 1963); and the Kaiser shipyard newspaper *Fore 'N' Aft* (1941–46).

39. Quoted in Mark S. Foster, *Henry Kaiser: Builder in the Modern American West* (Austin: University of Texas Press, 1989), p. 81.

5

The San Francisco Machinists and the National War Labor Board

Richard P. Boyden

In the fall of 1944, San Francisco machinists Martin Joos and Arthur Burke found themselves fired from their jobs and blacklisted. A member of Machinists' Lodge 68 since 1920 and a shop steward at Bodinson Manufacturing Company, Joos lost his job after protesting to management against members of another craft doing machinists' work. Burke was a wartime newcomer to the Bay Area and a union committeeman at the National Motor Bearing plant in San Mateo. The company dismissed him because he had prevented a machinist from being in the toolroom doing toolmaker's work. Both Joos' and Burke's actions consisted of routine performance of union business. Both men were fired by order of the U.S. Navy. Before being fired, each man was taken into a back room and questioned by Federal Bureau of Investigation (FBI) agents, because the navy hoped to have them prosecuted under wartime antistrike legislation.[1]

These actions were a part of one of the harshest set of federal government measures employed against any group of American workers during World War II. Pursuant to two executive orders by President Roosevelt in September 1944, the U.S. Navy took possession of the bulk of the machinery industry in San Francisco and the industrial suburbs south of the city. The existing multiemployer contract was suspended, as were collective bargaining rights, union recognition, dues payment, the hiring hall, and the right of union representation.

Joos and Burke were fired and blacklisted "for the duration" of the war. Others were referred to the Selective Service System for immediate drafting into the armed forces. Others had their ration cards for food and gas revoked. A large number of FBI agents fanned out through the working-class community, visiting and interviewing thousands of machinists in their homes. There was talk that the union leaders would be prosecuted under new federal and antistrike legislation.[2] What led up to these events, and what were some of their consequences?

During the war, the San Francisco and Oakland machinists' locals were known as the "stormy petrels of West Coast labor."[3] They were highly skilled, all-round mechanics who had a national reputation for militancy (and radicalism) going back to the turn of the century.

In recent years, social historians of the workplace have taken a fresh look at the role of skilled workers, who have been dismissed by many as labor-aristocratic defenders of craft privilege. David Montgomery argues that a mutualistic craftsmen's ethic radically clashed with managerial reform; Jeffrey Haydu, that American machinists devised limited classification systems that embraced the unskilled in alliance against scientific management; and Ronald Schatz, that skilled workers played leading roles as shop floor organizers for industrial unions in mass production plants during the Great Depression.[4] Others have shown that shop floor militancy in American industry during and after World War II shaped employers' and government efforts to create a new system of industrial relations.[5]

The San Francisco machinists, for their part, had long felt their skills and livelihoods to be threatened by technological and managerial revolutions: the introduction of jigs and fixtures and systematized authoritarianism as represented by Frederick Taylor's scientific management and similar schemes.[6] The result was a decades-long struggle with major employers, in which machinists helped to lead broad-based strikes of metal workers. For example, in 1919–20, a ten-month strike by 60,000 Bay Area shipyard workers was the fourth largest labor dispute in the nation during the postwar strike wave. In the ensuing open shop era, the machinists were able to maintain their wage scale and job control in most plants without signed agreements, through strong rank-and-file involvement and informal bargaining.[7]

During the 1930s, the machinists were again prominent in the revival of unionism and in radical opposition to national union leadership. In 1934, during the epochal unionization struggle of West Coast waterfront workers, the San Francisco machinists were the first of the old, established craft unions to push the idea of a general strike.[8] In 1936, the machinists defied their international union against the imposition of a low-paid "production worker" job classification. When the international union attempted to break a major strike over the issue, the Oakland machinists withdrew from the International Association of Machinists (IAM) and joined the Congress of Industrial Organizations' (CIO) Steel Workers Organizing Committee.[9] As a result, Lodge 68 and the new Steel Workers' Local 1304, which continued to work closely together despite interfederation warfare, may have been the first AFL-CIO in the country.

As the clouds of war darkened in the spring of 1941, the Bay machinists again struck, this time against the federal government's Shipbuilding Stabilization Committee in its efforts to limit wage increases to shipyard and other metal workers.[10]

During the war, the machinists would not relinquish bedrock conditions. After the first rush of patriotism in the early days of the war, and especially after the tide of war began to turn in favor of the Allies in 1943, machinists, like other workers, increasingly worried about what the end of the war would bring. If conditions were not defended now, they reasoned, workers might never get them back. Many remembered the aftermath of the last war, when unionized workers faced the open shop onslaught. They did not want to repeat the experience. They resented the disparity between swollen corporate earnings, wages frozen "for the duration," and a rising cost of living only weakly dampened by government price controls.[11]

Workers were combative and militant during the war, as large waves of strike activity prove. In the San Francisco Bay Area, the machinists exemplified this movement. What about the other unions? In the 1930s, the longshoremen led the labor movement. This was the famous union of Harry Bridges, the International Longshoremen's and Warehousemen's Union (ILWU). The ILWU leadership, believing that the defense of the Soviet Union and the defeat of Nazi Germany transcended all other issues, took the position that any strike, no matter what the cause, aided Hitler.[12] The leaders of the shipyard unions were conservative American Federation of Labor craft unionists whose treasuries were bulging with the dues of thousands of new war workers. Other union leaders, progressives in the New Deal mold, also believed that the war transcended almost all issues. None of these leaderships was about to give effective voice to the real and deeply felt grievances of their members.[13]

Discontent found expression in fairly numerous quickie strikes, but these rarely got past the "blowing off steam" stage.[14]

The machinists were different. They had grievances, a militant tradition, and rigorously democratic internal governance. Moreover, they had a large core of activists and an experienced and determined leadership. The outstanding leaders were Edward F. Dillon and Harry Hook, business agents of Lodge 68, and James P. ("Turkeyneck") Smith of Local 1304.

The National War Labor Board (NWLB) was established in early 1942 as an impartial arbitrator of disputes between capital and labor. This impartiality was soon nullified when the board was given responsibility for administering a wage freeze. Under the board's "Little Steel Formula" handed down in July, wage increases were not to exceed 15 percent of rates in effect on January 1, 1941. Because most organized workers had won substantial increases in the spring of that year, the NWLB's decision meant that they would receive few, if any, further wage increases during the war.[15]

In 1942, the San Francisco machinists received their only wage increase of the war by defying government policy. Their annual contract expired in April. The Shipbuilding Stabilization Committee had called a national wage conference for May, where labor would be called upon to accept a 5.5 percent increase, amounting to only half of the rise in the cost of living for the preceding year. At the same time, the government and the California Metal Trades Association (CMTA), which represented machine shop employers in the nonshipyard, so-called uptown shop sector, were together trying to tie wages in their negotiations to those mandated for the shipbuilding industry. Both the government and the CMTA exerted heavy pressure on the bulk of uptown shop employers not to accede to the machinists' demand for an 11 percent increase. Counterpressure from the machinists proved stronger, however, and by mid-April the CMTA agreed to the higher rate. This caused consternation in high government circles, because the new uptown machinist rate of $1.28 per hour threatened to spoil efforts to impose a $1.20 rate in West Coast shipyards. Thereafter, the government's wage freezing efforts became more effective.[16]

In the fall of the same year, management of the Joshua Hendy Iron Works attempted to impose a low-wage "production worker" classification in its very large Sunnyvale plant. This was one of the most important war factories in the country. Owned by a consortium of Kaiser, Bechtel, future Central Intelligence Agency Director John A. McCone, and others, the plant was producing fully one-third of all Liberty ship engines in the nation. The workers, represented by Lodge 68, rebelled against the new classification and kept the plant in turmoil for months while the NWLB tried to arbitrate the issues. These events also attracted additional unfavorable attention of high government officials to the San Francisco machinists. One of these, NWLB member Wayne Morse, characterized the machinists' stand as "exhibit[ing] a callousness with respect to our national crisis which borders on lack of patriotism and indifference to our war effort."[17]

Machinists received no further wage increases during the war. By early 1944, they grew restive as inflation eroded their incomes in a region with one of the highest costs of living in the country. In the meantime, the winding down of the war effort in industry weakened the patriotic consensus against strike action. On the other hand, the employers' group, the CMTA, was completely unresponsive to machinists' demands for a substantial wage increase. The "Little Steel Formula" was still in force. The union looked to possible changes in the war situation that might open the way for unrestrained negotiations. It did not want its hands tied by a year contract if the war should end. Lodge 68, therefore, proposed that the wage issue be compromised: in return for the dropping of wage demands, the CMTA agreed to reopen the wage issue every 30 days. Hook and Dillon presented the proposal to a large meeting of the local on March 26, five days prior to the contract's expiration. After heated debate, the machinists adopted the compromise.[18]

A few days later, when the union committee met with the CMTA to complete the contract negotiations, they were surprised to find an almost entirely new employer committee across the table. The employers proceeded to repudiate the previous agreement and even refused to agree to keep the old contract in force pending further negotiations. The workers greeted these moves first with dismay, then outrage. Having a strong tradition of refusing to work without an agreement, they voted on April 12 to ban all overtime in excess of 48 hours per week in the CMTA shops. Faced with this, the CMTA rushed to the NWLB for protection.[19]

Two days before the overtime ban was to go into effect, the parties met with a federal conciliator. After less than an hour, the employers broke off the meeting — over the objections of both the union and the conciliator. Within one hour, the NWLB in Washington, D.C., had assumed jurisdiction over the case. This violated board procedures, because the conciliator had not yet submitted his report. The uncommon speed with which the board had acted seemed to confirm the machinists' suspicion that the NWLB, especially the regional board in San

Francisco, was collaborating with the CMTA to prevent Lodge 68 from getting its contract demands. "This," said Dillon, "is a sample of the dispatch with which the board moves when the employers are getting hurt." The board, of course, justified its actions on the ground that they were necessary to forestall the threatened overtime ban, which, in its view, was tantamount to a strike.[20]

On April 17, 1944, the overtime ban went into effect, to remain in force for four months, during which all machinists quit work after eight hours and refused to work on Sundays altogether. They insisted that they were not on strike and that their action did not adversely affect the war effort. The slackening of the war economy had resulted in layoffs of over a thousand machinists in the uptown shops since the first of the year. Refusal to work overtime was a time-honored method of spreading the work. The big companies enjoyed the bulk of war contracts and needed ten-hour shifts. They were responsible for the CMTA's hard-line policy. If these employers remained intransigent, argued the machinists, the resulting production shortfalls could easily be made up in smaller, currently underutilized machine shops, 20 of which had signed the proposed union contract. The machinists also insisted that the ban violated no laws or legal government orders, because it conformed to Roosevelt's executive order mandating the 48-hour week in war industry.[21]

The NWLB was motivated by two sets of considerations in its fight with the San Francisco machinists, one national and one regional. On the national level, the board felt its authority challenged by the machinists' refusal to abide by repeated orders to rescind the ban. This was especially true in light of the NWLB's concurrent struggle against the Montgomery Ward Company's refusal to respect the collective bargaining rights of its employees. The federal government had recently seized Ward's properties and evicted its die-hard president Sewell Avery in a move that brought indignation from the business community. Board members now felt that unless the NWLB succeeded in cracking down on Lodge 68, it would be perceived as coddling labor while going hard on business. Just as important, the board feared that if the machinists won a new contract through the use of the overtime ban, other workers might also adopt the tactic as a way of evading the no-strike pledge. These fears were heightened by a Chicago printers' overtime ban the month before. As Fred Vinson, Roosevelt's economic stabilization czar, remarked, the San Francisco machinists were setting an example that must be "stamped out" before it spread across the entire country.[22]

In the Regional War Labor Board in San Francisco, there was consensus among government, labor, and business members that Lodge 68
must be brought to heel. This was especially true, strangely enough, of
the labor members, led by the leadership of the ILWU. The machinists
and the Communist-party-oriented ILWU had maintained a close
working relationship during most of the 1930s, but bitter animosity had
grown between them since the beginning of the war. The wartime ILWU
attitude toward the machinists was expressed by prominent San
Francisco labor attorney Aubrey Grossman writing to CIO national
counsel Lee Pressman in October 1944. According to Grossman, Lodge
68 had staged more strikes since Pearl Harbor than all the other unions in
the region combined. "Their strikes have not only done untold damage to
the war effort," he claimed, "but the publicity has immeasurably injured
the prestige of labor in California and swung large numbers of votes
from President Roosevelt and in favor of the infamous Proposition
12."[23]

The strongest voice inside the Regional War Labor Board for military
intervention against the machinists was that of ILWU vice-president
Louis Goldblatt. Goldblatt told a June 1944 closed session of the NWLB
in Washington that the machinists' overtime ban "is a strike . . . which
unless this board takes decisive action is going to spread. . . . It is
contagious; because you have many unions throughout the Region that
are pretty expert at job action, quickie strikes, and where for many years
prior to the war that was really the common form of economic action —
not the major strikes . . . and there are a number of forces within the labor
movement . . . who are not a bit adverse to going back to that type of
guerrilla warfare."[24]

Goldblatt then made the following remarkable statement, indicating
that he was not simply following a pro-Communist line but that he had
developed — in a profound break with the traditions of 1934 — a
genuine conservatism like that of many other union leaders: "We on the
labor side don't want to see any resumption in the San Francisco Bay
Area . . . of the type of collective bargaining that prevailed six or seven
years ago when you had a constant economic contest [and] one of the
best strike records that anybody ever had in the country. We think we
have had enough of that. . . . We don't want the resumption of guerilla
warfare which will inevitably result if this board fails to act, because
these employers will begin to fold one by one, and then you have taken
the lid off."[25]

Differences within the government delayed action for another six
weeks. The navy was especially resistant. It was not interested in

snatching the NWLB's chestnuts out of the fire, especially because the onus for repression would likely fall on them. The navy also claimed that the overtime ban was not actually hurting war production in the Bay Area and, in an effort to undermine the NWLB, leaked this information to the press. It was now clear that the real issue in the dispute was not damage to the war effort, but the prestige and authority of the NWLB itself.[26] Only after an overt strike was successfully provoked in one of the plants did the board succeed in getting action from the White House.[27]

If the navy had been hesitant in taking repressive action prior to seizure of the machine shops, all such misgivings were dispelled with the arrival in San Francisco of Vice-Admiral Harold G. Bowen, who believed that the machinists' union had long "been a thorn in the flesh of the people of San Francisco" and characterized Hook and Dillon as "labor racketeers." When Bowen met stiff initial resistance from the machinist rank and file to his orders to resume ten-hour shifts, he adopted a series of draconian measures to force compliance. Demanding that the FBI "take them two bastards into custody," Bowen sought to have Hook and Dillon prosecuted under the Smith-Connally Act.[28]

Although the navy was unable to jail the union leaders, it did succeed in wiping out most of Lodge 68's formal union rights and in cowing the workers individually with the threat of severe punishment. Coordinated by the Office of Economic Stabilization in the White House, the government cancelled the machinists' collective bargaining agreement, grievance procedure, union shop, dues collection, and hiring hall. Sanctions were applied against workers who refused to work over eight hours per day. For many months prior to the seizure, the NWLB had repeatedly asserted that no individual worker could be forced to work the longer hours. All that the board wanted from Lodge 68 was a rescinding of the ban so that each worker could decide for himself whether to work overtime. This promise was now forgotten. Faced with mass refusal, Admiral Bowen turned over 58 machinists to their draft boards for induction into the armed forces. The gas rations of others were cancelled. Bowen ordered the firing of eight workers, including Arthur Burke and Martin Joos. They and others were blacklisted by the War Manpower Commission (WMC). Bowen publicly vowed that these workers would remain jobless "for the duration" of the war.[29]

These measures succeeded in ending the overtime ban and in preventing the machinists from getting the contract language they sought, but they did not have the desired effect of breaking the union. A number of factors explain this. First, however much leaders of the local labor movement had previously wanted government seizure, they had not expected the navy to take such blatantly antiunion sanctions as instituting an open shop and blacklisting individual workers. Labor now reacted strongly against these measures. Nor were the employers particularly happy about navy occupation, because of their concern about the continuing power of the machinists to regulate production, which they proceeded to do with great effect. Ed Dillon summed up the workers' attitude in a still-potent Wobbly idiom: "We're just sawing wood, let the other fellow do the talking."[30]

Through the use of such informal pressure, the machinists maintained their organization in the shops as strongly as ever. Dues collection, enforcement of the union shop, and grievance processing continued on an informal basis almost as if there had been no navy presence at all. In addition, the navy quietly retreated from its victimization of individual workers. Except in the highly publicized Joos and Burke cases, all the fired workers soon returned to their jobs, and not a single machinist was drafted. Joos and Burke became the center of a lengthy appeals procedure and a lawsuit by the union against the federal government.[31]

A detailed examination of the cases of the two men reveals much about the complex political relationships affecting the outcome of government seizure. As soon as the machinists had been blacklisted, the navy informed them that although they had the right to appeal to the WMC, their appeals would be denied. At this point, the American Civil Liberties Union intervened on their behalf. In answer to angry inquires from the American Civil Liberties Union, the San Francisco WMC office claimed that appeals would have to be delayed pending a decision from Washington on whether the cases would be heard there or in San Francisco. Meanwhile, the same San Francisco officials were telephoning Washington to try to get the cases "lifted" to the national level! If hearings were held locally, they said, Joos and Burke would win their appeals. The navy's cases against both men were weak. Both men had been fired on orders from the navy, allegedly for interfering with production and violating navy orders; in fact, both dismissals resulted from each man's routine attempts to enforce union rules at companies long known for their hard-line antiunion policies. Just as important, both labor and employer representatives on local hearings panels were annoyed with what they viewed as the high-handedness of Admiral Bowen and his staff. If the men won their appeals, the navy, having vowed to blacklist them for the remainder of the war, would suffer a humiliating blow to its authority.[32]

Only after Lodge 68 had filed suit against the federal government did the WMC hold local hearings for Joos and Burke. After the local panel had ordered their reinstatement, national WMC chairman Paul McNutt violated his own regulations by retroactively denying the panel's right to make findings in the case. McNutt then upheld the blacklistings but limited them to 60 days. A federal judge in San Francisco sustained McNutt's order and dismissed the union's suit. Meanwhile, Lodge 68 had paid Joos' and Burke's wages, in keeping with an old tradition embodied in the local's "laws" that members victimized for union activity "shall have the full protection of the Organization."[33]

The machine shops remained under nominal navy occupation until the end of the war. The results were mixed from the government's point of view. Most employers had wanted to reach agreement with the union. Now the day of reckoning was merely postponed. "If I know the membership of Lodge No. 68," wrote Dillon, "then the Admiral can make arrangements for a permanent address in San Francisco and we will see the employers after the war and do it the hard way."[34]

In the cases of Martin Joos and Arthur Burke, we can see a dauntingly complex set of forces and events resulting in what was ultimately an ineffectual victimization of these union activists. First, the machinists were a compact group of skilled workers with powerful traditions and interests they perceived to be seriously threatened. They proved ready to challenge their employers and, if need be, the U.S. government. Second were major employers, intent on curbing labor's power precisely in the arena where the machinists excelled: job control on the shop floor. Third was the government, which proved to be internally divided and slow to act.

Finally, much of the leadership of the regional labor movement opposed the machinists. Fearing that pent-up grievances would lead to strikes and strikes to an antilabor backlash in public opinion, many regional labor leaders pursued the limited strategy of working with the NWLB to wrest concessions from management. The machinists threatened this position, both because they seemed oblivious to the political danger of backlash and, more importantly, because they posed an implied alternative leadership strategy to that of the moderates. Galvanizing opposition to the machinists within the labor movement was the Communist party.[35] Under Hook and Dillon, its former allies in the progressive wing of the labor movement, the machinists' union had become a major threat to the party's goal of promoting labor peace and "national unity" in the cause of Allied victory.[36] The conflict between the Communist party and the machinists' union would continue into the postwar period, with tragic consequences.

Edward Dillon's prophesy came true: the end of the war in the fall of 1945 saw the machinists confront the employers "the old fashioned way." They walked off their jobs in shipyards and machine shops in San Francisco and Oakland, demanding, like the autoworkers who struck against General Motors three weeks later, a 30 percent wage increase. Although 12,000 machinists struck, some 45,000 nonstriking members of other metal craft unions honored the picket lines.[37] However, the strike divided the labor movement: union officials, including ILWU leaders, attacked the strike and undermined it behind the scenes. Because of this lack of official union support, 45,000 nonstrikers received no strike benefits.

After five months on the picket lines, the strike was broken when the IAM national leadership, at the employers' urging, arrived in San Francisco, placed Lodge 68 in trusteeship, and induced other metal craftsmen, who had been without strike benefits for five months, to return to work.[38] Over the next five years, the IAM, supported by the courts and employing a small army of "goons," carried out a systematic and often violent purge of Hook and Dillon and their many followers. This effort succeeded, in part, because of the acquiescence and support of the official labor movement, including Harry Bridges and the Communist party. These events contributed to a crisis in the party, with the expulsion of many of its machinist members for supporting the strike and the subsequent exodus of about one-half of its membership in the region.[39] (However, that is a story for another day.)

NOTES

1. Jack H. Sapiro (IAM Lodge 68 attorney) in Transcript of Appeal Hearing, case of Martin Joos, October 9, 1944, Appeals Cases, Region XII, Records of the War Manpower Commission, RG 211, National Archives — Pacific Sierra Region, San Bruno, California (hereafter cited as Joos Trans., WMC XII, NA-Pac. Sierra).

2. *San Francisco Chronicle*, August 17, 1944; Harold G. Bowen, *Ships, Machinery, and Mossbacks: The Autobiography of a Naval Engineer* (Princeton, N.J.: Princeton University Press, 1954), pp. 285–89; Edward F. Dillon to Harvey W. Brown (IAM International President), September 3, 1944, in Lodge 68 File, International President's Files, International Association of Machinists Papers (microfilm), Wisconsin State Historical Society, Madison, Wisconsin (hereafter cited as IAM Papers).

3. *San Francisco Call Bulletin*, March 7, 1947; Katherine Archibald, *Wartime Shipyard: A Study in Social Disunity* (Berkeley: University of California Press, 1948), p. 142.

4. David Montgomery, *Workers' Control in America: Studies in Work, Technology, and Labor Struggles* (New York: Cambridge University Press, 1979); Jeffrey Haydu, "Factory Politics in the British and American Metal Trades: Changing Agenda for Protest, 1890–1922" (Ph.D. diss., University of California at Berkeley, 1984); Ronald Schatz, *The Electrical Workers: A History of Labor at General Electric and Westinghouse, 1923–60* (Urbana: University of Illinois Press, 1983).

5. Nelson Lichtenstein, *Labor's War at Home: The CIO in World War II* (New York: Cambridge University Press, 1982); Howell John Harris, *The Right to Manage: Industrial Relations Policies of American Business in the 1940s* (Madison: University of Wisconsin Press, 1982).

6. Ira B. Cross, "Machinists' Local 68," handwritten notes, October–November 1914, Folder 51, Carton II, Cross Collection, Bancroft Library, University of California, Berkeley.

7. Delegate Carberry (Lodge 68), 1920 IAM Convention Proceedings, p. 226; Louis Goldblatt (member Tenth Regional War Labor Board and vice-president of the Longshoremen's and Warehousemen's union) in Executive Sessions of the National War Labor Board (hereafter cited as Exec. Sess.), June 2, 1944, p. 427.

8. Levon Mosgofian interview, March 30, 1984; Lodge 68 Minutes, June 13 and 20, 1934, in custody of IAM Local 1327, Oakland, California.

9. Harvey Brown to George Adams (Lodge 284), July 14, 1936; Walter Galenson, *The CIO Challenge to the AFL: A History of the American Labor Movement, 1935–41* (Cambridge, Mass.: Harvard University Press, 1960), pp. 502–4.

10. Horace Drury, *History of Shipbuilding Stabilization: A Study of Industrial Relations in a Key War Industry:* Part II, *Stabilization in the Framework of National Defense* (typescript, Office of Defense Management, Washington, D.C., 1954), pp. 207–22, copy in RG 254, Records of the Shipbuilding Stabilization Committee, National Archives.

11. Lichtenstein, *Labor's War at Home*, pp. 119–20; Levon Mosgofian interview, February 2, 1984; Ralph Miller interview, October 6, 1985.

12. *Daily Worker*, March 3, 1942; Harry Bridges, *Longshoremen's Bulletin* (ILWU Local 10, San Francisco, California), March 10, 1942.

13. Archibald, *Wartime Shipyard*, pp. 131–41; Richard Claire interview, July 22, 1985.

14. For example, there were at least 30 longshore job actions on the San Francisco waterfront during the war, none of them sanctioned by union officials. Minutes of Joint ILWU-Waterfront Employers Association Labor Relations Committee, San Francisco, California, in Local 10, May 10, September 8 and 18, 1942, and passim.

15. Harris, *The Right to Manage*, p. 47; "Wages: Squaring the Vicious Circle," *Fortune* 27 (May 1943): 88; Melvyn Dubofsky and Warren Van Tine, *John L. Lewis: A Biography* (New York: New York Times Books, 1977), pp. 418–19; Lichtenstein, *Labor's War at Home*, pp. 150, 159; Art Preis, *Labor's Giant Step: Twenty Years of the CIO* (New York: Pioneer, 1966), p. 161.

16. Sidney Hillman to Metal Trades Councils and Shipbuilding Employers of the West Coast, March 25, 1942, in San Francisco Machinists Locals 68 and 1304 file, file code 37/3, Subject Classified Central Files, Records of the Shipbuilding Stabilization Committee, RG 254, National Archives; Frank Knox (Secretary of the Navy to all

District Commandants, March 25, 1942, in San Francisco Bay Area file, file code unknown RG 254; Ralph Bard (Assistant Secretary of the Navy) to Frances Perkins, May 22, 1942, file code 58/544, RG 254.

17.	Ralph Miller interview, October 6, 1985; Wayne Morse, NWLB Opinion, January 1, 1943, cited in Sam Kagel, Union's Opening Brief, pp. 89 ff., in Case 665, *Lodge 68* vs. *California Metal Trades Association*, in Records Relating to Dispute Cases, national War Labor Board Region X, San Francisco, RG 202, in "Clark Kerr Collection," San Francisco Labor Archives and Research Center, San Francisco State University.

18.	E. F. Dillon to H. W. Brown, January 7, 1944, IAM Papers; Harry Hook and E. F. Dillon to H. W. Brown, April 9, 1944, IAM Papers; Minutes of Special Called Meeting, Lodge 68, March 26, 1944, in Lodge 68 Minutes.

19.	E. F. Dillon to H. W. Brown, April 27, 1944, IAM Papers; Dillon, quoted in *San Francisco Chronicle*, August 3, 1944.

20.	Dillon to Brown, April 27, 1944, IAM Papers; Fred Hewitt (editor, *Machinists Monthly Journal* and alternate labor member of the NWLB) in Exec. Sess., May 2, 1944, pp. 186–88; H. W. Brown to William H. Davis (chairman of the NWLB), May 5, 1944, IAM Papers; H. A. Schrader (IAM International) to George W. Lawson (AFL member, NWLB), May 10, 1944, IAM Papers; H. A. Schrader, statement before the NWLB, May 10, 1944, p. 70, IAM Papers; E. F. Dillon to H. W. Brown, April 27, 1944, IAM Papers; Lloyd Garrison (public member, NWLB), in Exec. Sess., May 10, 1944, p. 325.

21.	Lodge 68 Resolution, April 26, 1944, in Lodge 68 Minutes; Mr. Keezer in Exec. Sess., May 10, 1944, p. 306; J. H. Sapiro (Lodge 68 attorney) in NWLB hearing, May 10, 1944, p. 18; *San Francisco Chronicle*, May 7, 1944.

22.	Thomas F. Neblett (chairman, NWLB Region X, San Francisco) to Lodge 68, telegram announcing directive order, April 20, 1944; the union enforced a ban on overtime at Union Iron Works in the 1930s. Lodge 68 Membership Minutes, April 1, 1936; Lewis Gill (public member, NWLB) in Exec. Sess., May 2, 1944, p. 202; George Taylor (public member, NWLB) in Exec. Sess., May 31, 1944, p. 100; Vinson, quoted in Bowen, *Ships, Machinery, and Mossbacks*, p. 283.

23.	Aubrey Grossman to Lee Pressman, October 28, 1944, in Pipefitters' Local 590 File, Papers of Gladstein, Leonard, Patsy, and Anderson, Bancroft Library, University of California, Berkeley.

24.	Exec. Sess., June 2, 1944, pp. 397–98.

25.	Ibid., p. 401.

26.	Lloyd Garrison in Exec. Sess., June 2, 1944, pp. 363–64; Lewis Gill in Exec. Sess., June 2, 1944, pp. 48, 366; and *New York Times*, July 9, 1944.

27.	*New York Times*, August 1 and 22, 1944; *San Francisco Chronicle*, August 1, 2, 3, and 4, 1944; E. F. Dillon to Harvey W. Brown, September 3, 1944, IAM Papers.

28.	Bowen, *Ships, Machinery, and Mossbacks*, pp. 282, 284, 305, and passim; Dillon to Brown, September 3, 1944.

29.	*New York Times*, August 16, 1944; *San Francisco Chronicle*, August 19 and 20, 1944; Garrison in Exec. Sess., August 18, 1944, p. 596, and Lt. Barrett (USN), in Exec. Sess., August 18, 1944, pp. 623; *San Francisco Chronicle*, August 18 and September 3, 1944; Bowen, *Ships, Machinery, and Mossbacks*, p. 299; *San Francisco Chronicle*, August 27, 1944.

30.   Anthony O'Brien (War Manpower Commission, San Francisco office) in telephone conversation with Bernice Lotwin (War Manpower Commission, Washington, D.C.), September 15, 1944, verbatim transcript, Arthur Burke file, Appeals Cases, Region XII, Records of the War Manpower Commission, Record Group 211, NA-Pac. Sierra (hereafter cited as WMC XII); Bowen, *Ships, Machinery, and Mossbacks*, p. 285; K. C. Apperson to Roy Brown, August 31, 1944, IAM Papers.

31.   Ibid.; Dillon to Brown, September 3, 1944, IAM Papers; Bowen, *Ships, Machinery, and Mossbacks*, p. 303; Dillon to Brown, September 3, 1944, IAM Papers; *San Francisco Chronicle*, September 14, 1944.

32.   O'Brien to Lotwin, WMC XII; Statement of William A. Edwards, late August–early September 1944(?), File 663, ACLU of Northern California Papers, California Historical Society; O'Brien to Lotwin, WMC XII.

33.   J. H. Sapiro, Brief of October 16, 1944, pp. 6–7, in *San Francisco Lodge 68, International Association of Machinists* vs. *Forrestal, et al.*, Case No. 23721G, U.S. District Court, Northern District of California, RG 21, NA-Pac. Sierra; Paul V. McNutt, "In the Matter of the Appeal of Arthur B. Burke: Chairman's Findings of Fact and Decision," p. 10, in File 663, ACLU of Northern California; Lodge 68 Minutes, September 13, 1944.

34.   Dillon to Brown, September 3, 1944.

35.   For example, at the start of hearings in Washington, D.C., Dillon informed IAM headquarters staff that Goldblatt was lobbying officials of other international unions in the capital against the San Francisco machinists' cause. E. F. Dillon telegram to Eric Peterson, general vice-president, International Association of Machinists, June 1, 1944, IAM Papers.

36.   Harry Bridges, "On the Beam," *ILWU Dispatcher*, 1941–46, passim.

37.   *San Francisco Chronicle*, October 30, 1945.

38.   The role of the employers is discussed by leading employer representative, Paul St. Sure, in his oral history. According to St. Sure, a committee of major Bay region employers sat the IAM international executive board down in Berkeley's Claremont Hotel and told them how to place Lodge 68 under receivership and break the strike. "Some comments on Employer Organizations and Collective Bargaining Since 1934. An Interview Conducted by Corine Gilb for the Institute for Industrial Relations Oral History Project" (typescript, University of California at Berkeley, 1957), p. 357.

39.   For opposition to strike by the metal trades and the San Francisco Central Labor Council, see *San Francisco Chronicle*, October 21, 25, and 30, and November 2, 1945; the Communist party's San Francisco newspaper, *People's World*, November 1, 2, and 5, 1945. Dissident elements within the Communist party succeeded in printing their criticisms of the ILWU leaderships' efforts to undermine the machinists' strike in the *People's World* in the fall of 1945. See Harrison George (author of many of these articles), "Crisis in the CPUSA" (Los Angeles, self-published, 1947). The author's 1984 interviews with Levon Mosgofian, a prominent rank-and-file Communist machinist who was expelled from the party for supporting the strike and the Lodge 68 leadership, have also been instructive. For Louis Goldblatt's version of his role in the

strike, including the opposition he encountered from the ILWU membership, see his oral history "Louis Goldblatt — Working Class Leader of the ILWU" (Bancroft Library, University of California, Berkeley, 1974), pp. 336–40.

6

Who Controls the Hiring Hall? The Struggle for Job Control in the ILWU during World War II

Nancy L. Quam-Wickham

For historians of the twentieth-century labor movement, one paradox centers on that fundamental question: did rank-and-file militancy in the new industrial unions of the 1930s diminish rapidly in the 1940s?[1] Many recent scholars have focused on the role some union leaders played in suppressing independent rank-and-file action during World War II. In particular, these labor leaders adopted the no-strike pledge and promised speed-ups in their attempts to maximize production during the war years. According to the critical interpretations, the inevitable consequences of these policies of class collaboration were "apathy toward the unions and disaffection with union leaders." Left-led unions have fared quite poorly in these accounts. Because radical unionists were among the most vociferous proponents of maximized production schemes, shop-floor militancy and rank-and-file independence are presumed to have languished in the war years, casualties of these same radical politics. Even in some of the most balanced accounts, the pro-Communist leaders of the International Longshoremen's and Warehousemen's Union

This chapter originally appeared in Steve Rosswurm, editor, *The CIO's Left-Led Unions* (New Brunswick, N.J.: Rutgers University Press, 1992). Reprinted with permission.

(ILWU) have been characterized as administering the union's affairs during the war "in ways that best served the CP [Communist party] line," not the union's members.[2]

Difficult times, of course, demanded difficult decisions. Expanded union bureaucracies with their stronger disciplinary rules surely contained some rank-and-file dissent during the war years. Focusing on the alleged role productionist labor leaders had in smothering rank-and-file militancy does not fully explain workers' relative quiescence during the war. Union leaders' motivations for cooperating with the state in war production boards have been only partly explored by historians. In addition, as David Brody suggested several years ago, scholars must also turn to the rank and filers themselves to uncover "what was inherent in the labor militancy of the 1930s that gave it so short a life."[3]

For historians interested in the ILWU, labor's experience must be viewed with eyes alert to both the novelties of the war and the continuities of class struggle. Indeed, the continuity of industrial conflict forcefully shaped the pattern of wartime labor relations. The union did cooperate in attempts to increase production during the war, but it also protected significant gains made in the union struggles of the 1930s. Moreover, the ILWU's participation on the regional War Production Board and its subsidiary, the Pacific Coast Maritime Industry Board (PCMIB), did not disfranchise the rank and file.

Neither bureaucratic change within the union's structure nor the union's new relationship of formal accommodation to employers and the state upset many ILWU members. Instead, momentous changes in the larger society, especially the changing racial composition of the organized work force, challenged the prewar concept of rank-and-file "independence." A two-front battle within the ILWU revolved around the question of who would control the hiring hall. The union's leadership fought to maintain the integrity of the hiring system, defending the hall against attacks by boardroom bosses and the armed forces. On the other side, the leadership resisted, often unsuccessfully, the tendencies of some rank and filers to use the hall as an exclusionary device against African-American and Latino workers. In order to understand the character of rank-and-file militancy during the war years, we must briefly consider how the maritime workers' complex class and racial consciousness developed before the war.

THE GENERATION OF 1934 AND
THE ILWU BEFORE THE WAR

After 1934, Pacific coast longshoremen and warehouse workers, under the leadership of Harry Bridges, fashioned one of the most democratic labor unions in the country. The cornerstones of that democracy were rank-and-file control of membership requirements, work rules, local union committees and offices, and, especially, the hiring process. The longshore hiring halls were established by arbitration after the 1934 strikes; the hiring hall system in warehousing was instituted at the local level and then enforced by job action in 1935–36. Although the hiring halls were run jointly by employers and the union, unionists essentially controlled the hiring process through a variety of methods. By transferring the process of hiring workers from the employers' prerogative to the union's purview, workers and their union fundamentally transformed the structure of the labor market in Pacific coast longshoring and warehousing operations. No longer could employers arbitrarily refuse to hire individuals or certain groups of workers based on race, ethnic background, political orientation, or union beliefs. The ILWU's screening of applicants for jobs dispatched through the hiring hall vested tremendous power in the local union. As one ILWU publication put it, "the hiring hall *is* the ILWU."[4]

The ILWU gained a solid reputation in the 1930s as a left-wing union in which rank-and-file activism supported the leadership's ideological commitment to radical politics.[5] This relationship between shared experience, political radicalism, and rank-and-file militancy and independence on the job fostered a fierce sense of community among West Coast longshoremen. The generation of 1934, remembered dockworker Al Langley some five decades later, was "a fraternal outfit. . . . You felt that you had to protect one another. You know, that boss, you hated him so bad, you did anything to get even with him, even if you had to work your head off."[6]

Rank-and-file fraternalism, moreover, extended to union leadership, regardless of political differences, and continued in spite of increasing attacks on both the ILWU and Bridges. Rank-and-file efforts to build a truly industrial union of all maritime workers, as embodied in the formation of the Maritime Federation of the Pacific, foundered after the 1935 tanker strike was broken by oil employers — leaving the longshoremen's union increasingly isolated and intensifying hostilities between Harry Bridges and other trade unionists.[7] The press's criticism of both the union and Bridges stepped up during the growing conservative national mood after the 1938 congressional elections. In that same year, the federal government began the first of four attempts to deport Bridges. To most of the ILWU's membership, though, he was indisputably still "for the working guy." One longshoreman even remembered that these attacks triggered greater aggressiveness among the rank and file: *"that* was when we became strong and militant."8

THE COMING OF WAR AND THE ILWU

The ILWU became aware of the power of the newly united force of industry and the federal government that occurred as a result of war preparedness even before the latter broke the North American Aviation strike with army troops in June 1941. During the spring of 1941, the union began receiving reports of repeated attempts, often successful, by the military and private employers to subvert the union hiring process. In April, the union received notice from the U.S. Army and the Waterfront Employers Association that "certain stevedores" henceforth would be "denied admission to the Army Transport Docks," allegedly for security reasons. When the union protested that its members were being discriminated against for political reasons and that this action breached established union hiring procedures, the army replied tersely that its decision was "not subject to review by any organization outside the Government."9

By August, union officials also were expressing concern about the army's plan to train a "Negro Battalion of 600" for longshore work at an army dock in Oakland. Secretary of War Henry Stimson's response to the Congress of Industrial Organizations (CIO) and ILWU did little to allay their fears that union workers soon would be replaced by army troops. The training and eventual use of troops on the docks, according to Stimson, was necessary "to insure the successful outcome of military operations"; citing safety concerns, he insisted that "military personnel must be used for this task."10

This was an alarming message to the union. In war, much of the cargo being loaded on vessels in Pacific coast ports would be military cargo destined for the South Pacific. Would the military eventually extend the use of army longshoremen to other docks in the Bay Area or to other ports on the coast? The challenge for the union was how to maintain its presence, especially its control over the hiring process, in the face of military demands.

One answer to these demands was the union's outright unwillingness to cooperate with the military. In August 1941, the dispatcher at

Local 10's hiring hall received a call to provide six winch drivers for work on an army transport ship at the Benecia Arsenal. Because winch drivers could neither load nor discharge a ship's cargo without longshoremen and because no orders for dispatch of longshoremen to the job had been issued by the army, the dispatcher refused to fill the order for the winch drivers. Later that day, an army captain at the Benecia Arsenal admitted, after questioning by union officials, that "civil service employees would handle the cargo in the hold and on the dock." The union then refused to provide the six winch drivers to the army.[11]

ILWU support for the establishment of a tripartite wartime production board constituted yet another response to the coming of war. In November 1941, Bridges, who previously had proposed, then shelved, a similar plan, brought the issue of increasing production back to the ILWU membership. He appealed to union members to endorse the "Murray Plan," a scheme linking the "establishment of a joint labor relations committee for each basic industry in the United States" to increased production. He urged ILWU members to write their "respective Congressmen," recommending adoption of the Murray Plan, "in the interests of national defense, and as a step towards strengthening genuine collective bargaining and to offset passage of anti-strike and anti-labor legislation" then pending in Congress.[12]

Later that month, Bridges was in Washington promoting his version of a defense plan. On November 26 and 27, he met with U.S. Maritime Assistant Commissioner Edward Macauley, Sidney Hillman of the Office of Production Management, steamship company executive Roger Lapham, and labor arbitrator Wayne L. Morse, all of whom "expressed approval" of Bridges' plan. As then formulated, the plan would establish a tripartite labor relations board in order to "secure maximum production" and guaranteed no strikes by labor "for the duration."[13]

Bridges returned to San Francisco a few days after the attack on Pearl Harbor and presented his plan to the employers' association. The employers quickly accepted the provisions of the plan, but within a week they recanted their endorsement, intimating that the plan was nothing but a "maneuver" by Bridges to obtain a "favorable deportation decision." They insisted that "as a result of seven years of . . . almost deliberate sabotage in the industry through slowdowns, violations of agreements," they could not trust the union's "honesty or sincerity in presenting this plan." Management went on opposing the defense production plan (by now commonly called the Bridges Plan), and the impasse between employers, the government, and the union over implementing it continued. The Bridges Plan did not become policy until mid-February 1942.[14]

Earlier, the ILWU rank and file had refused to abandon their commitment to nonintervention. Shortly after the Nazis invaded the Soviet Union on June 22, 1941, a Communist "club" within warehouse Local 6 introduced at a regular membership meeting a resolution advocating wholehearted support for the "war of liberation" against the Nazis. Yet, without the support of the local leadership, the resolution suffered a stinging ten to one electoral defeat. The membership clearly rejected CP-sponsored proposals on certain issues at certain times. However, later developments also attest to the leadership Bridges provided: at the next membership meeting in July, Bridges, in an hour-long speech, introduced a similar resolution to the membership. This time the resolution passed nearly unanimously.[15]

In later months, the ILWU rank and file was more willing than business and government to endorse such provisions as the no-strike pledge and the oath to speed production. Several recent historical works quote at length the story of how Bridges, when he outlined the ILWU's official stance on the no-strike pledge and wartime speed-up, was laughed at and nearly booed off the stage of the Wilmington Bowl in southern California by rank-and-file members of Local 13. As the account goes, after the union president outlined his plan, a rank-and-file member of the local chided Bridges, "Just because your pal Joe Stalin is in trouble, don't expect us to give up our conditions to help him out." This anecdote is meant to illustrate the depth of antagonism between a "class collaborationist" labor leader, who both cooperated with government and industry and was sympathetic to the CP, and militant rank-and-file unionists who were unwilling to swallow the CP line on wartime production increases.[16]

There was, of course, antagonism between some union members and their leader, but more happened at the meeting in Wilmington in 1942 than that oft-repeated tale indicates. As "Chick" Loveridge remembered it, Bridges was, in fact, "booed unmercifully" by the audience of dockworkers. However, then, following a long wait in line, Bridges returned to the podium and "after he hit that [microphone] and talked for forty-five or fifty minutes, people wanted to polish his head and shine his shoes and bow to him and everything." Similarly, in an extensive series of oral histories of rank-and-file ILWU members, remarkably few recalled any opposition to the no-strike pledge. Ruben Negrete, a San Pedro longshoreman, remembered during the war, "[W]e worked our asses off [because] we were helping our country. . . . How Harry made that promise that we wouldn't strike, and at the time, we all listened to Harry. We still do. . . . I don't think there was too much turmoil here, the

guys were patriotic and all." Art Kaunisto, whose immigrant father had
been blacklisted for radical union activities, put the issue within its
historical context. "During them days," he said, "it was right after Pearl
Harbor, there wasn't much said about it. You'd do your work and that
was it."

Others remember more practical twists to the lack of criticism over the
no-strike pledge. Elmer Gutierrez recalled that no matter what the
membership thought, Bridges "was pretty well known for getting what
he wanted." "Of course we couldn't say anything, 'cause a lot of us had
brothers, uncles [in the service] and we had to go with the war effort,"
asserted Elmer Mevert; "there was no such thing as dissension." Al
Langley remembered the reaction to the no-strike pledge was "generally
favorable," although "a lot of people gave more consideration to the
monetary gain [increased production would bring] than to the war effort
that we were actually trying to accomplish. Ninety-eight percent of the
membership coastwide supported Harry."[17]

Few members, by the same token, who were interviewed could recall
any hostility toward the wartime speed-up. Pete Grassi argued that work
"was faster and everything; we wanted to win the war." Kathryn Young,
remembering her days as a bottle labeler in a San Francisco warehouse,
stated that "[I] worked like a son-of-a-gun" during the war yet could not
recall any opposition to the speed-up by women working in that bottling
plant. Likewise, Charles Hackett reported that "no one [in Local 6] was
opposed to the [speed-up]. We even worked extra overtime, which was
against our [union's] principles!"[18]

A general availability of work at the union's lucrative overtime rates
of pay, hinted at in Hackett's testimony, suggests one possible reason
why union members did not object strenuously to the speed-up. Bill
Castagnasso, a union member and supervising foreman on the waterfront, testified to the changes in the pace of work during the war. In the
early years of the war, when "we started getting all these [new] guys out
of the hall," he told an interviewer,

We started giving what we called "deals." We'd tell a gang, "OK, now look, for
every [railroad] car of [200 oil] drums that you unload . . . you get one hour
credit." So the gangs would come to work in the morning and . . . knock off
their cars as fast as they could. . . . I have seen gangs go home at 12 o'clock with
eight double-decked cars [unloaded] . . . and get paid for eight hours. Many,
many times we'd have guys go home at four in the afternoon with twelve hours
pay — eight straight and four hours over[time]. And this happened straight
through the war. Guys were working hard.[19]

There are still other reasons why ILWU rank and filers remained relatively quiescent during the war. On the docks, some rank-and-file ILWU members and employers made informal deals over work processes, in the evolution of the "four on, four off" system, where only half of the workers in an eight-man gang would be working at any given time. Few stevedoring companies objected to this system, because it padded the payroll, making cost-plus contracts all the more lucrative. For workers accustomed to the prewar pace of work on the docks and in the ships, cost-plus was a welcomed change. Longshoreman Frank Sunstedt explained that his fellow workers were well aware of the relationship between four on, four off and cost-plus contracts: "[The employer] would say, 'Hey, we don't need this many men down here. Why don't two or so of you guys go get a cup of coffee or something.' Well, you'd see that it would be readily acceptable to the men." Remembered Langley, "that was supposedly *our* privilege. . . . The employer never ever complained."[20]

Few employers or military officials interpreted workers taking advantage of four on, four off as slowdowns or work stoppages. On the other hand, the union's international leadership denounced the corruption inherent in the four on, four off system, equally blaming "labor hoarding" bosses and "deliberate shirkers" within the ranks for the continuing practice.[21] However, local union officials often took the complaints as more nuisances than serious problems that should be addressed. John Mitchell remembered one such objection to the longshoremen's new wartime pace of work by a "goldbraid . . . a little old stinking ensign." As his local's president, Mitchell simply instructed the union members to get back "on their feet." Bridges could not stop the four on, four off system, given the reluctance of local union officials to end the practice. As two workers commented later, in the four on, four off system the employers "created a monster" that "they couldn't eliminate after the war"; longshoremen later paid the price in extensive employer surveillance of work processes on the postwar docks.[22]

The uses of this corrupt system reveal as much about the longshoreman's sense of community as they do his concepts of class conflict. John Martinez remarked that "all of us fellows had families, and during the war our sons were overseas. These fellows that worked for me, their sons would come home and I'd say, 'You go ahead and stay there. I'll take care of the job.' We would carry the guy." Four on, four off also allowed workers to complete chores that otherwise would have required a day off work: looking for an apartment, visiting the rationing board, shopping for scarce goods. In accepting this new work pace, longshoremen, in the words of one sociologist, "torn by the conflicting loyalties of nationalism and class, ultimately determined the proper mix of accommodation and resistance on the docks during the war."[23]

The union initiated its own forms of workers' control. With the international's help, ILWU warehousemen were able to consolidate gains made during the previous few years. The ILWU's great "March Inland" of the 1930s had been halted largely by the teamsters; part of the truce from those jurisdictional battles stipulated that teamsters could not deposit their cargoes more than 20 feet from their trucks or inside ILWU warehouses. In the spirit of maximized production, ILWU leaders rescinded this agreement with the teamsters. To "speed up the war effort," teamster truck drivers could cross well-defined jurisdictional boundaries to place their cargoes anywhere in ILWU warehouses or on ILWU docks as long as such cargoes were designated with a "T" (teamster) ticket. ILWU warehousemen would then rebuild those "T-ticketed" cargoes, even if they were already palletized and ready and scheduled for immediate loading on board a ship. One Local 6 business agent later characterized the practice of "T-ticketing" as make work that did nothing to increase production or speed the movement of cargo. The practice was adopted solely as a way of espousing productionist rhetoric while maintaining jurisdictional prerogatives.[24]

THE BATTLE FOR THE HIRING HALL: CHALLENGE FROM THE OUTSIDE

Once war was declared, the prospects of employment in defense industries promised opportunities for economic prosperity. "Buster" Hanspard, who had spent most of the previous two decades working on railroad and levee labor gangs in Mississippi and Louisiana, described the mood of cautious optimism in early 1942. "At that time," he remembered, "people was going everywhere then. People were scouting out everywhere." Yet, paradoxically, as wartime employment in general began to increase in 1942, the ILWU became engaged in ever more serious battles to retain control over those jobs that it had before war was declared. On several fronts, the union's hiring system again was under attack by the military, which intended to use army personnel and civil service employees as longshoremen and warehousemen all along the coast, as happened both in San Diego and Seattle. Seattle unionists also worried that another "colored battalion" of army longshore trainees would take over more civilian jobs then held by union members.[25]

Both private employers and the military sought to institute "preferred" status for certain groups of workers in order to create "steady, specialty gangs that stay made up and work together all the time." The union's leadership responded by refusing to oblige both the military and private employers. As Bridges argued, "preferred gangs would disrupt the union, destroy morale and arouse bitterness" among men who worked rotated jobs out of the hiring hall.[26]

Opposition to the institution of "preferred status" workers was not limited to union leaders. In December 1942, the membership of longshore Local 10 unanimously rejected a motion by its executive board to supply 20 steady longshoremen to the Army Transport Service (ATS) for loading ammunition at Richmond. A motion was then presented to supply the ATS with 50 gangs — of 18 men each — of steady longshoremen for ammunition loading at the same terminal! That motion, too, was unanimously rejected. Instead, after a "lengthy discussion," another motion was proposed and carried "unanimously that Local 1-10 of the ILWU will positively dispatch safe and efficient gangs when requested by the Army and Navy Transportation Service," with no mention of steady, "preferred" status.[27]

Requests for "preferred" gangs was just one aspect of a continuing effort to supersede unions that grew into a bitter, running battle between labor and industry throughout the war years. On army docks up and down the Pacific coast, government clerks, who allegedly were "secured from the Veterans of Foreign Wars and blanketed into civil service for the emergency, but without examination," replaced union clerks, who were laid off.[28]

Groups of "dock seamen," like civil service employees, replaced longshoremen on docks and warehouse workers in (railroad) carloading operations over the protests of the ILWU. These dock seamen, the union protested, were hired by the army via the "State Employment Office or off the street" to work at "longer hours, no overtime, [and] lesser rates of pay." The union's response was characteristic: organize these workers. These efforts, however, often were hampered by the military's bureaucratic "hostility and a determined effort to prevent union participation in the war effort." In mid-1942, for example, the union unsuccessfully proposed that dock seamen be permitted to register as permit longshoremen, that a special permit longshoremen's hiring hall be set up, and that an ILWU member be hired as dispatcher for that hall.[29]

The military's outright hostility greeted ILWU efforts to organize dock and warehouse workers, because the armed services often hired non-union civil servants to replace union members.[30] Homer Dunlap was

fired from his civil service job at an ATS dock in 1943 but returned to
work at another military establishment as an ILWU warehouseman and
union organizer. His "secret" task was to organize civil servants. One
day, while piling freight on the dock, he recalled, "here come the Captain
and the Colonel and the Army. [It was] nothing but brass caps coming
down. They took me across the road . . . and the Colonel did all the talking. [He] says, 'I got all these stripes around my arms and I don't want to
lose them.'" Orders had come down from Washington to fire Dunlap for
his organizing activities. When the union agreed to take him off the job,
he was relieved. Fearful that his draft deferment would be canceled for
his organizing activities, Dunlap later recalled that he "didn't want them
to throw me in the army — you know, that's what they'd do to you." The
ILWU also collected numerous affidavits from unionists who had been
proselytized by military officials. An indignant union member resented
the implication that patriotism and union affiliation were not compatible:
"[I] was approached on three different occasions and it was suggested to
me I drop my Union affiliations and join the Naval Supply Depot under
civil service and a bright future was assured me by doing so. I am an ex-
serviceman from the first World War and a CIO member."[31]

The patterns of wartime labor relations paralleled the prewar experience, at least in part, because of those recruited to perform the military's
managerial functions. One high-ranking officer involved in San Francisco ATS operations was a former district manager for a steamship
company, who had, it was reported, recruited scabs during the 1934
strike. Additional reports indicated that other military officers were formerly superintendents and supervisors of local steamship and stevedoring companies. This antiunion bias extended to the top of the military
as well. Rear Admiral Emory Land, head of the War Shipping Administration, once remarked that all union organizers during the war "ought to
be shot at sunrise."[32]

A shortage of workers plagued the longshoring and warehousing
industries on the Pacific coast by mid-1942. In San Pedro, the dearth of
longshoremen was so acute that stevedoring companies resorted to
calling the local high school in order to find enough workers to unload
perishable and nonessential cargoes from vessels in the harbor. In ports
up and down the coast, servicemen on leave were allowed to work temporarily as permit longshoremen and warehouse workers. By the summer
of 1944, the War Manpower Commission endowed its top priority rating
on longshore work in the San Francisco Bay Area. As the eventual outcome of the war seemed assured by autumn of that year, moreover, war

workers in search of peacetime jobs "fled" the Pacific coast at an astonishing rate.[33]

Employers, who conflated the general shortage of civilian workers in the latter years of the war with the allegedly inherent inability of the union, through its hiring hall, to provide enough competent workers, sought to solve labor shortages by recapturing the hiring process. They argued that civilian labor "pools" ought to replace inefficient union hiring halls. In reply, union leaders admonished locals to do better at fulfilling labor needs and requested longshoremen themselves to assist in recruiting new workers. Only concerted action by union members would "offset recruiting efforts by all public agencies." Despite the union's best efforts to recruit new workers, however, employers' threats did not cease. In June 1945, Henry Schmidt warned international Vice-President Rosco Craycraft that "there have been some threats [from employers] . . . that they will be forced to set-up their own civilian longshore pools and thus circumvent the hiring hall or employ military labor battalions."[34]

Employer representatives on the PCMIB, as part of their campaign against the hiring halls, in 1943 took away the screening privileges formerly held by the union as part of its hiring procedure. In December 1942, the ILWU had initiated a recruiting and training program for new workers that functioned separately from the PCMIB. By mid-1943, however, Chairman Paul Eliel and employer members of the board seized control of this program and replaced its ILWU director with another "labor representative," John Kelly of the Web Pressman's Union, an American Federation of Labor affiliate. The ILWU leadership, which vehemently opposed this move, argued that not only must experienced waterfront workers evaluate the fitness of prospective applicants for union work but also "new workers coming on the waterfront must be . . . educated in union organization principles by our union." The union, furthermore, insisted that only ILWU officials, in properly screening the applicants, could "keep an eye open to see that no undesirable elements opposed to the principles of labor may be fed into our union by employer interests." Finally, in a letter to the president of the Web Pressmen's Union, J. Vernon Burke, Bridges appealed to strictly traditional union concerns: "It would be very hard for us to understand, and possibly for your organization also, if under similar circumstances a longshoreman was put in charge of recruiting and training of apprentices for the industry over which your union has jurisdiction and contracts. We would think there was something very wrong underneath it all if such a situation occurred."[35]

By late 1944, the PCMIB had placed another official in charge of its recruiting and training, but the union also found this arrangement unsatisfactory. The board stationed its recruiting officer at the U.S. Employment Service (USES). Laborers who came to the USES for jobs, many of whom had recently been laid off from work in shipyards, were screened by the board's agent. Once an applicant passed this review, he or she was sent upstairs to "four gentlemen representing employers of labor" who screened the applicant again. If the applicant passed this inquiry, only then was he or she sent to the union hiring hall to apply for work. Unionists were nearly powerless in preventing abuses of this system, even when prospective workers were openly discriminated against. Near the end of the war, the union members of the board protested when two job applicants were turned down because they were Chinese-Americans. However, their objections were overruled because, as one employer representative stated flatly, "it developed that the work was too heavy," even though the men were not given the opportunity to try it. Not only was the union in jeopardy of losing total control over the hiring process but also the PCMIB and the state, through the USES, sanctioned racial discrimination in employment, despite Executive Order 8802 (prohibiting racial discrimination in employment) and the formation of the Fair Employment Practices Commission.[36]

Finally, management also attempted to enlist the government's aid in winning its battle against the union. During the war, employers and their representatives continually tried to force a confrontation between the military and the union over hiring procedures. One such incident occurred when San Pedro longshoremen, members of Local 13, balked at increasing the sling-load limit of cement from 21 to 31 hundred-pound sacks while loading navy vessels. Eliel, openly allied with employers on the board, threatened to order "U.S. troops . . . to work the ships."[37]

THE BATTLE FOR THE HIRING HALL: CHALLENGE FROM WITHIN

Wartime labor shortages figure prominently in the history of the ILWU. For the leadership, the conflict was clearly framed in class terms: who would control hiring — workers or industry? Yet, the rank and file fought the battle on two fronts. Workers fought capital on one side and other workers on the other side. ILWU leaders had to recruit new workers during the war in order to meet manpower requirements and, thus, stave off the bosses' attack on its hiring halls. In the warehouse division, at least one new worker in five was African-American or

Mexican-American; in the longshore division, the percentage of minorities was even higher. White workers often did not take kindly to this influx of nonwhites, especially after recruiting efforts intensified at the end of 1942. Many slowdowns and work stoppages came about as whites resisted the entry or promotion of minority workers on the job.

The ILWU's leadership drastically underestimated the extent and potency of racist beliefs among its rank-and-file members. A good example of this is a 1942 *Dispatcher* editorial in which Bridges chided members for "some incidents" of racism. Declaring that "discrimination against Negroes is anti-labor, anti-American and anti-white," Bridges attributed racist assaults on black workers to three things. First, the attacks were the "sabotage" actions of a few "appeasers, Trotskyites and other such Hitlerian fifth column elements" striving to "disrupt the whole war effort." Second, he asserted, in typical left-wing prose, that "Southern Bourbon labor-haters" were fomenting "Negro hatred and discrimination" in order to "create and keep a cheap labor market"; he continued, "'Divide and make profits,' is their open slogan." Third, Bridges blamed African-Americans themselves: "Negro workers, lacking experience and discipline and nursing past wounds, have needlessly antagonized some older members of the union and have thus furnished fuel for the sabotage work of the deliberately disruptive minority elements."[38]

The ILWU leadership, however, made only limited efforts to enforce its dedication to the "economic and political equality" of all races. Officially, the ILWU's leadership openly denounced racist discrimination on the job, in the union, and in the larger society. In 1942, for example, Louis Goldblatt, an ILWU member, a Communist, and secretary-treasurer of the California State Industrial Union Council, CIO, illustrated this ideological commitment in his condemnation of the wartime internment of Japanese-Americans. Many ILWU leaders, furthermore, like other trade unionists, intellectuals, and political activists of the time, saw parallels between the race hatred of white Americans and the Aryan supremist beliefs of the Nazis. However, what distinguished the racist actions of many ILWU members and probably made those acts more tolerable to the international leadership is that it often was hard to distinguish among job consciousness, union pride, and flagrant racial discrimination.[39]

ILWU members looked to their own experiences in order to interpret racial antagonism on the docks and in the warehouses: the result was often a blurring of the distinctions between racism and class antagonism. Henry Gaitan, a Mexican-American who labored on the racially segregated lumber docks in San Pedro during the 1930s, recalled that waterfront employers had pitted one ethnic group against another in order to increase production in the prewar years. "What the company used to do," he remembered, was "to hire Italians over there, and then hire a group of Mexicans over here, and then a group of something else over there . . . and then say, 'Look, those guys can do a better job than you guys.'" Through this lens, he contended that it was the employers who, during the war, were "bringing these blacks from Texas. The idea was to break the union, weaken the union. . . . The [employers' association] was one of the instigators of it." Eugene Lasartemay, an African-American engineer, remembered how ship owners had traditionally used black workers as strikebreakers; Bridges constantly played upon this awareness to remind ILWU members that they should "learn how to work with [blacks] now" because employers had imported "blacks to break the strikes" of 1919 and 1934.[40]

The inability to draw a sharp distinction between job consciousness and racism was still apparent to Walter Williams over 40 years after the war. Williams, a CIO organizer who came to the waterfront after a bitter struggle over the training and upgrading of black tradesmen in a large shipyard, found the situation "almost confusing." "You had to wonder," he said, if whites resented black workers "because they considered us to be invaders, because we weren't there in large numbers when the union first organized . . . or whether it was just out-and-out racism."[41]

This "confusion" between race pride and union pride is superbly illustrated in an incident involving one of the first Mexican-American ILWU walking bosses and an all African-American eight-man gang. Mexican-Americans had faced much prejudice on the docks before the war — so much so that several remembered the increased presence of blacks "took the pressure away from us Mexicans." Anti-Mexican-American sentiment did not, however, disappear and John Martinez had "a lot of problems" with both white and African-American longshoremen. Martinez, who knew well the sting of white workers' bigotry through decades of experience as a dockworker, finally reached the breaking point. "One day," he recalled, "I had enough of it." He stopped all work on the ship after being insulted all morning by an all-black gang of longshoremen who were angry because Martinez had docked them an hour's pay apiece the previous day. The exchange that followed reveals much. The gang in the hold, recounted Martinez, said, "Hey there's that SOB. . . . What does [he] know about working? [He] never worked a day in [his] life!" Martinez stopped the winch and told them, "Now look, you mothers. You say I never worked a day in my life on this waterfront. I'll tell you, back in '33 and '34, and in '36 and '37, [in] '40, I pounded the bricks for this union, when you all were still back in Africa!"[42] The fact was, however, that several of those African-Americans in the ship's hold that day were not "back in Africa" in 1934 when the ILWU was formed. They were experienced longshoremen who had come to San Pedro during the war from the Gulf Coast, where, as members of segregated "Jim Crow" International Longshoremen's Association locals, they had been relegated to only the most noxious work. Nor were they alone. A significant percentage of black dockworkers new to the ILWU during the war had been members of the International Longshoremen's Association in the South before the war.[43]

In other cases, however, the source of discrimination was easily discerned: it was "out-and-out racism." One dockworker found himself in a gang with a black man who "nobody else wanted to work with" but learned to respect that man's skill while loading bales of cotton and wool with him in a ship's hold; they remained partners throughout the war. He later placed the blame for this hostility on the local union. "Corky" Wilson found that even though some blacks were "nice guys" and good, hardworking "old-time stevedores," he just "couldn't cope with the colored people." So, he formed his own gang of eight men, no less than half of whom were family members. Williams described one common response of "regular 'longies'" (longshoremen) to black workers: some whites would say, "'I'm going to call me a damn replacement' if they saw a black guy coming down into the hold. And they would call a replacement rather than work with us." Joe Stahl also remembered that many "old-timers wouldn't work with a black guy. [They] would turn around and call a replacement."[44]

Joseph H. Tipp, assistant to the PCMIB, noticed similar sentiments among longtime members of the union who felt threatened by the admission of black workers into longshore jobs. Tipp, in a series of reports to the board, observed widespread complaints on the San Francisco waterfront against "too many replacements, mostly colored, [who] have slowed down efficiency and production in most of the old-time, good gangs, according to the walking bosses." However, in his reports on declining production rates, Tipp never differentiated between inexperienced and experienced black dockworkers. Rather, he noted a general resistance among whites to all black workers. Henry Schmidt also remarked that many members of the generation of 1934 "were opposed to those people coming in. The typical, popular idea was that, 'We shouldn't start with this.'"[45]

Tipp further indicated that racism was sometimes masked by concerns about union conditions. "Many old-timers in regular gangs," Tipp wrote, objected to working with "colored boys, not because of their color, but because most of them are shiftless and lazy, folding up after a few hours . . . leaving most of the work in the hatch to the old-timers — but they draw the same pay." Like Williams and Stahl, Tipp also noted that many whites avoided working with blacks by calling replacements or dissolving their gangs. In 1942, the union, primarily in response to gang instability brought on by rampant racism, decreed that all gangs had to stay together for a minimum of 30 days. Shortly thereafter, Tipp observed that some old-timers subverted the new gang rule by deliberately "getting fired from a job for doing slow work in order to get rid of the gang."[46]

Incidents of racial antagonism were not limited to the docks. Before the war, the management of a Colgate plant in the East Bay, whose workers were organized in the ILWU warehouse division's Local 6, allegedly maintained a "gentlemen's agreement" with the union to limit African-Americans to a few poorly paid janitorial positions. These race barriers were broken in 1939, but only after one black man's bid to gain a better position in the plant was put to a vote of the union members at Colgate. The testimony of the vice-president of the local, seven Colgate stewards, and the man bidding on the job, Eugene Lasartemay, was required before the membership voted to abolish racial restrictions on job advancement. This action, however, did not eradicate race hatred in the plant during the war. Fannie Walker, a former domestic, was the "very first Negro colored girl at Colgate." She endured racial slurs, faced racial segregation in the lunchroom, was prevented from using the water fountain, and repeatedly had her lunch put on the floor, where "the dogs ate," by her fellow workers. Virginia Wysinger, another black worker at Colgate during the war, found that white workers harassed her by sabotaging the production process to make her look incompetent. Both women recalled that although some white workers supported them, racial harassment was curtailed only through the actions of the ILWU warehouse division's leadership.[47]

Yet, what is important about these examples is not that racial prejudice existed, or that, as Bridges would have had it, the consequences of that bigotry were absenteeism and a slowdown of production, but that whites who did not want to work with African-American and Mexican-American workers could easily manipulate the union hiring system to their advantage. All a worker had to do was to return to the hiring hall where there were other jobs waiting to be had. This powerful instrument of workers' control — the hiring hall — clearly was misused by the reactionary and the racist to further job-conscious, not class-conscious, unionism.

Rank and filers often found themselves in direct opposition to their national leaders, especially on racial issues. Many ILWU leaders supported the hiring of black workers through local union halls, but direct action by the International in settling racial disputes among the rank and file was often limited by other, more practical, considerations.[48] In December 1943, a longshore local in Portland, Oregon, refused to accept a black man as a full member "solely because he was a Negro." Yet, outside of a letter from Bridges asking the membership "to eliminate any form of racial discrimination from your ranks," the International took no action. Concerted direct action to prevent race discrimination would have necessitated a drastic modification in the operation of the hiring hall system, a measure the International was not prepared to take.[49]

The Portland incident contrasts sharply with another episode of racism nearly two years later, where practicality led the leadership in a different direction. In June 1945, ILWU warehousemen in Stockton, California, refused to work with Japanese-Americans recently released from internment camps. This incident was not only a political and social embarrassment to the International leadership but also threatened the ILWU's organizing drive in Hawaii, where a substantial number of workers were Japanese-Americans. The International resolved the crisis by revoking the Stockton local's charter until the members accepted Japanese-American workers into their local. The hiring hall system, moreover, was not jeopardized by this action, because in the last days of the war the union was faced with a surplus, not a shortage, of workers.[50]

There is little evidence that the ILWU leadership actively contested racism within the rank and file. Instead, local autonomy prevailed. Locals screened applicants for membership through their "investigating committees." Even during the war, new applicants were quizzed about their backgrounds: What did they do during the 1934 strike? Had they ever been strikebreakers? What did they think about the union? What experience did they have? The answers to these and other questions were taken seriously; most applicants were required to document their claims. The investigating committee was, recalled Paul Ware, "a very important committee. It was the structure of the union." To Mickey Mahon, who applied for membership during the war, the investigating process posed some problems. The committee members, "all '34 guys, good, solid men," demanded of Mahon that he verify his whereabouts during

the 1934 strike; after a delay, the committee granted him union membership only after Mahon had somehow proven where he was in 1934 —
unemployed, "living off the land: bumming water, food, panhandling, . . .
washing dishes, [and] hang[ing] around Pershing Square" in Los
Angeles. Few African-American workers made it to, let alone through,
the investigating committee process. Instead, remembered Williams,
African-American dockworkers were offered the chance to work only
after they had signed "a commitment to work there in a temporary status
and to approve of being terminated after the war."[51]

The promotions committee was also a locus of rank-and-file control.
Unlike many unionized workers, ILWU longshoremen were not
promoted on a seniority basis alone. Instead, workers not only had to
have both job seniority and job knowledge but also had to prove it to
their peers before they were considered for promotions. Frank Sunstedt,
chairman of the San Pedro longshore local's promotion committee
during the war, noted that his local used the committee to deny African-
Americans promotions: "No black member had ever been given a
gang. . . . Every time a black man was about ready to get a gang, the
[other] promotions committee members would go around and entice
anyone else to get a gang, just to keep a black man out. . . . These guys
used to . . . go through these files and any application of a black man,
they'd throw it in the wastebasket." In an interview recorded almost 40
years after the war ended, Kaunisto expressed his enduring frustration
about how his local's promotions committee functioned during the war.
When African-Americans applied for gang boss ratings to the promotions committee, the committee members "would just kind of roust them
around. A bunch of guys would ask them, 'Can you do this? Can you do
that?' Christ, you're not supposed to be a college man to work on the
waterfront."[52]

The wartime labor emergency compelled at least one promotions
committee to revise its criteria for upgrading workers, in the direction of
greater racial exclusivity. In 1945, Langley was the job dispatcher in
Local 13's hiring hall, and, when he could not locate any available and
qualified white longshoreman, he sent a black man, Rice Sims, out on a
job as gang boss. When Sims arrived at the job site that evening, the gang
of "white Navy kids" refused to work for him and walked off the job.
The company fired Sims because his gang would not work, and Langley
was reprimanded by the chief dispatcher for sending a black man out on
a gang boss job. The union, afraid that it would be vulnerable to antidiscrimination lawsuits if it refused to dispatch other qualified black men to
bosses' jobs, took the Sims case to arbitration. The resolution to this

problem was "simple" and was extended coastwide as formal policy. "The employers and the union agreed that no man could be a boss unless he had five years in the industry [on the Pacific coast]. . . . We weren't ready for the blacks as a boss [sic]. They had to agree to something to keep down the fuss on the waterfront. . . . The blacks had then begun to get acclimated, and they knew their stuff. . . . They wanted to be part of the industry, too."[53] By establishing this rule, management and the union effectively restricted African-American and Mexican-American workers to lower-paying hold and deck jobs, because most of these workers were hired during the war and, thus, did not have the requisite ILWU seniority to qualify for the more prestigious skilled jobs.

The hiring hall and the investigating and promotions committees unquestionably endowed longshoremen and warehouse workers in the ILWU with a high degree of workers' control over the social relations of production. As such, they were invaluable weapons in labor's arsenal for the class-based battle against industry. However, they also were exceptionally effective exclusionary devices through which workers could determine which elements of the working class their union would represent.

CONCLUSION

Despite the ILWU's productionist orientation, the fundamental dynamics of interaction between employers and the union did not change after Pearl Harbor. What changed was not so much the essential conflict as the degree to which both the union and employers sought state intervention in resolving that conflict to their respective satisfaction.

There were work slowdowns and even occasional work stoppages, but these events, important indices of "shop-floor disaffection," seldom involved a direct confrontation between the leadership and the rank and file over either the no-strike pledge or a speed-up in production. The ILWU leadership, motivated by both pro-Communist political consider- ations and the exigencies of more "traditional" unionism, enacted mea- sures designed to maximize production but refused to sacrifice the real economic and contractual gains of the previous decade. The ILWU's wartime production record remains in dispute; most reports record a 10–15 percent rise in productivity over prewar levels, but others assert that little speed-up actually occurred. It must be kept in mind, furthermore, that immediate prewar productivity levels, the standard against which wartime rates were measured, were far below pre-1934 levels.[54]

The real struggle within the ILWU revolved around the question of who would determine the vision and direction of the union in the war years. This process did not involve a clash between economic self-interest and patriotic support for the fight against fascism. It, instead, involved a struggle over the best way to protect the achievements of the 1930s. For the leadership, preserving the hiring hall system demanded some cooperation with the state. Yet, many workers sought to protect the gains of the 1930s by preventing new workers from enjoying those very same benefits. In this context, rank and filism meant racism; if the leaders had more aggressively attacked racism, it would have meant attacking the rank and file and control at the point of production. Many racial exclusionists in the union were not stereotypical "war babies" — young workers who "came from non-union, rural, conservative backgrounds" — but, rather, "old-timers," many of whom created the militant, left-wing union in the 1930s.[55] Does their behavior during the war say something about the character and limits of working-class militancy before the war? In considering the actions of the ILWU rank and file, we must ask: for whom, really, was the class struggle waged? Many rank-and-file members of the ILWU, acting contentiously to preserve job control and their sense of community during the war, placed real constraints on the leadership's ability to pursue a radical political agenda. In time, the ideological commitment to racial equality among left-wing ILWUers triumphed, but only after many highly contested and costly battles in the postwar period — battles that then, too, were fought over the hiring hall.

NOTES

    1.   David Brody, "Radical Labor History and Rank-and-File Militancy," in *Workers in Industrial America: Essays on the 20th Century Struggle* (New York: Oxford University Press, 1980), pp. 146–58; Maurice Isserman, *Which Side Were You On? The American Communist Party During the Second World War* (Middletown, Conn.: Wesleyan University Press, 1982), pp. 137–38.

    2.   For the quotation, see Nelson Lichtenstein, "Ambiguous Legacy: The Union Security Problem During World War II," *Labor History* (hereafter *LH*) 18 (Spring 1977): 227; Nelson Lichtenstein, *Labor's War at Home: The CIO in World War II* (New York: Cambridge University Press, 1982); James Green, "Fighting on Two Fronts: Working-Class Militancy in the 1940s," *Radical America* 9 (July–August 1975): 7–48; Michael Torigian, "National Unity on the Waterfront: Communist Politics and the ILWU During the Second World War," *LH* 30 (1990): 432.

    3.   Brody, "Radical Labor History and Rank-and-File Militancy," p. 157.

    4.   Paul Heide, "A Warehouseman's Reminiscences," interviewed by Frank N. Jones, Earl Warren Oral History Project, University of California, Berkeley, Regional

Oral History Office, 1969, p. 7; Harvey Schwartz, *The March Inland: Origins of the ILWU Warehouse Division, 1934–1938* (Los Angeles: University of California, Institute of Industrial Relations, 1978), p. 90; International Longshoremen's and Warehousemen's Union, *Union Busting: New Model*, quoted in Charles P. Larrowe, *Shape-Up and Hiring Hall: A Comparison of Hiring Methods and Labor Relations on the New York and Seattle Waterfronts* (Berkeley: University of California Press, 1955), p. 139.

5.   Bruce Nelson, *Workers on the Waterfront: Seamen, Longshoremen, and Unionism in the 1930s* (Urbana: University of Illinois Press, 1988); Howard Kimeldorf, *Reds or Rackets? The Making of Radical and Conservative Unions on the Waterfront* (Berkeley: University of California Press, 1988).

6.   Al Langley, interviewed by Harvey Schwartz, November 19, 1981, ILWU–National Endowment for the Humanities Oral History Project, in the ILWU Archives, San Francisco (ILWUA). Unless otherwise noted, all interviews referred to below are part of this project, which interviewed 244 rank-and-file members from eight ILWU locals, recorded between 1981 and 1986. Most of those interviewed were members of the union during World War II; many had been active in the union's formation in the 1930s.

7.   On this point, see Jeff Quam-Wickham and Nancy Quam-Wickham, "The American Plan, the 1935 Tanker Strike, and the Maritime Federation of the Pacific," unpublished paper presented at the Southwest Labor Studies Association annual meeting, California State University, Dominguez Hills, May 1990.

8.   Dave Gonzales, interviewed by Schwartz, January 4, 1983; L. L. Loveridge, interviewed by Schwartz, December 9, 1983.

9.   Major R. H. Wylie to Henry Schmidt, April 25, 1941, World War II History (hereafter, WW2 History), Box 1, folder Bridges Plan; Statement of C. E. McMillin (1941), WW2 History, Box 2, folder Waterfront Security; Wylie to Schmidt, April 25, 1941. All manuscript materials cited in this chapter are located in the ILWUA.

10.   Schmidt to Bjorne Halling, August 18, 1941, WW2 History, Box 1, folder General History; Stimson to Allen S. Haywood, August 4, 1941, Pacific Coast Maritime Industry Board (hereafter PCMIB), Box A-3, folder Army Reports; Stimson's anti-labor attitude is well documented in Paul Koistenen, "Mobilizing the World War II Economy: Labor and the Industrial-Military Alliance," *Pacific Historical Review* 42 (1973): 443–78.

11.   Schmidt to Halling, August 18, 1941.

12.   Irving Bernstein, *The Turbulent Years* (Boston: Houghton Mifflin, 1971), pp. 752–67; Bridges to all ILWU Locals, November 13, 1941, WW2 History, Box 1, folder Bridges Plan.

13.   [H. Bridges] Memorandum [to CIO President Philip Murray] Re Plan to Increase production in Longshore Industry [1941], WW2 History, Box 1, folder Bridges Plan.

14.   Ibid. It is unclear why employers and the government finally adopted the Bridges Plan. Larrowe attributes it to the rumors of sabotage in the destruction of the troopship *Normandie* on the New York waterfront. The poor progress of the war in the Pacific was likely a contributing factor. Charles P. Larrowe, *Harry Bridges: The Rise and Fall of Radical Labor in the United States* (New York: L. Hill Company, 1972), p. 254.

15.   Richard Criley, interview with author, September 30, 1990.

16.   This story is recounted in Larrowe, *Harry Bridges*, pp. 255–56; Lichtenstein, *Workers on the Waterfront*, p. 265.

17.   Loveridge interview; Bill T. Ward, interviewed by Schwartz, October 27, 1981; Ruben Negrete, interviewed by Daniel Beagle, May 11, 1983; Arthur Kaunisto, interviewed by Schwartz, September 23, 1982; Elmer Gutierrez, interviewed by Schwartz, December 6, 1983; Loveridge interview; Elmer Mevert, interviewed by Schwartz, September 23, 1982; Al Langley, interviewed by Schwartz, November 19, 1981.

18.   Pete Grassi, interviewed by Schwartz and Beagle, January 20, 1983, and April 20, 1983; Kathryn Young, interviewed by Schwartz, June 17, 1983; Charles Hackett, interview with author, November 7, 1988.

19.   Bill Castagnasso, interviewed by Schwartz, October 8 and October 27, 1982.

20.   Sunstedt interview; Langley interview; Grassi interview.

21.   *Dispatcher*, March 26, 1943, p. 5.

22.   John Mitchell, interviewed by Schwartz, May 23, 1984; Kaunisto interview; Ed Thayne, interviewed by Schwartz, December 8, 1983.

23.   Martinez interview; Kimeldorf, *Reds or Rackets?*, p. 138.

24.   Bill Burke, interviewed by Schwartz, February 26, 1986.

25.   Hiram ("Buster") Hanspard, interviewed by Schwartz, March 25, 1983; Kagel and Halling to Commander G. Keller, February 3, 1942, WW2 History, Box 1, folder Bridges Plan; Rosco Craycraft, "Notes on Meeting with Col. Ross, Seattle, April 21, 1942," WW2 History, Box 2, folder Waterfront Security.

26.   Bridges to Kagel, January 23, 1942, WW2 History, Box 1, folder Labor Relations Committee & Pacific Maritime Industry Board Correspondence, 1941–42 (hereafter folder LRC-PCMIB Corr., 1941–42); Leon Bick, "The Longshore Hiring Hall in San Francisco," (M.A. thesis, University of California, Berkeley, 1948), pp. 139–43; Bridges to Kagel, January 27, 1942, WW2 History, Box 1, folder LRC-PCMIB Corr., 1941–42.

27.   George May to Paul Eliel, Chairman, PCMIB, December 22, 1942, PCMIB, Box A-3, folder PCMIB Corr. from locals, 1942–44.

28.   Memorandum to the PCMIB from C. Jackman and H. Schmidt, May 11, 1942, PCMIB, Box A-4, folder PCMIB Manpower Proposals.

29.   Bridges to Kagel, January 27, 1942; "Statement of Louis Goldblatt, April 23, 1943, at San Francisco, before the Special Subcommittee of the U.S. Senate Committee on Military Affairs," WW2 History, Box 1, folder Downey Committee Hearings; Cole Jackman, "Utilization of Present Dock Seamen," July 6, 1942, WW2 History, Box 2, folder Waterfront Security.

30.   For example, more than 400 of 700 ILWU members working at the Naval Supply Depot in Oakland were replaced by nonunion civil servants between September 1943 and February 1944. Louis Goldblatt, "Investigation of the Naval Supply Depot at Oakland," February 3, 1944, WW2 History, Box 1, folder LRC-PCMIB Corr., 1943–45; "Statement of Louis Goldblatt . . . before the Senate Committee."

31.   Homer Dunlap, interviewed by Schwartz, March 18, 1983; Goldblatt, "Investigation."

32.   "Personnel in Charge of ATS Port of Embarkation, San Francisco" (n.a., n.d.), PCMIB, Box A-3, folder Dock Seamen; National Maritime Union *Pilot*, October 23, 1942, quoted in Albert Bendich, "A History of the Marine Cooks' and Stewards' Union," (M.A. thesis, University of California, Berkeley, 1953), p. 120.

33. Ward interview; "Longshoremen Needed," *Business Week*, July 22, 1944, p. 96; "Closing the Hole," *Business Week*, October 28, 1944, p. 90.

34. *Bosses' and Stewards' News Letter*, No. 9, May 19, 1945; telegram, Schmidt to Craycraft, June 14, 1945, PCMIB, Box A-3, folder PCMIB Corr. all locals.

35. Bridges to Burke, August 20, 1943, PCMIB, Box A-3, folder PCMIB Corr., 1942–44.

36. Frank Gregory, quoted in the PCMIB, "Minutes of Meeting, March 13, 1945," pp. 16–17, PCMIB, Box A-1, PCMIB Transcript Proceedings binder, January–April 1945. In Los Angeles, employers also used the USES to circumvent established union hiring procedures and discriminate against African-American workers. Here, however, a coalition of black community organizers (led by Reverend Clayton Russell's Victory Committee) and black labor activists (many of them longshoremen who would go on to form the Afro-American Labor Protective Society in 1946) were somewhat more successful than their white union counterparts in San Francisco in pressuring the USES into sending black applicants out to jobs. See Walter Williams, interviewed by Schwartz, March 30, 1984.

37. Bridges to Eliel, October 27, 1942, PCMIB, Box A-3, folder PCMIB Corr. all locals.

38. *Dispatcher*, December 18, 1942, p. 7.

39. C.f. Harvey Schwartz, "A Union Combats Racism: The ILWU's Japanese-American 'Stockton Incident' of 1945," *Southern California Quarterly* 62 (1980): 161–75.

40. Henry Gaitan, interviewed by Daniel Beagle and David Wellman, May 14, 1983; Eugene Lasartemay, interviewed by Schwartz (?), 1981(?). The Pacific Maritime Association was the postwar employers' association.

41. Williams interview.

42. Walking bosses were ILWU members who supervised dock operations. John Martinez, interviewed by Schwartz, March 29, 1984.

43. Joe Stahl, who was on the same dock the day that Martinez confronted his men, supplies this information about those workers. Stahl, interviewed by Schwartz, December 7, 1983. Odell Franklin, quoted in Victor Silverman, "Left-Led Unions and Racism: A History of the Integration of ILWU Local 10, 1940–1960," unpublished seminar paper, University of California, Berkeley, 1983.

44. Gaitan interview; Wilson interview; Williams interview; Stahl interview.

45. Tipp, "Daily Inspection Report," December 30, 1942, PCMIB, Box A-3, folder PCMIB Corr., 1942–46; Henry Schmidt, "Secondary Leadership in the ILWU, 1933–1966," an oral history conducted from 1974 to 1981 by Miriam F. Stein and Estolv Ethan Ward, Regional Oral History Office, University of California, Berkeley, 1983, p. 228.

46. Tipp, "Daily Inspection Reports," September 30, 1942, and November 25, 1942, PCMIB, Box A-3, folder PCMIB Corr., 1942–46.

47. Lasartemay interview; Fannie Walker, interviewed by Schwartz, October 6, 1982; Virginia Wysinger, interviewed by Schwartz, October 13, 1982.

48. Louis Goldblatt noted that warehouse hiring hall dispatchers simply referred "the same man back and back and back" to a job until the employer "would get the point — if he didn't hire this man, he wasn't going to get anybody." Goldblatt, "Working-Class Leader in the ILWU, 1935–1977," an oral history conducted from

1978 to 1979 by Estolv Ethan Ward, Regional Oral History Project, University of California, Berkeley, 1980, pp. 189–90.

49.   Bridges to Brother Member of ILWU, Local 8, December 21, 1943, PCMIB, Box A-3, folder PCMIB Corr. Local 8.

50.   Sanford Zalburg, *A Spark is Struck! Jack Hall and the ILWU in Hawaii* (Honolulu: University Press of Hawaii, 1979), pp. 16, 122; Goldblatt, "Working-Class Leader," pp. 316, 319–20; Schwartz, "A Union Combats Racism."

51.   Paul Ware, interviewed by Beagle, February 14, 1982; John ("Mickey") Mahon and Pete Grassi, interviewed by Schwartz, April 20, 1983; Williams interview.

52.   Gutierrez interview; Frank Sunstedt, interviewed by Schwartz, March 26, 1984. A gang head, or gang boss, serves as the leader of his gang, often determines the pace of work, and acts as intermediary between his gang and the walking boss; Kaunisto interview.

53.   Langley interview; Local 13 *Bulletin*, July 16, 1945.

54.   In some cases, production was down 50 percent between 1934 and 1941. Kimeldorf, *Reds or Rackets?* pp. 113, 132.

55.   Joshua Freeman, "Delivering the Goods: Industrial Unionism During World War II," *LH* 19 (1978): 587.

III

RACE, GENDER, AND COMMUNITY

7

"Her Husband Didn't Have a Word to Say": Black Women and Blues Clubs in Richmond, California, during World War II

Shirley Ann Moore

Before World War II, Richmond, California, was merely a dot on the California map. Located on the east side of the San Francisco Bay, Richmond's population numbered only 23,000 in 1940. Its mild climate, deep harbor, and vast tracts of unused land led Richmond city founders to pursue a dream of becoming the industrial center of the Pacific coast, the "Pittsburgh of the West." Moreover, Richmond developers' offers of tax incentives and assurances of a plentiful, docile labor force made the city even more attractive to prospective industries. Within a decade of its incorporation in 1905, Richmond had wooed and won major industries like Standard Oil, the Santa Fe Railroad, the Pullman Coach Company, and the American Standard porcelain factory. However, although early city boosters looked forward to a burgeoning industrial base, many were ambivalent about the consequences of full-scale industrialization and urbanization. Expecting that change in the city could be held to a "slow, gradual and comforting process," civic and political leaders were determined that city neighborhoods would remain "familiar" and "tidy."[1]

Richmond's leaders expected that political and economic power would remain in the hands of a small group of native-born whites who had dominated the city's political and economic life since the city's founding. Although wealthy Richmond boosters like founder A. S.

MacDonald and developer Fred Parr chose not to live in Richmond, an influential group of professionals and industrial executives provided active leadership in the development of the city and shaped its political, economic, and civic life. For example, Henry Creeger, a native-born manager of the American Standard Company, served on the chamber of commerce and as a trustee of the Richmond high school board. He also belonged to the influential Elks' Club and sat on the city's blue-ribbon wartime committee, which was established to lure war industries to the city. Edward Downer, founder and president of the Mechanic's Bank of Richmond, and John Galvin, publisher of the Richmond *Independent*, the town's leading newspaper, also were part of Richmond's "informal ruling council." On the eve of World War II, most of Richmond's public officials had held their positions for many years. By 1940, for example, the city manager had been in office for 20 years, the superintendent of schools had been at that post since 1901, and the chief of police had been on the force since 1915.[2] Thus, despite its rapid industrialization and standing as a "workingman's town," Richmond retained a small-town ambience and had acquired a reputation as a politically stagnant, cultural backwater among other Bay Area cities on the eve of World War II.

African-Americans had resided in Richmond along with their white, Asian, Mexican, and Native American counterparts since the town's founding. According to census figures, "nonwhites" comprised about 2 percent of the city's population (6,802) in 1910, and African-Americans accounted for 29. By 1920, the city's population more than doubled to 16,628, with a total of 33 black residents. The 1930 census indicated that African-Americans numbered 48 in Richmond's total population of 20,093. By 1940, their presence had grown to 270 and the city's total population stood at 23,642. Although Richmond's prewar industries, factories, and foundries attracted black residents and workers from surrounding Bay Area cities, all of them encountered workplace discrimination that consigned them to the lowest, most menial occupations. Moreover, some Richmond industries, like Standard Oil and the Filice and Perrelli Company, the city's largest produce cannery, did not employ blacks at all. One longtime Richmond black resident explained, "You see, if you were just brute strength, they would hire you for lifting pieces of steel, but if you had a little bit of education, they would not hire you."[3]

In addition to these limitations, prewar black Richmondites found that their place of residence and lack of a middle or professional class stigmatized them as "backward" in the eyes of other Bay Area blacks who resided in the larger, more prestigious Bay Area cities. For example, when Ivy Reid Lewis' family moved from Oakland to Richmond in the 1930s to get away from what her father considered to be the artificiality of black middle-class society in Oakland, her relatives voiced their disapproval: "When we moved to Richmond, I know my aunt would come and say she thought it was a shame [my father] moved us back there in Richmond with all those backwards, backwoods people. She was always mad about it and my grandmother didn't like it either."[4]

As early as 1910, Oakland's black population of 3,055 (the city's largest minority) contained a middle class that resembled a "beehive of industry." By 1929, for example, African-Americans in Oakland owned and operated more than 100 businesses, including "16 real estate brokers, 16 barber shops, 15 restaurants and cafes, 13 beauty parlors, 11 billiard and pool parlors, 8 dressmakers, 8 tailoring shops, 5 printers, 5 furniture stores, 4 candy shops, 3 garages, 2 jewelers, 2 undertakers, 2 insurance companies, and a pharmacy." In the nearby university town of Berkeley, African-Americans owned businesses that included "law practices, real estate agencies, a dentist, painting, plastering and bricklaying services, carpenters, beauty parlors, and plumbers." Although San Francisco's black business enterprises were overshadowed by the black entrepreneurial activity in the East Bay, it, too, produced a prominent black middle class early in the century.[5]

In contrast to these Bay Area communities and to most black communities of the East coast and midwest, Richmond's middle and professional class developed much later in the twentieth century, emerging only after World War II. One longtime black resident recalled that "before the war there weren't no colored doctors, dentists or lawyers in Richmond." Although one or two black-owned businesses operated in Richmond as early as 1905, Samuel Rogers' contracting and paving company, established in 1918, held the distinction of being the city's most successful prewar black-owned business. More typical of black business entrepreneurship in Richmond was the small, chronically undercapitalized North Richmond grocery store established in 1919 by Louisiana natives Joseph and Betty Griffin. The Griffins' store offered its customers a limited selection of food and "sundries." More importantly, the Griffins frequently extended credit to their customers "when they run short." Generally, however, black Richmondites preferred to do their "big shopping" in the larger downtown markets in Richmond or Oakland. One resident recalled, "we'd get in our little car and go shopping at the Housewives [Market] in Oakland."[6]

Because Richmond residence connoted undesirability and lower-class status, most blacks in the Bay Area had no desire to live there. They were less reserved about seeking employment in Richmond, however. African-American women, compelled by economic necessity to enter the work force, were, like their male counterparts, relegated to low-paying, menial labor. For instance, many of Richmond's produce and fish canneries relied on the labor of African-American, Filipino, Mexican, Portuguese, and Italian women. However, the overwhelming majority of Richmond's prewar black female labor force were employed as domestic or "day workers," earning $2 to $5 a week in the homes and kitchens of affluent whites living in Richmond, Berkeley, San Francisco, or the surrounding East Bay suburbs. These women labored under a triple yoke of oppression, confined by racism to the lowest rungs of the employment ladder, stigmatized by their presumed lower-class status because of their residency, and further constrained because of gender bias. For example, Irene Batchan, who settled in Richmond in 1926, recalled that in the years before the war: "Most women who weren't too old were working in white folks' kitchens, cleaning and cooking. If you were married and your husband had a steady job, you might stay at home; you did that. But most had to work and the men seemed to think that only day work or housework was suited to a black woman."[7]

Everything changed, however, when Richmond developers persuaded industrialist Henry Kaiser to locate four shipyards in Richmond in 1940. As the United States geared up to become the "arsenal of democracy," the Kaiser shipyards dominated the life of the city, churning out Liberty ships at an astounding rate and transforming Richmond from a "sleepy little backwater" to a wide open, 24-hour-a-day industrial "boomtown." In just three years, Richmond's population of 23,000 soared to over 123,000 by 1943. The black population increased about 5,000 percent (to over 15,000 by 1943). African-Americans poured into the city primarily from Texas, Arkansas, Louisiana, Oklahoma, and Mississippi. Like their white counterparts, they were eager for an economic shift upward through shipyard employment. They took jobs as welders, burners, riggers, or general laborers in the highly mechanized Kaiser yards. Black women were part of that work force. In contrast to black migration elsewhere in the United States during World War II and to the earlier Great Migration, women made up the majority of black migrants to the Bay Area, by a ratio of 53 to 47 percent. Twice as many females in the 15- to 24-year-old age group migrated. Moreover, these black newcomers to the Bay Area were young (23.13 years), and most were married. African-American sociologist Charles S. Johnson's contemporary study of black wartime migrants to San Francisco concluded that this atypical female-to-male migration ratio was due to the "relatively large proportion of males of this age group who may have migrated to the city as civilians and have since been drafted." In addition, because San Francisco served as a port of departure for servicemen going overseas, young wives followed their soldier husbands and remained in the area to work. Finally, black female workers benefitted from the Bay Area's chronic labor shortage in the defense industries.[8]

Shipyard work represented a significant economic shift upward for the majority of black workers, even though black workers faced racism in employment in the yards. African-Americans comprised 25 to 30 percent of the Kaiser shipyards' work force. However, despite their high hopes for social and economic freedom in California, black workers encountered blatant discrimination from the powerful shipyard unions (most notable the Boilermakers' union), who fiercely resisted admitting blacks to full membership. Black workers, male and female, routinely were assigned to the lower-paying unskilled job categories. Although white shipyard workers generally made an hourly wage of $1.25 per eight-hour shift, black workers earned about 90 cents an hour per eight-hour shift.[9]

Nevertheless, the experience of migration and entry into the urban industrial work force via the shipyards helped African-American women move away from the deferential racial and stereotypical gender roles to which they had been confined by giving them an economic alternative. For example, one African-American woman explained that she took a job as a shipburner at Kaiser's Richmond shipyards "because, number one, I needed work; number two, I'd had bad experience in jobs before where I hadn't felt any pride in the kind of work I was doing; number three, there was a war on and the people were all enthused about helping out in every way they could."[10] Now wartime work offered an escape from low-paying, dead-end domestic employment that racism and gender bias had reserved for black female workers. A Marshall, Texas, woman explained her reasons for migrating to Richmond: "I'll tell you. You see, I am a colored woman and I am forty-two years old. Now, you know that colored women don't have a chance for any kind of job back there except in somebody's kitchen working for two or three dollars a week. I have an old mother and a crippled aunt to take care of, and I have to make as much as I can to take care of them. . . . I got my neighbors to look after my mother and aunt and came out here on the bus. I went to work for Kaiser and saved enough money to bring my aunt and mother out here."[11]

African-American women not only took the initiative in migrating but also, in many cases, supplied the impetus for migration. For example, Arkansas native Margaret Starks, who worked as a cook in Pine Bluff, recalled that after seeing a Kaiser shipyard recruiting advertisement in her hometown newspaper, she demanded that her husband "go to California and get a job [then] send for me later." Within a few weeks of her arrival in Richmond, Margaret Starks became a laborer in the Kaiser shipyards. When she learned that she was pregnant and that "my husband was playing around on me," she decided to take matters in her own hands once again: "I knew I couldn't go back to Pine Bluff. I had an abortion, divorced him and with the money I earned from the shipyards I started a life of my own." In addition to holding down a shipyard job, Starks began to publish Richmond's first black newspaper, *The Richmond Guide*, in 1943. She also became active in the newly established Richmond branch of the National Association for the Advancement of Colored People (NAACP), serving as the branch secretary. Thus, shipyard work could have a liberating effect on the lives of black female workers. They now had a chance to "do something different."[12]

Despite the economic shift upward that Kaiser shipyard work represented for most African-American women, some found the choice between the shipyards or "somebody's kitchen" still too restrictive. Although the shipyard unions denied all black workers membership or shunted them into segregated auxiliaries, where they paid union dues but had no voice in policy, black female workers faced dual discrimination in the shipyards. In 1944, the manpower utilization division of California's War Manpower Commission reported to President Roosevelt's Fair Employment Practices Commission (FEPC) that "there is considerably more discrimination against Negro women than men" in the Kaiser shipyards at Richmond. Unlike their male counterparts, black women were constrained by a double standard that appealed to their patriotism and to their "domestic obligations." They were expected to do their part for the war effort by laboring in the shipyards, but at the same time, many felt pressure from spouses, children, and society to fulfill their "real womanly duties." One woman noted that this was "doing double duty, sometimes triple duty." A shipyard worker from Texas recalled, "You'd be so tired when you got home you just didn't want to do anything else and then you had to get up and start all over again." Therefore, some enterprising black women sought other avenues of independence and found them in North Richmond, where most of the area's black population now lived.[13]

One-third of North Richmond lay inside city limits while the rest of the area was located in the unincorporated county. It had few street lights, it was in close proximity to a garbage dump, and its unpaved streets became muddy quagmires in the rain. Prior to World War II,

North Richmond was a rural, ethnically diverse area where blacks lived alongside Portuguese-, Italian-, and Mexican-Americans. In contrast to their white counterparts, black newcomers looking for places to live were directed to North Richmond or to the city's wartime public housing, where waiting lists overflowed. White residents of North Richmond fled as more blacks moved in. By 1943, North Richmond had become virtually all black. In 1947, over 14,000 African-Americans lived in Richmond, and nearly one-fifth of them resided in North Richmond. Initially, African-American newcomers lived in tents, trailers, and other makeshift dwellings. A considerable number eventually were able to purchase land and build houses there. Because of the war, North Richmond became a black community complete with houses, businesses, churches, and several legal and illicit business enterprises. African-American women were instrumental in the development of some of these businesses, which catered to black newcomer preferences for "traditions from home."[14]

The African-American migrants who came to California from the South during the war years brought with them not only an expectation of economic and social mobility but also a need for cultural continuity that included the music and food that had been part of their lives in the South. North Richmond's blues clubs accommodated these desires and became profitable for a few black working-class women. In contrast to the more sophisticated, "streamlined" "supper clubs" and "lounges" that dotted Seventh Street, Oakland's bustling black commercial and entertainment corridor, North Richmond's blues establishments were "rough places that catered to a hard-drinking, fast-living black clientele." Some black people referred to the Richmond clubs as "honky tonks," "juke joints," or "buckets of blood." Most of the Bay Area black middle class looked down on those establishments. One black Richmondite recalled, "If someone of some kind of stature went out there, they'd generally have to sneak to go out there." Nevertheless, many Bay Area "black gentry" frequented the clubs, because "that's where you went if you wanted to hear good music."[15]

Employing skills traditionally considered "women's work," a handful of African-American women established some of the North Richmond blues and "after-hours" clubs that would become legendary in the Bay Area and throughout the United States. The exact number of female-owned and/or -operated blues and after-hours clubs in North Richmond is impossible to ascertain given the illicit and transitory nature of some of the enterprises and the paucity of materials documenting the African-American female experience in Richmond. Four such establishments are known to have existed in North Richmond and its environs. Although the women represented only a small minority of the African-American female work force in Richmond, their mere presence attests to the profound transforming impact World War II had on the lives of working-class African-American women in Richmond and throughout the United States. Their activities illustrated, as Margaret Starks noted, that the "whole world had changed."[16]

North Richmond's blues clubs, with names like Tappers Inn, Savoy Club, the B and L Club, and Minnie Lue's Club, and the more clandestine after-hours establishments provided channels through which some African-American women were able to carve out a degree of economic and personal autonomy outside the industrial labor force or the domestic service sphere. Minnie Lue Nichols, who opened her restaurant and club in North Richmond in 1948, explained, "It was just easier to take care of a club, give them music in a club, than it was to work all day and night in the yards, then turn around and work at home taking care of babies. Besides, if women were going to cook, they could make some real money off it."[17]

Too little is known about the black female entrepreneurs to draw a composite profile, but it appears that the most well-known shared some common characteristics. For example, all were migrants from the South (Texas, Arkansas, and Georgia) who settled in Richmond during the war or the immediate postwar period. They had been employed in traditional domestic or service work in their home states, and some had worked for a time in the Kaiser shipyards. Most of these women were married for at least a portion of the time they operated the clubs. At least one, Billye Strickland, married into a prewar black Richmond family. Billye, whose migrant status is unclear, co-owned and operated the North Richmond B and L Club with her husband, Lawrence Strickland, whose family had resided in the city since 1916. In addition to the B and L Club, the Stricklands operated a trailer court and a 14-room motel that catered to newly arrived black shipyard workers. When Lawrence was drafted and shipped overseas during the war, Billye became sole proprietor.[18]

Willie Mae "Granny" Johnson, an Arkansas migrant and sister-in-law of Missouri-born blues pianist and singer Jimmy McCracklin, operated the Savoy Club in North Richmond during the 1940s and 1950s. Blues greats such as Lowell Fulson, Sugar Pie DeSanto, L. C. "Good Rocking" Robinson, and Jimmy McCracklin performed at the Savoy.[19] Patrons recalled that its decor resembled an "old road house," with oilcloth tablecloths on wood tables. Blues performer Lowell Fulson described the Savoy as a "one room country shack." The Savoy could accommodate about 300 people at one time, and the room-length bar sold beer and wine. Patrons could purchase "home-cooked" meals of "greens," ribs, chicken, and other Southern cuisine in the club. Johnson was firmly in charge, doing not only all the cooking but also "all the hiring and firing." Lowell Fulson recalled that Johnson's husband, Deacon, worked a "day job . . . didn't have anything to do with it."[20]

Minnie Lue Nichols' club opened in North Richmond three years after the war's end. Nichols, a native of Atlanta, Georgia, moved to New York, where she worked as a cook in various restaurants and developed considerable culinary skills. Following a visit to her cousin in North Richmond, she moved there in 1948. Although Nichols had little formal education, she proved to be an astute businesswoman. After sampling the uninspired cooking at a local North Richmond restaurant, Nichols approached the proprietor, "Mr. Brown," and asked for a job as a cook. Instead, he offered to lease her his sagging business for $90 a month. Lacking the funds to lease, she struck a deal, promising to cook in the restaurant for three days and improve business; in return, she would obtain the lease. Nichols explained that "I didn't have any money to start with and I didn't have anything to lose." Instead, she relied on her talent for cooking and her outgoing personality to fill the restaurant with "customers [who] kept the juke box going day and night." The $60 earned from the jukebox alone in those three days was more than they had "collected from that box in a month previously." Brown was "so enthused over the amount of money she had made in three days that he did not hesitate to let her have $40.00 to buy the food she needed" to continue operating the restaurant. Eventually, she opened her own restaurant and club in North Richmond. In 1958, hers became the first black establishment there to obtain a "full liquor license."[21]

Minnie Lue's was an immediate success with black Richmondites, who came to partake of her "soul food" and the cultural solidarity implied in the music performed by artists such as Lowell Fulson, Charles Brown, Johnny Fuller, and jazz great Louis Armstrong. Nichols described the camaraderie that could develop in a blues club: "Well, if you've never felt the blues, I can't hardly explain. You know how it *feels*! It was a blues crowd, a beautiful crowd. When the house is full and they're rocking with members of the band, you just enjoy it!"[22]

Although Minnie Lue's Club remained a community fixture, Tappers Inn became the most popular night spot in North Richmond during the war years until the mid-1950s. Tappers offered black shipyard workers and others a variety of services, including round-the-clock barber and beauty shops and an all-night service station. Patrons recalled that it was a "very lavish place." Sometimes "it got so crowded on weekends that we had to take the bar stools out and the people just stood three and four deep at the bar." While patrons "jitterbugged" or "slow dragged" out on the dance floor to a band or the jukebox, others engaged in illegal gambling or played the slot machines "in the back room."[23]

Tappers Inn was owned by East Indian entrepreneur George Bally, who many black residents called "The Hindu." However, Arkansas native and former shipyard worker and cook Margaret Starks was hired by Bally as the manager. She routinely carried a .38 pistol as she fulfilled her duties as peacekeeper in the club. Starks handled all the business and talent booking for Tappers and other North Richmond clubs, booking blues greats like Charles Brown, Mabel Scott, and Ivory Joe Hunter. Her extensive community involvement earned her the title of "Mayor of North Richmond." Although the Richmond NAACP branch was located in various sites around the city (including in the wartime government projects that housed thousands of black shipyard workers), Margaret Starks conducted a great deal of NAACP business from the blues clubs she managed. She explained that "everyone knew where to find me if they needed something or had something to tell me. Everyone came through those clubs. We plotted many strategies there." Thus, many black migrants to the city were introduced to their first political activism through North Richmond's blues clubs. For example, Starks recalled that some of the NAACP-led desegregation campaigns of the late 1940s that successfully attacked downtown businesses that barred black patrons were organized in club offices.[24]

Blues clubs also provided many working-class African-Americans with a social oasis where, in contrast to the outside world, the rules were straightforward and consistent. The prevailing club etiquette dictated that "it didn't matter what you did outside on your job or who you were. If you acted right, nobody was better than anybody else." The blues clubs provided black newcomers with a welcome refuge from the racial hostility that permeated the world in which they earned their livelihood. Moreover, North Richmond's clubs also blunted some of the intraracial class conflict that pitted black newcomers against black longtime residents. Black longtime residents often characterized the black newcomers as unsophisticated, uncouth troublemakers, but even though the rough-and-tumble atmosphere of the North Richmond clubs implied "lower-class" status, club patrons tended to subscribe to, if not scrupulously honor, the culture of egalitarianism that prevailed in the North Richmond blues clubs. Thus, blues club culture offered working-class black people a refuge from some of the harshness of urban industrial life and eroded intraracial class conflict as well. Margaret Starks explained: "Those people didn't have too much, so they weren't about to let go of the music and good times they were used to. It made them feel better. I remember one lady from Louisiana, had gold all in her mouth, told me that she loved to hear that music because listening to that music in Tappers made her forget all that stuff in the shipyards. She always felt better when she left."[25]

Like the urban saloons that catered to European immigrants who poured into the United States in the nineteenth and early twentieth centuries, the blues clubs helped orient African-American newcomers to the urban industrial workplace during World War II. Although both institutions served similar functions for their patrons, the earlier white saloons, or "working men's clubs," generally restricted women to rigidly defined, subservient roles. In contrast, North Richmond's blues clubs were relatively free of such gender limitations. Black women not only participated as patrons and performers in the clubs, but also, as shown, a few could become club owners and managers.[26]

These business women often served as information sources and power brokers in their communities. The blues clubs catering as they did to newcomer cultural tastes, had a substantial economic impact on the larger African-American community as well. Club owners served as employers and informal employment agents for black Richmondites and blacks in other Bay Area cities. Their clubs provided employment for a cross section of black workers from musicians, bartenders, cooks, bookkeepers, and custodians to peacekeepers and private security guards. Although the small number of workers who found jobs through the clubs cannot compare with the thousands of workers employed in the shipyards, this function became more critical when Kaiser abruptly shut down and left the city in 1946. African-Americans were once again thrown out of work at higher rates than their white counterparts and were forced to rely on their own resources. Margaret Starks noted that Tappers and Minnie Lue's "kept some fellows with money in their pocket" by providing them "little sweeping up jobs and things like that." Club owners and operators, who had to contend with obtaining liquor licenses, building permits, and bank loans, acquired a considerable amount of expertise in dealing with the white business and financial establishment and gained access to the larger white community. These African-American women frequently were called upon to negotiate financial and governmental bureaucracies not only for themselves but also for the inexperienced and less well-connected members of the African-American community. In this way, some African-American women were able to attain influence and power beyond their immediate communities. They were able to step outside the traditional economic and social spheres to which racism, class stratification, and sexism confined most of their sisters.[27]

North Richmond's blues club scene was one area in which a small group of black women could achieve a degree of economic and social autonomy in their lives and regulate the economic life of their community by controlling white access to it. Illegal high-demand services such as prostitution and gambling flourished in the boom town atmosphere of World War II Richmond.[28] North Richmond's blues clubs attracted a significant white clientele who were eager to participate in these activities. African-American women who operated the clubs established the rules by which whites could gain entry into their world. Margaret Starks explained the rules laid down for white club patrons: "Well, the whites were scared to come out here. The blacks didn't allow them just to come out here anytime. If they came out, they said they were Mexicans. A taxi couldn't bring them. I didn't allow a white taxi cab company out here because they [the cab companies] were prejudiced. . . . When whites came, I told them to come 'round through the back."[29]

Capitalizing on the exotic allure that North Richmond held for many whites, after-hours clubs, catering to whites and blacks, flourished during the war and postwar years. More clandestine than the regular blues clubs, several after-hours clubs operated out of private homes. Most featured blues "jams," with musicians coming from all over the Bay Area and the country to play. Patrons could purchase home cooked meals, and liquor flowed. Gambling and prostitution were mainstays of the clubs. Although most served a racially-mixed clientele, a few catered to whites only. Whites from some of the Bay Area's most prominent families were able to indulge in sexual liaisons with prostitutes of various races. Margaret Starks recalled a visit to an after-hours club where a group of white World War I veterans known as the Last Man Club came to "carouse": "It was nice. Nice little furniture and everything. It had a bar and one of these Magnavox things. They'd come there and party. Sometimes they had live music. I was there one time and I saw all these Last Men, all these married men, lawyers and doctors."[30]

By the early 1960s, only a few North Richmond blues clubs remained. Changes in the political and social mood of African-Americans and shifting musical tastes caused blues music to undergo a transformation that made the musical expressions of the agrarian South seem anachronistic to the postwar generation of African-Americans living in the urban industrial United States. Moreover, a postwar law enforcement crackdown on gambling and vice shut down many of the North Richmond clubs. Finally, the impact of television and the widespread commercialization and dissemination of African-American music lessened the importance of the clubs as musical venues and cultural refuges. Ollie Freeman, resident of North Richmond since 1929 and owner of a popular record store in the 1950s, explained the decline: "People are seeking a little different class of night life. . . . Today there has come a different trend in music. People watch TV and accept a different class of entertainment. If they can't go out and find this type of excitement for themselves, they don't want this other thing. They label it lowbrow. 'I don't want my kid to listen to that crud,' they will say. 'That blues sickens me. I don't want no blues.'"[31]

The black migrants who came to work in the Richmond shipyards were no longer newcomers to the urban industrial arena. They had gained more confidence in their ability to survive. Few blues clubs were able to adapt to all these changes in the postwar era. By the late 1950s and early 1960s, Tappers Inn and the Savoy Club had shut their doors, victims of the changing political and cultural climate. Minnie Lue Nichols' club survived as a community fixture as she shrewdly decided to emphasize the restaurant, "upgrade" the music, and make her place a "community center" and meeting place for civil rights groups. Her club continued to function on a very reduced scale until her death in the 1980s.

When the Kaiser shipyards pulled out of Richmond at the end of the war, Richmond's white power structure hoped that most black residents would "go back where they came from." African-Americans remained in Richmond, but the economic shift upward created by shipyard employment could not be sustained. Some 1,000 workers a day were thrown out of work at the yards, and black workers were hit disproportionately hard. African-American women remained in the work force in numbers higher than white women after the war. However, black women now found themselves in competition with white men, white women, and black men. In addition to racial discrimination, it appears that African-American women in postwar Richmond were faced with hostility from a number of their male counterparts, who feared that black men now would be given lowest hiring priority for the scarce "nontraditional" jobs that remained in the postwar era. Some African-American men believed that white employers would give preference to black women, who were viewed as more docile and willing to work for lower wages. Columnist Lewis Campbell, writing for the Oakland-based black newspaper the

California Voice, warned that when the shipyards pulled out, the "good jobs" would be filled with "women and Chinese boys."[32]

The postwar employment reality for African-American men and women, however, was different. The majority of black workers were compelled to settle into a cycle of low-paying domestic work or seasonal factory and cannery employment. Yet, a few African-American women waged their own personal battles against racial, gender, and class limitations by employing the experience and money that they had gained as club operators. They were able to upgrade their work and educational skills in this way. For example, on the strength of experience as an after-hours club manager, one black Richmond woman was hired as a "bookkeeper" for a chain of brothels that operated throughout California and the Pacific Northwest. She later opened her own "legitimate book-keeping service and made a good living." Similarly, a Richmond mother and daughter team challenged the constraints of race, class, and gender when they put themselves through nursing school with the money they earned operating an after-hours club. They were among the first black nurses in Richmond. Residents recalled that "they're good nurses, some of the best Contra Costa [County] ever had too, and their husbands didn't have a word to say about it."[33]

Thus, the blues clubs of North Richmond that flourished during World War II afforded a number of African-American women the opportunity to achieve a measure of economic and personal autonomy. These female-owned and -operated enterprises were sustained by the influx of black southern migrants who came to California in the Second Great Migration looking for an economic shift upward and cultural continuity. Although the clubs were anchored firmly in black working-class culture, they helped erode the racial, gender, and sexual proscriptions that kept most African-American women at the bottom of the socioeconomic hierarchy. Not only did the clubs provide a cultural and economic bridge that facilitated African-Americans' transition from rural agrarian laborers to the urban industrial arena, but they also helped some black women gain a measure of power and influence at a time when most black working-class women had little access to either.

NOTES

1.   Joseph C. Whitnah, *A History of Richmond, California: The City That Grew From a Rancho* (Richmond, Calif.: Richmond Chamber of Commerce, 1944), pp. 8, 18–31, 46–48, 78, 84–85; Eleanor Mason Ramsey, "Richmond, California between 1850–1940: An Ethnohistorical Reconstruction" (unpublished monograph, San

Francisco, 1980), pp. 7–15; Susan D. Coles, *Richmond: Windows to the Past* (Richmond, Calif.: Wild Cat Canyon Books, 1980), pp. 51–52; *The Richmond Independent Newspaper*, "The Woman's Edition," (Richmond Historical Association, 1910), pp. 8, 15, 17, 21; "Burg Brothers Real Estate Company for the Pullman Townsite, Burg Brothers, Exclusive Agents," pamphlet, 1910; F. J. Hulaniski, ed., *History of Contra Costa County, California* (Berkeley, Calif.: The Elms Publishing Co., 1917), pp. 35, 336; Hubert Owen Brown, "The Impact of War Worker Migration on the Public School System of Richmond, California from 1940 to 1945" (Ph.D. diss., Stanford University, 1973), pp. 18, 37–40.

2.   Brown, "The Impact of War Worker Migration," pp. 38–40; Whitnah, *A History of Richmond*, pp. 28–55.

3.   Wilbur and Vesper Wheat, Richmond residents since 1942, interview with author, January 24, 1987; Irene Batchan, Richmond resident since 1926, interview with author, September 14, 1985. I am indebted to Susan Hirsch of Loyola University, Chicago, for sharing some of her work on black workers and labor unions in the Pullman Company with me: Hirsch, unpublished manuscript on the Pullman Company, especially chapters 2 and 4; Newberry Library (Chicago) holdings, *Proceedings of the Meeting between the Pullman Company and the Pullman Company Employees Association of the Repair Shops*, August 1940, Box 39-250, p. 46. See also Shirley Ann Moore, "Getting There, Being There: African American Migration to Richmond, California, 1910–1945," in *The Great Migration in Historical Perspective: New Dimensions of Race, Class, and Gender*, ed. Joe William Trotter, Jr. (Bloomington: Indiana University Press, 1991), pp. 106–26; Lawrence P. Crouchett, Lonnie G. Bunch, III, and Martha Kendall Winnacker, *Visions toward Tomorrow: The History of the East Bay Afro-American Community 1852–1977* (Oakland: Northern California Center for Afro-American History and Life, 1989), pp. 17–19; United States Department of Commerce, Bureau of the Census, *Thirteenth Census of the United States (1910) Statistics for California Supplement*, pp. 118, 614; United States Department of Commerce, Bureau of the Census, *Fourteenth Census of the United States, 1920*, "Population," Vol. III, pp. 118–19; United States Department of Commerce, Bureau of the Census, *Fifteenth Census of the United States, 1930*, "Population," Vol. III, Part 1; United States Department of Commerce, Bureau of the Census, *Sixteenth Census of the United States, 1940*, "Population," Vol. II, p. 610.

4.   Ivy Reid Lewis, Richmond resident since the 1930s, interview with author, July 29, 1987.

5.   Edward E. France, "Some Aspects of the Migration of the Negro to the San Francisco Bay Area Since 1940" (Ph.D. diss., University of California, Berkeley, 1962), pp. 18–21; Douglas Henry Daniels, *Pioneer Urbanites: A Social and Cultural History of Black San Francisco* (Berkeley: University of California Press, 1990), pp. 18–24, 46–48; 1910 Census; Crouchett et al., *Visions toward Tomorrow*, pp. 17–21.

6.   Crouchett et al., *Visions toward Tomorrow*, p. 17; Irene Batchan, interview with author, September 14, 1985; *Pacific Coast Appeal*, circa January 3, 1905; *Western Outlook*, July 24, 1925; Oakland *Independent*, December 14, 1929; William Malbrough, interview with author, September 14, 1985.

7.   Irene Batchan, interview with author, August 18, 1985.

8.   Moore, "Getting There, Being There," pp. 111, 118–20; Charles S. Johnson, *The Negro War Worker in San Francisco* (San Francisco, Calif.: n.p., 1944), pp. 5–7.

9.   Moore, "Getting There, Being There," pp. 111, 118–20.

10.   Miriam Frank, Marilyn Ziebarth, and Connie Field, *The Life and Times of Rosie the Riveter: The Story of Three Million Working Women During World War II* (Emeryville, Calif.: Clarity Educational Productions, 1982), p. 17; Frances Mary Albrier, *Determined Advocate for Racial Equality* (Berkeley: University of California, Regional Oral History Office, 1977–78), pp. vi, 132–33.

11.   Cy W. Record, "Characteristics of some Unemployed Negro Shipyard Workers in Richmond, California" (unpublished monograph, University of California, Library of Economic Research, September 1947), pp. 9, 31.

12.   Margaret Starks, interview with author, April 2, 1988; Albrier, *Determined Advocate*, pp. vi, 132–33. Approximately 18 million women were in the labor force during World War II. The majority of the female work force remained in "traditional women's occupations," but some 3 million women found work in war industries. African-American and other women of color comprised between 10 and 19 percent of those who worked in defense centers. Although the shift into wartime work had a dramatic economic and social impact on the lives of African-American women, millions of white female war workers experienced a similar "liberation" as they escaped low-paying, unstimulating "pink collar ghetto" jobs and began to enjoy the "benefits of being part of an organized work force." See Frank et al., *Rosie the Riveter*, particularly "Women and Work, Women and War," pp. 13–27.

13.   Sam Kagel, acting state manpower director, Northern California (signed by A. L. Sharee, liaison officer, Manpower Utilization Division), letter to Edward Routledge, examiner-in-charge, FEPC, "Non-White Employment — ES270 Reports, Richmond, California, June 9, 1944, FEPC Records, Region 12, Record Group 228, box 11, entry number 68; Albrier, *Determined Advocate*, pp. vi, 132–33; Margaret Starks, interview with author, April 2, 1988; Vesper Wheat, interview with author, January 24, 1987.

14.   Irene Batchan, interview with author, August 18, 1985; Edwin P. (Red) Stephensen, *Transition: White Man in a Black Town, 1950–1967* (Berkeley: University of California, Regional Oral History Office, 1975), pp. 27–28; Ivy Reid Lewis, interview with author, July 29, 1987; Sherrill David Luke, "The Problem of Annexing North Richmond to the City of Richmond" (Master's thesis, University of California, Berkeley, 1954), p. 3; Lee Hildebrand, "North Richmond Blues," *The East Bay Express, The East Bay's Free Weekly*, February 9, 1979, pp. 1, 4; William Sokol, "From Workingman's Town to All American City: The Socio-Political Economy of Richmond, California During World War Two" (unpublished monograph, Richmond Public Library, June 1971), p. 34; Robert Wenkert, *An Historical Digest of Negro-White Relations in Richmond, California* (Berkeley: University of California Survey Research Center, 1967), pp. 21–22.

15.   Lee Hildebrand, "Oakland Blues," *East Bay Express*(?), n.d., p. 3; Hildebrand, "North Richmond Blues"; Bill Thurston, Mississippi migrant to Richmond in 1944, interview with author, September 8, 1983; Margaret Starks, interview with author, June 29, 1988; Ivy Reid Lewis, interview with author, July 29, 1988.

16.   Margaret Starks, interview with author, April 2, 1988.

17.   Minnie Lue Nichols, interview with author, August 1981.

18.   Minnie Lue Nichols, interview with author, January 6, 1980; Margaret Starks, interview with author, June 29, 1988; *Directory of Leading Colored Citizens, 1916–1917* (Richmond, Calif.: n.p., ca. 1917); Tilghman Press, *We Also Serve*

(Berkeley, Calif.: Tilghman Press, 1945), pp. 59, 61, 66; Tilghman Press, *We Also Serve: Armed Forces Edition* (Berkeley, Calif.: Tilghman Press, 1945), p. 38.

19. Jimmy McCracklin immortalized Richmond's Savoy Club when he wrote and recorded the hit "Club Savoy" in the mid 1950s: "Now Richmond, California is a great little town / And I live there and, Jack, / I gets around. / If you ever go there and you want to jump for joy, / I'll tell you where to go — that 's the Club Savoy." Lyric quoted in Hildebrand, "North Richmond Blues."

20. Hildebrand, "Oakland Blues"; Hildebrand, "North Richmond Blues"; Bill Thurston, Mississippi migrant to Richmond in 1944, interview with author, September 8, 1983; Margaret Starks, interview with author, June 29, 1988; Tilghman Press, *We Also Serve*, pp. 59, 61, 66; Tilghman Press, *We Also Serve: Armed Forces Edition*, p. 38; Joseph Malbrough, interview with author, August 18, 1985; Lowell Fulson, telephone interview with author, January 21, 1993.

21. Eldreadge Wright, "An Interview with Minnie Lue," (unpublished paper, March 24, 1972); Hildebrand, "North Richmond Blues"; Minnie Lue Nichols, interview with author, January 6, 1980.

22. Minnie Lue Nichols, interview with author, January 6, 1980.

23. Joseph Malbrough, interview with author, August 18, 1985; Margaret Starks, interview with author, June 29, 1988; Tilghman Press, *We Also Serve: Armed Forces Edition*, p. 38.

24. Margaret Starks, interview with author, April 2, 1988; Margaret Starks, letter to Noah W. Griffin, executive director NAACP, West Coast Region, May 4, 1945; Noah Griffin, memo to file, November 9, 1945; Noah Griffin, letter to Margaret Starks, April 13, 1943; Noah W. Griffin, letter to Margaret Starks, April 14, 1945, in NAACP, West Coast Region Records, ca. 1946–70, carton 16, University of California, Berkeley, Bancroft Library (hereinafter called NAACP Papers).

25. Margaret Starks, interview with author, April 2, 1988.

26. A notable exception to the male-dominated immigrant saloons of the nineteenth century were the "shebeens" or small drinking establishments that were run by Irish women who brewed and sold beer. Shebeens flourished in the 1840s but went into decline by 1890 as the liquor business in the United States became dominated by large corporate monopolies. Some nineteenth-century male-owned immigrant saloons allowed women to use the "ladies entrance" or side door if they wished to enjoy the saloon's "free lunch," attend the numerous social functions held in the "back room," or wanted to purchase a pail of beer to take home. For more on women's roles in immigrant saloons, see Roy Rosenzweig, *Eight Hours for What We Will: Workers and Leisure in an Industrial City, 1870–1920* (Oxford: Cambridge University Press, 1983), Chap. 2, pp. 35–64; Perry R. Duis, *The Saloon: Public Drinking in Chicago and Boston, 1880–1920* (Urbana: University of Illinois Press, 1983). For the social function of the immigrant saloons' "back room," see Upton Sinclair, *The Jungle* (New York: New American Library, 1980 edition of 1906 publication), pp. 7–25. I am indebted to Madelon Powers for her discussion of immigrant saloons and working-class women. See Madelon Mae Powers, "Faces Along the Bar: Lore and Order in the Workingman's Saloon, 1870–1920" (Ph.D. diss., University of California, Berkeley, 1991), pp. 23–36.

27. Walter White, executive secretary, NAACP, letter to Noah W. Griffin, July 16, 1945, NAACP Papers, carton 16, "Miscellaneous Papers," 4 folders, 1944–59; Minnie Lue Nichols, interview with author, August 1981; Wright, "An Interview with

Minnie Lue," pp. 3–5; Joseph Malbrough, Richmond resident since 1926, interview with author, August 18, 1985; Margaret Starks, interview with author, April 2, 1988.

28.   Oakland *Tribune*, "Vice Is Held Rampant in North Richmond Area," October 12, 1949; Bill Thurston, interview with author, September 8, 1983; Ivy Reid Lewis, interview with author, July 29, 1987; Margaret Starks, interview with author, April 2, 1988.

29.   Margaret Starks, interview with author, April 2, 1988.

30.   Ibid.

31.   Quoted in Hildebrand, "North Richmond Blues," p. 5.

32.   *California Voice*, August 1, 1941.

33.   Irene Batchan, interview with author, September 14, 1985.

8

African-American Migrant Women in the San Francisco East Bay Area

Gretchen Lemke-Santangelo

For much of this century, African-Americans have been highly mobile, moving from farm to farm, from the rural South to southern towns and cities, and from southern cities to northern and western metropolitan areas. For migrants, these journeys have served as imagined or actual passages to something better. As such, they provide examples of African-American agency and resistance and offer insight into how new communities are established and maintained. Historians, long recognizing the incredible drama and poignancy of these mass population movements, have produced a rich and varied migration literature.

A number of excellent studies document black migration during the first two decades of the twentieth century and describe the impact of male migrants on the communities that received them.[1] However, migration during World War II and the particular experience and contributions of black women migrants have received little attention. Similarly, the literature on women and World War II, although discussing labor force participation, employment discrimination, and shifting gender roles, only partially reconstructs how African-American women experienced the war.[2]

In defense centers across the nation, most black women were workers and migrants. As they made the transition from field and domestic work to jobs in an industrial economy, they struggled to keep their families together, establish new households, and create community-sustaining networks and institutions. Although white women negotiated the double burden of wage labor and housework, African-American migrant women shouldered substantially more. Filling defense jobs and caring for their families, they also performed many of the tasks associated with relocation and community building: finding schools and housing, locating markets, churches, and medical services; establishing new institutions; building relationships with other migrants; and maintaining ties to those back home. White migrant women, although facing some of the same challenges, did not have to contend with racial discrimination, a burden that forced black migrant women to create new institutions and multiplied their housing and employment difficulties. Finally, black migrant women facilitated chain migration by encouraging friends and relatives to join them and providing newcomers with food, shelter, and emotional support until they found their own jobs and housing.

This chapter examines the migration and community-building efforts of African-American women who moved from the South to the San Francisco Bay Area during World War II. Drawing upon the life stories of four migrant women — stories that are interwoven with 46 additional oral interviews that were conducted with former migrants — this chapter describes who these women were, how they experienced the migration, and how they used their southern cultural traditions to keep their families together and establish new communities in the East Bay Area. I will also examine migrant women's wartime and postwar employment, emphasizing their efforts to define "work" and assign value to their own labor. Filling the least desirable, lowest paying jobs in the labor force, migrant women created alternate sources of status and identity as homemakers, church women, and community workers. Defining their labor on behalf of family and community as "real" work, migrant women resisted efforts to categorize them as menial or marginal laborers. At the same time, however, much of their community work directly challenged employment discrimination, complementing their workplace resistance and suggesting that their labor force participation was, in fact, an important source of identity and self-esteem.

During World War II, thousands of African-Americans migrated from the South to the San Francisco East Bay Area in search of social and economic mobility associated with the region's expanding defense industry and reputation for greater racial tolerance. Prior to World War II, the black population in the East Bay was small and highly insular. However, the wartime economic boom, fueled by federal investment in shipbuilding, changed all of this. African-Americans from the South, hearing of defense jobs from labor recruiters, railroad workers, employment bureaus, newspapers, and, most importantly, word of mouth, joined white workers in a westward exodus. As a consequence, the East Bay's black population grew significantly — up to fivefold in many communities. In Richmond, for example, the African-American population grew from 270 in 1940 to 10,000 in 1945. Similarly, Oakland's black population grew from 8,462 to over 37,000 during the same period.[3] Of the African-Americans who joined the migration to the East Bay, most came from Texas, Louisiana, Mississippi, Arkansas, and Oklahoma. Roughly half were women.[4]

The stories of Ethel Tillman, Lacey Gray, Olive Blue, and Bertha Walker illustrate the similarities and differences among migrant women. They, and the majority of other migrant women who were sampled, came from deeply religious, two-parent, working-class families. Only 30 percent were reared on farms, and of this number, most had parents who owned or rented their land. Whether rural, urban, or from small towns, a majority had fathers and brothers who worked full-time or seasonally in skilled or semiskilled trades and industries. Among the fathers of this group, 30 percent worked as skilled craftsmen — a disproportionately high percentage when compared with the South's black population as a whole. Migrant women, their mothers, and their sisters also worked for wages as domestic servants, cooks, cateresses, dressmakers, and, less frequently, in southern industrial occupations. These findings are consistent with several wartime surveys that characterized migrants as predominantly urban, relatively skilled members of an expanding black, southern working class.[5]

Ethel Tillman, born in rural Mississippi in 1900, is about 15 years older than the average migrant woman in the sample. Reared on a farm that her family initially rented and then purchased in 1915, Ethel remembers a childhood of hard work but relative freedom from grinding poverty. Her father supplemented farm income by working as a carpenter. Her mother, in addition to performing the tasks of a farm wife, worked as a seamstress, domestic servant, and cateress. Ethel and her six siblings helped on the farm and, when old enough, also went out to work. Bertha Walker, in contrast, was reared in an urban environment. Born in Houston, Texas, in 1919, she grew up in the city's predominantly black Fifth Ward. Her father worked at a cotton seed compress, while her mother did domestic work. Bertha's brothers contributed to family income by shining shoes and sorting salvageable cotton out of damaged bales. Bertha started domestic work when she graduated from high school, although she longed to go to college.[6]

Lacey Gray, born in Longleaf, Louisiana, in 1916, remembers how her father farmed 80 acres of his own land while working full-time at a sawmill. When she was nine, she began to chop cotton and hoe corn, and at 14, she went out to work as a domestic servant. "Would get to work by eight and stay until one. Didn't work all day, but the money was still so low. I worked for a dollar and a quarter a whole week." She and her brothers, who worked at the sawmill, turned every other paycheck over to their mother. Olive Blue, born in 1918 and reared in New Orleans, Louisiana, had a more sheltered girlhood. Her father, a cotton compress worker, and her mother, a seamstress, made enough income to keep their three daughters at home. "My parents kept me at home until I was married . . . didn't want me to work." Their protectiveness was not uncommon. If at all possible, parents attempted to protect their daughters from the harsh and often demeaning world of domestic service.[7] Moreover, several informants reported that their parents went to extraordinary lengths to educate them, building schools or sending their daughters to board with relatives who lived closer to educational facilities. Lacey Gray, for example, attended a school that was built by her community. In this manner, black working-class parents often subverted white Southerners' efforts to deprive black children of decent educational opportunities.[8]

Church and family formed the center of migrant women's girlhoods. Ethel Tillman, like other women who were sampled, experienced a life-altering conversion in her early teens and remained deeply religious throughout her life. Church, which she and her family attended all day Sunday and several evenings during the week, reinforced the values she acquired from her parents of hard work, loyalty to family, respect for elders, and concern for a wider community. Similarly, Lacey Gray recalls how church was the center of family life. Her father, who donated land for the neighborhood church, served as its head deacon. Her mother, who baked the communion bread, was a stewardess. "My parents were very religious people. Children then were not like they are now. We would do as we were told. And when we got old enough for boys to come and see us, we wouldn't go alone. We walked ahead, and she [mother] walked behind. And she'd see us to church and back and everything."[9]

In the home and the church, migrant women learned that their survival was linked to the well-being of friends and neighbors. Ethel's mother regularly quilted with neighbor women, donating the quilts to poorer community members. In addition, Ethel's mother liberally shared her garden produce with needy families. Similarly, Lacey's mother was a traditional medical practitioner, using folk remedies derived from roots, barks, and herbs. "She was known for helping people. Wasn't for money either; it was for love." This ethic of care was quite different from black middle-class notions of racial uplift — institutional forms of charity that frequently reinforced class distinctions. Rather, the type of giving that Ethel and Lacey learned was based on the idea that little separated their families from those they helped, and indeed, little did.[10]

This ethic of care coexisted with a fierce desire for economic independence from white people. Migrant women recall how their parents counselled them to "own your own." Many went on to reflect that it was their churches, businesses, schools, and economic independence that insulated them from the hardships and humiliations of Jim Crow. Olive learned at an early age that church was the foundation of her community, providing fellowship, personal affirmation, and essential social services. Sustained by women like Olive's mother, the church and other community-sustaining institutions taught Olive essential organizing skills that she later used to establish new institutions in California. Although both men and women learned about the virtues of hard work and economic independence, women prided themselves on their ability to create and sustain reciprocal relationships within formal and informal settings. Olive and other migrant women learned by watching their mothers to create the networks that were essential to emotional well-being, feeding and clothing families, finding help with childcare, obtaining medical advice, and maintaining churches and schools.[11]

In their late teens and early twenties, most migrant women married men who, like their fathers, worked in skilled or semiskilled trades and industries. For this generation, marriage and childbearing coincided with the wartime economic boom on the West Coast. For young adults starting new families, the Bay Area was particularly attractive, holding the promise of economic opportunity and relative freedom from the harsh realities of Jim Crow. Not surprisingly, most of the women in this sample were neither bitterly poor nor members of the middle class. Unlike their poorer neighbors, they had the resources to leave, and unlike the middle class, they had less economic stake in their communities of origin.[12]

Had they remained in the South, few migrant women could have expected more than a domestic service job paying $2 or less per week. However, fate and human initiative intervened. This particular generation reached young adulthood during an extraordinary time. By 1940, almost 2,000 miles from their homes, defense industries were transforming the East Bay Area into a virtual Canaan for both skilled and unskilled workers. Migrant women, confronting futures limited by segregation, seized this rare historical advantage. They would soon learn, however, that the promise was imperfect, raising new and equally painful barriers in place of the old.

Ethel Tillman married a man who worked on his family's land while augmenting farm income with seasonal work in nearby southern cities. After six years, the young couple left the farm and moved to Vicksburg, Mississippi. There, Ethel did domestic work and cared for their growing family while her husband worked as a skilled tradesman. When the war began, Ethel's husband left Vicksburg to find defense work in southern Mississippi, sending money home to his family. It was there that he heard about employment opportunities in the East Bay's expanding shipbuilding industry. By the time Ethel and her husband decided to move to the Bay Area — a decision they made jointly — they had been married 15 years and had ten children.[13]

Most migrant women came West with their husbands, and the majority were young and only recently wed. Bertha Walker married a Houston longshoreman in 1943, at the age of 24. At that time, she was working for a white couple from California "who treated me nice and talked to me like I was a person. And they told me about California and how I would like it." Her new husband, who had just lost his job on the waterfront, heard "about there being good longshore work out West." Bertha, like most migrant women in my sample, was eager to leave. "You don't know what it was like in the South. They [white people] would try and make you feel like you weren't human. You'd have to get off the sidewalk, even for children in certain areas. And if you didn't they would knock you off."[14]

Lacey Gray married her husband, a sawmill worker, in 1937. Living in a two-room company house, Lacey took in washing and ironing while caring for her two young daughters, born in 1939 and 1942. Early in 1943, Lacey's husband moved to Alexandria to find a better paying job, and Lacey returned to her parent's home. In the meantime, Lacey's sister and brother-in-law moved to the East Bay Area and found defense jobs, writing home about their good fortune and encouraging Lacey and her husband to join them. Throughout the south, employment discrimination forced many husbands and fathers to leave home for prolonged periods in search of better-paying jobs. For the Grays and many other migrant couples, the move West held the promise of family reunification.[15]

Olive Blue married in 1936 at the age of 18. Just after her first child was born, her husband enlisted in the military and was sent to Pearl

Harbor. Reeling from their separation, Olive suffered a second loss, the death of her father. A cousin, who had moved to the Bay Area, encouraged Olive to join her. To Olive, migration was a way to escape her pain and grief — "to get away from where my father had died."[16]

Typically, men moved to the Bay Area first, finding jobs and sending for their wives and children. Similarly, single women, either unmarried or with husbands away in the military, rarely made the trip unless they had friends and relatives waiting for them with offers of temporary support. Ethel Tillman's husband moved to the East Bay first, finding a job at the Mare Island shipyard while Ethel remained behind to prepare her family for the move. Like other migrant women in my sample, Ethel was concerned with preserving her cultural and familial history. She was proud of her southern heritage, seeing it as a source of strength and something that she wanted to pass on to her children. Thus, she packed practical items as well as her great-grandmother's Wedgewood serving platter and cast iron washpot. She also packed a trunk with canned fruit and vegetables, unwilling to part with such a tangible reminder of home and her own labor.[17]

Bertha Walker's husband moved West three weeks ahead of his new bride. During his first day in the Bay Area, he looked unsuccessfully for work on the San Francisco waterfront. He had better luck the second day, securing employment that allowed him to send for Bertha. Asked whether she was afraid to leave her home and family, Bertha responded that she was ready to move and had confidence in her husband. Similarly, Lacey Gray's husband left Louisiana in July 1943. After finding a job and a rented room in Richmond, he sent for Lacy in November.[18]

Most women made the trip across country by train. The most powerful moment of the journey came after the train crossed the line separating the segregated South from the more racially tolerant West. Lacey Gray, travelling with her two small children, "took sick on the train" after drinking some contaminated water and was assisted by some friendly soldiers. Although ill, she was acutely aware of changing trains in El Paso. At that point, she was able to move out of the Jim Crow car into more comfortable and less crowded seating.[19]

Bertha Walker rode out of Texas on a Jim Crow car packed with servicemen. In El Paso, she changed trains, and a soldier told her that she could "relax because we've crossed the line and the great white father has to look up to you now." Arriving in the Bay Area in October 23, her birthday, an exhausted Bertha hugged and kissed her husband, exclaiming that she was so tired that she wished she had stayed home. Years later, her husband told her that this remark had deeply hurt him.[20]

The journey, although exciting, was emotionally and physically exhausting. Many migrant women had never left the towns and cities where they were born, and California, despite its golden image, raised fears as well as hopes. Throughout the journey, women carried anxieties about starting a new life in a strange environment: finding jobs and housing, being reunited with loved ones after prolonged separations, and facing the possibility of temporary dependence upon friends and relatives. Finally, those who came with small children found the trip physically exhausting. Weariness heightened the emotional intensity of the journey and eroded the composure of even the most confident.

Fears frequently intensified in the first days following arrival. The East Bay grew significantly during the war years, taking on the characteristics of a boom town. Richmond, in particular, looked wild and unkempt, with government housing projects, trailer parks, cafes, bars, and clubs springing up on swampy, vacant lots to the north and west of the city. New arrivals, unable to find housing, slept in cars and parks. Throughout the East Bay, the existing housing stock was strained beyond capacity. For black migrants, it was worse. Housing segregation was rigidly enforced by racist landlords, unfair housing practices on the part of real estate agencies, and threats to personal safety. Migrants were, thus, forced into already overcrowded and older housing in existing black communities that often lacked adequate plumbing and cooking facilities.[21]

The burden of transforming substandard housing into reasonably comfortable accommodations fell largely upon women. Moreover, routine chores like cooking and laundry were time-consuming without adequate facilities. While women struggled to "make do," they also performed the orientation tasks associated with a major move: enrolling children in schools, locating markets and medical services, negotiating public transportation, finding churches, and securing better housing.

After arriving in Richmond with her two infants, Lacey moved into the room that her husband had rented in advance for his family. For an entire month, Lacey, her husband, and their two children shared the same bed, but as Lacey soon discovered, they at least lived in a real house, even if they had to share a kitchen and bath with other renters. Until women like Lacey found more permanent housing, which took from 1 to 12 months, they struggled with minimal resources to care for their families. Bathing, cooking, cleaning, childcare, and washing clothes all required ingenuity, versatility, and additional labor in the absence of proper facilities. Moreover, women devoted more time and effort to emotional housekeeping — maintaining family peace and unity — in an environment characterized by its newness and lack of privacy.[22]

Women's efforts to create stable homes and friendships were heroic, given what little they had to work with. Wartime housing investigators documented some of the difficulties migrant women faced. One family, unsuccessful at finding better housing, lived in a basement where: "There is no bathroom, no tub, and the whole family seem[s] to wash in the kitchen sink. The place is infested with rats, and when it rains the place is immediately inundated because neither doors nor windows can be shut tightly. . . . The place is unaired and dimly lighted. For these [sic] extremely unsanitary, dirty, overcrowded place the family pays weekly $16.25."[23]

Such conditions were the norm. Over 40 percent of new arrivals lived in buildings that contained no bathroom. Of those who did have bathrooms, a fourth lacked showers or tubs. Most dwellings did have kitchens, but not in individual units. "The most characteristic arrangement was for all families . . . to share a common kitchen."[24]

Most migrants moved from temporary housing into one of several government war housing projects in the East Bay. These projects, flimsily constructed as temporary structures, deteriorated rapidly from overcrowding, lack of maintenance, and underprovision of necessary services such as trash collection, proper drainage, recreation facilities, and street lighting. Moreover, most were completely or partially segregated. Despite these deficiencies, migrant women preferred the projects to the single rooms that they recently had vacated. Women also expressed satisfaction with indoor plumbing, space heat, hot and cold running water, and modern cooking and refrigeration facilities, amenities many had never had. Indeed, several women commented that the projects were the nicest place they had ever lived.[25]

Lacey Gray, whose two-room company house in Louisiana had lacked modern plumbing, was jubilant when her family's name came up for war housing. For $35 per month, which included utilities, she received more space than she had ever had: a living room, bedroom, kitchen, and full bath. Above all, government housing was woman-centered, spatially conducive to the formation of helping networks. The projects, in addition to housing large concentrations, of migrants, contained common yards and laundry facilities. In these shared areas, women assisted each other with tasks such as finding markets, churches, and social services. There, women watched children, made friends while doing laundry, and exchanged garden produce and recipes.[26]

Ethel Tillman, whose family secured government housing after doubling up with friends for their first two weeks in the Bay Area, "made friends with neighbors right away." Her popularity grew along with her generosity. "We sponsored dozens of other families while we were still in the projects, putting them up until they could find a house and a job. . . . We have fond memories of the different people who came through — family, strangers, couples, children, single men and women." Ethel and an aunt, who accompanied the Tillmans to California, also shared food with their neighbors, provided medical advice, and helped care for the children of working mothers. Life in war housing also facilitated institution building. Ethel and her husband soon learned that other former residents of Vicksburg had formed their own social club and mutual aid organization. Ethel recalled how women from this club "decided we just had to have some cornbread. Used Cream of Wheat and it was a good substitute." She went on to explain "how stockings were the hardest thing to find, and they were the ugliest colors. Us African women learned how to change them. Put them in oil and boiled them and it would make them the loveliest color."[27]

Olive, while still in the projects, began attending the only black Baptist church in town. "But it was hard to get to by 9:00 a.m.," so she and some friends from the project organized a new congregation. Lacey Gray, who came later, joined this new church and, along with Olive and other members, purchased land to build a permanent meeting place. Eventually Olive left and helped found a third Baptist church, which Lacey later joined as well. Other migrant women, like Ethel and her aunt, joined existing congregations, tripling and quadrupling church memberships, initiating church-based services for newcomers, and making it possible for congregations to purchase land and buildings.[28]

Whether they established their own churches or joined existing ones, migrant women formed the backbone of these institutions, raising money to pay pastors and purchase buildings, teaching Sunday school and Bible study, cooking church dinners, attracting new members, and forming the loyal core of congregations. Migrant men were also active church members. However, church work was widely recognized as women's work. As Joseph W. Scott and Albert Black have noted, "church values and norms are those of female-centered kin networks [which] emphasize the preservation of home and family." Berkeley's St. Paul A.M.E., for example, grew from 72 to 185 members between 1942 and 1943, with women forming 72 percent of the total congregation. In church and elsewhere, the migrant population reshaped institutions to meet their needs. Indeed, the prewar black communities of Richmond, Oakland,

and Berkeley were largely absorbed by the southern migrant community. There was never a question of migrants assimilating into existing institutions or communities. Viewed as unassimilable outsiders by most established white and black residents, newcomers found a sense of solidarity with other migrants and used their southernness as the currency of group identity and cohesiveness.[29]

As migrant women created new homes and institutions for their families with their unpaid labor, they also contributed to family income through wage work. Indeed, most women began to look for paid employment soon after moving to the Bay Area. Thus, the physical and emotional stress of relocation was often compounded by the demands of beginning a new job. However, unlike decent housing, jobs were relatively easy to find. Migrant women heard about them from friends, relatives, neighbors, newspaper ads, employment bureaus, and fellow passengers on trains and trolleys. Word of work was everywhere — electrifying the atmosphere of streetcars, markets, theaters, diners, and dance clubs.

Jobs were not only easy to find, they were also good. In the past, most gainfully employed African-American women worked in domestic service, but during the war, migrant women found other, higher paying jobs. For the first time in their lives, many had other options: industrial jobs in defense industries, clerical work in an expanding governmental sector, service employment on military bases and in defense plants. However, even as the war produced greater economic opportunities for migrant women, their economic status in relationship to other workers remained the same. As Karen Anderson observed, "Whatever the hierarchy of preference . . . black women could always be found at the bottom."[30]

During the war, defense industries hired white women first, training them to fill better paying, less dangerous jobs. A Department of Labor study revealed that: "There was a considerable scattering of white women in a broad range of jobs, a very large number appearing in the clerical occupations. The racial minorities, however, were markedly concentrated in a limited number of occupations. Thus, 63 percent of the Negro women were engaged as welders trainees and laborers. . . . In contrast only 6 percent of white women were engaged as laborers, 9 percent as welders trainees, and 9 percent as electrical trainees." By the time black women were hired, white women had already received training and taken the best jobs, "working as inspectors, painters, shipfitters, electricians, welders, machinists, assemblers, truck drivers, tank sealers, loaders and unloaders." White women not only worked at better paying jobs but also held jobs longer. Just as large numbers of black women were hired in 1943, war production peaked and declined within a year.[31]

Relegated to the least skilled, lowest paying, and most dangerous jobs, migrant women also had to contend with hostility from white workers and supervisors, union discrimination, and lack of advancement and promotions, but however bad these jobs were, migrant women relished the fact that "we were at least getting paid for putting up with it. In the South it had been nothing but hard work and bad treatment. Here I was making more in a day than I made back home in a month." Thus, although they filled the least desirable jobs in the defense economy, their employment represented a tremendous improvement over the domestic service jobs they had previously held.

Olive Blue and the sister who accompanied her out West found work at the Kaiser shipyards in Richmond. She signed up to be a scaler, smoothing out welds by removing stray drops of metal, but was reassigned to issue tools and mark time cards because she wrote clearly. However, scaling paid better, and Olive convinced her supervisor to give her back her old assignment. "After a while I began to show other ladies how to work. I worked days, swing, and grave, and rotated shifts. I enjoyed it, but didn't stay long. My mother came out to visit and she liked to die . . . said she wouldn't go back as long as we [Olive and her sister] were working in the shipyards." In the meantime, Olive's mother found out that the post office was hiring women and encouraged her daughters to apply. "So that's what I did — went to San Francisco and took the civil service exam. I always feared what the Bible said, and that was to obey your parents." Olive not only passed the exam and received the job but also began giving classes in her Richmond housing project, teaching others how to take the test. "My sister got into it [the post office] and friends got into it, and it was just nice."[32]

Ethel Tillman found a job at Mare Island, sorting scrap metal into different piles according to composition. While she worked the swing shift, her aunt cared for all ten children and for many others whose mothers also worked in the defense industry. During off hours, Ethel had her hands full, shopping, washing clothes, preparing meals, and making certain the children were doing well in school. Bertha Walker, who did not have children, still took major responsibility for household chores and cooking although she worked full time at American Can Company, stacking cans as they came off the line.[33]

Lacey Gray, unlike most women in my sample, passed up the opportunity to make extra money during the war years. Her husband found work in the Kaiser shipyards and, for the first time during their marriage, made enough to support the family on one salary. Lacey enjoyed staying at home with her children, a luxury that few working-class African-American women felt they could afford. Only after her children began school did Lacey take part-time jobs outside the house.[34]

Most migrant women experienced employment discrimination during the war years. One woman, a welder, "never saw a black leaderman in welding. I had a black woman friend who was a leaderman, but only over those ladies who swept up." Her observation was correct. In 1942, 102 black workers, including at least 30 women, filed a complaint with the Fair Employment Practices Commission (FEPC), claiming that their employer, Permanente Metals Corporation of Richmond, failed to promote or upgrade them and, in some cases, asked them to train white employees who became their supervisors. Just a month later, 173 workers, including 27 women, filed a similar complaint against Richmond Shipyard #1.[35]

Migrant women also filed complaints against unions, which turned away black members or relegated them to auxiliaries. One woman, writing to the FEPC, bitterly protested this type of discrimination:

Mr. President

Honorable Sir,

I wish to call your attention to a very disgraceful and UnAmerican situation that now exists in the Boilermakers and Welders Union Local 513 of Richmond Calif. I am a Negro girl. Three weeks ago I and lots of others enrolled in the National Defense Training Classes to become welders. I applied for a job at the yards several times. But each time myself and others of my race were given the run around. . . . [B]ecause of being Negro I was not allowed to join the Union. Now Mr. President there are a great many Negroes in Defense Training as myself who upon completion of the course will be subjected to the same treatment as myself. We are all doing what we can to assist in winning the war. I sincerely feel that this is no time for our very own fellow citizens to use discrimination of this type.[36]

Other women protested employment discrimination by refusing to take demeaning jobs. Beatrice Morris, for example, applied for an opening as a power machine operator at the California Manufacturing Company in Oakland. The company hired her but placed her in a less skilled job. When she asked to be reclassified as a power machine operator, she was told that "the white power machine operators objected to having a Negro seated among them." She immediately quit her job and filed a complaint with the FEPC.[37]

Although the majority of married migrant women in my sample worked for wages during the war, most identified themselves as wives, mothers, and "community" women rather than as "workers." Ethel Tillman, for example, was visibly proud of her job at Mare Island but, nevertheless, described it as "helping out" — supplementing the wages of her husband, who, regardless of his contribution to family income, claimed the breadwinner role. By defining their community or family work as "real" work, women not only preserved traditional gender roles and family peace but also created a dignified category of labor that they alone controlled.

As church women, neighborhood mothers, medical practitioners, and social service providers, they contributed to the health, stability, and permanence of migrant communities while creating an alternate source of status and identity. Through their church work, women raised money for scholarships, established drug rehabilitation programs, mentored the young, and provided material assistance to the needy. Several migrant women in this sample established or participated in community service projects. Maude Green and Canary Jones, for example, founded a grass roots development project in Richmond that funded a food co-op, recycling program, job training program, credit union, and food stamp distribution center. Their organization also built a neighborhood play center and documented employment discrimination in downtown Richmond.[38] Yet, however they defined it, migrant women's paid employment was central to the economic stability of the black working class, frequently providing half or more of family income. Even when women's employment was irregular and supplemental to that of primary wage earners, their wages enhanced family security and quality of life.

By 1945, most migrant women had lost their wartime jobs. Having earned between $0.90 and $1.50 per hour, several times what they had made as southern domestic workers or school teachers, most hoped to find other industrial jobs. For them, work was more than a patriotic duty; it was an economic necessity. A Women's Bureau survey of Bay Area women found that 95 percent of nonwhite women employed during the war years planned to continue working after the war. In contrast, 67 percent of white women expressed the same desire.[39]

After the war, most migrants continued to be forced into occupations well below their skill levels, necessitating two wage earners in most families. Few migrant women returned to domestic service, a majority worked in food processing industries, apparel factories, or institutional settings as nurse's aides, custodians, and cooks — a new form of domestic work. In 1948, only one-fifth of black women in the Bay Area held clerical, managerial, or professional jobs, compared with three-fourths of all employed Bay Area women. Those who did find clerical jobs usually worked for the government. The post office, for example, employed several women in this sample. Indeed, government employment continued to expand throughout the postwar period, providing better job security, wages, and benefits than all other Bay Area jobs open to migrant women. In Oakland alone, government employment expanded 28 percent between 1960 and 1966, employing 29 percent of the city's civilian employed black population by the end of that period.[40]

Bertha Walker lost her job at American Can Company "the last part of 1945 when men started coming back." Unable to find another industrial job, she returned to domestic service, cleaning homes and providing childcare. "My husband was afraid he'd lose his longshore job after the war too, because he didn't have as much seniority as other workers. But Harry Bridges stood up for the newer workers, and he kept his job. But for a while my husband kept saying we'd have to go home." The Walkers weathered this period of postwar economic uncertainty and, in 1966, purchased a home in Oakland with their combined income.[41]

Olive Blue lost her postal service job following the war but found another clerical position at the Oakland Naval Supply Center, handling insurance claims for military personnel. She held this position for 36 years, retiring in 1984. Her husband joined her in the East Bay Area after his discharge from the military, but they soon negotiated an amicable divorce after he insisted upon returning to Texas. Olive remarried and, with her new husband, built a home in Richmond in 1948.[42]

After the war, Lacey Gray's husband lost his shipyard job and then found employment as an elevator operator and doorman at an Oakland bank. When her daughters started school, Lacey worked part-time at a bakery. By the mid-1950s, they had saved enough to buy a home and began to look for a safe, family-oriented neighborhood. Realtors steered them to North Richmond, a predominantly black section of town, "but it was segregated and I didn't want a place there." Agents then took them to a new suburban development called Parchester Village and "said it was going to be black and white together. But they had but one white lady living in a model home, and when black people had all moved in, she moved out. And it was nothing but a black settlement." The Grays, like Olive Blue, eventually built their own home on a lot that they purchased in 1955. "When we bought it, there were only a few houses in the neighborhood and a few white people. But they moved out when we moved in." She, and other migrant women, dreamed of living in an integrated neighborhood, only to discover that as they moved in, whites left for the growing suburbs.[43]

Following the war, Ethel Tillman and her husband had enough combined income to purchase a home in Berkeley. She became a full-time homemaker, while her husband found a well-paying, secure job at U.S. Steel. Although her hands were full with her own children, Ethel became a neighborhood mother — a person everyone came to for medical advice, help with personal problems, and assistance with childcare.[44]

Now permanent residents, migrant women turned to creating permanent institutions within their communities. Church, rather than the common space once afforded by war housing, became the single most important outlet for women's community work. Other women in the sample formed neighborhood associations, organized boycotts of local businesses that refused to hire black citizens, registered voters, led school desegregation campaigns, created new chapters of the National Association for the Advancement of Colored People (NAACP) and National Council of Negro Women, and staffed community development projects funded by the Johnson administration during the 1960s.

Olive Blue, one of the more active women in the sample, not only helped establish two new churches, as cited above, but also served as secretary of the Richmond NAACP and the Richmond branch of the National Council of Negro Women. In her church, she served as secretary, president of Pastor's Aid, and active member of the Usher's Board, choir, Missionary Society, and Christian Aid Board. She also joined the Richmond Democratic Club and helped with several political campaigns. Asked to relate her philosophy, Olive stated "be dedicated. I think we should love what we do. Do it, whether it is a great task or small. Do it well or not at all. Stand up. And just because everything doesn't go the way we hope, or the way we desire it to go, doesn't mean the effort wasn't worthwhile." She went on to reflect that "short comings are given unto each life. Into each life some rain is going to fall. Some days are going to be dark. And many times we'll weep . . . but weep not like those who have no hope, because weeping comes in the night, but joy comes in the morning."[45]

Lacey Gray joined the NAACP, Vicksburg Club, and Daughters of the Eastern Star. She, too, became active in her church, attending several nights a week, teaching Sunday school, and serving as secretary and captain of its fundraising board. Her advice to the young is "to patternize your life after someone who is doing good." Bertha Walker became an adoptive mother to several young children in her neighborhood, providing guidance, nourishing food, and a safe place to study and play. She is proud of the fact that her adoptive children call her "grandma to this day." Similarly, Ethel Tillman served as a neighborhood mother. She and her husband also became active in their church, helped establish a local senior center, and retained their membership in the Vicksburg Club, currently helping to care for sick and housebound members.[46]

Beginning at the end of the war and increasing during the 1950s, white residents began to leave East Bay cities and relocate to the suburban fringe. This white flight coincided with a sharp reduction of manufacturing jobs in the urban core, as industry followed white residents to the suburbs. Between 1960 and 1966, for example, Oakland lost one-fourth of its manufacturing jobs — jobs traditionally a source of upward mobility for minority workers. In brief, deindustrialization, which captured the attention of the white public in the 1980s, has been a longstanding problem within East Bay black communities. The migrant generation, however, was less affected by this structural shift than younger workers because of their longer employment histories, union seniority, and relatively high skill levels.[47]

As jobs were leaving the East Bay inner cities, poorly planned redevelopment schemes further eroded the economic vitality of migrant communities. In West Oakland, transportation officials razed single family homes and the black business district to make room for new freeways and the Bay Area Rapid Transit System. Finally, neighborhoods that were spared the wrecking ball were separated from vital services and resources and, then, targeted for public housing development.

In the absence of sustained societal commitment to providing jobs and housing for black communities, working-class migrants were called upon to stabilize their neighborhoods in the hard economic times of the postwar era. Their helping ethic, desire for economic independence, and commitment to institution building — all pieces of a southern cultural legacy that allowed their forbears to resist the economic hardships and dehumanization of Jim Crow — were now turned to helping communities resist chronic unemployment and its accompanying dislocations. In the end, their efforts to provide for their families and neighbors support Jacqueline Jones's contention that "embedded in the historical record of ordinary families . . . is a powerful refutation of the culture of poverty or culture of dependency thesis."[48]

Olive, Ethel, Lacey, and Bertha, who are representative of other women in the sample, were actively involved in individual and collective efforts to create community-sustaining institutions — efforts that reveal a common, historically rooted desire for independence and self-determination. East Bay black communities, although facing severe problems, also had considerable resources. A majority of residents, poor and working class, continued to draw upon southern cultural traditions to keep their families together, build community-sustaining institutions, and challenge racial stereotypes and restrictions. The experience and contributions of migrant women counter generalizations about inner city communities that obscure their agency and diversity and the historical processes that led to urban poverty.

NOTES

1. See for example, Peter Gottlieb, *Making Their Own Way: Southern Black Migration to Pittsburgh 1916–1930* (Urbana: University of Illinois Press, 1987); James Grossman, *Land of Hope: Chicago, Black Southerners and the Great Migration* (Chicago: University of Chicago Press, 1989); Carole Marks, *Farewell We're Good and Gone: The Great Black Migration* (Bloomington: Indiana University Press, 1989); Joe Trotter, *Black Milwaukee: The Making of an Industrial Proletariat, 1915–1945* (Urbana: University of Illinois Press, 1985).

2. Marilynn S. Johnson's *The Second Gold Rush: Oakland and the East Bay During World War II* (Berkeley: University of California Press, 1993) is one of the first published studies detailing the demographic, cultural, and political transformation of the San Francisco East Bay Area during World War II. Although this is a more general study of wartime migration to the East Bay Area, emphasizing the experience of white migrants, it contains richly descriptive sections on black migrant labor, housing, and civil rights activism. Johnson's work suggests that a full-length study of wartime East Bay black migration would be an important addition to the literature. Shirley Ann Moore's forthcoming history of African-Americans in Richmond, California, containing sections on wartime migration, will also contribute to our knowledge of this subject. For an overview of women's experience during World War II, see William Chafe, *The Paradox of Change: American Women in the Twentieth Century* (New York: Oxford University Press, 1991); Karen Anderson, "Last Hired, First Fired: Black Women Workers During World War II," *Journal of American History* 69 (June 1982): 82–97; Karen Anderson, *Wartime Women: Sex Roles, Family Relations and the Status of Women During World War II* (Westport, Conn.: Greenwood Press, 1981); Susan Hartman, *The Homefront and Beyond: American Women in the 1940s* (Boston: Twayne, 1982); Sherna Gluck, *Rosie the Riveter Revisited: Women, the War, and Social Change* (Boston: Twayne, 1987).

3. Gerald Nash, *The American West Transformed* (Bloomington: Indiana University Press, 1985), pp. 26, 66, 67; Robert O. Brown, "Impact of War Worker Migration on the Public School System of Richmond, California from 1940–1945" (Ph.D. diss., Stanford University, 1973), pp. 109, 110; U.S. Congress, House Committee on Naval Affairs, Subcommittee of the Committee on Naval Affairs, *Investigation of Congested Areas*, 78th Cong., 1st Sess., 1943, Vol. 1, Pt. 3, p. 855;

Edward E. France, "Some Aspects of the Migration of the Negro to the San Francisco Bay Area Since 1940" (Ph.D. diss., University of California, Berkeley, 1962), p. 24.

4.   Charles S. Johnson, *The Negro War Worker in San Francisco* (San Francisco, Calif.: YWCA and the Race Relations Program of the American Missionary Association, 1944).

5.   Aggregate statistics from 50 oral interviews conducted with former migrants between 1990 and 1991; Henry S. Shyrock, Jr., "Wartime Shifts of the Civilian Population," *Milbank Memorial Fund Quarterly* 25 (July 1947): 269–82, found that the majority of migrants to the West coast were from towns and cities. Only 13 to 19 percent were former farm residents. Other studies point to the relatively high skill levels of black migrants: Cy W. Record, *Characteristics of Some Unemployed Negro Shipyard Workers in Richmond, California* (Berkeley, Calif.: Institute for Governmental Studies, 1947); U.S. Department of Labor, Bureau of Labor Statistics, Labor Force in Durable Goods Manufacture in the San Francisco Bay Area, 1943, *Monthly Labor Review*, October 1945; Johnson, *The Negro War Worker in San Francisco*.

6.   Ethel Tillman, interview held in Berkeley, California, September 21, 1990; Bertha Walker, interview held in Oakland, California, March 4, 1991.

7.   Lacey Gray, interview held in Richmond, California, May 21, 1991; Olive Blue, interview held in Richmond, California, May 5, 1991.

8.   Lacey Gray interview; Aggregate statistics; Johnson, in *The Negro War Worker in San Francisco*, pp. 7–8, reported migrants' education levels nearly equaled those of the nonmigrant black population and migrant white population and were higher for black migrant women than for black migrant men. His statistics were based on a larger sample than mine and are probably more reliable. In his sample, 74 percent of all migrant women completed eight years of school, 65 percent had some high school, 35 percent completed high school, and 9 percent had college or professional training.

9.   Ethel Tillman interview; Lacey Gray interview; William E. Montgomery, *Under Their Own Vine and Fig Tree: The African American Church in the South, 1856–1900* (Baton Rouge: Louisiana State University Press, 1992); Johnson, *The Negro War Worker in San Francisco*, p. 87.

10.   Ethel Tillman interview; Lacey Gray interview; see Paula Giddings, *When and Where I Enter: The Impact of Black Women on Race and Sex in America* (New York: William Morrow, 1984); Lynda F. Dickson, "Toward a Broader Angle of Vision in Uncovering Women's History: Black Women's Clubs Revisited," *Frontiers* 9 (1987): 62–68; Jacqueline Anne Rouse, *Lugenia Burns Hope: Black Southern Reformer* (Atlanta: University of Georgia Press, 1989), pp. 89–90; Linda Gordon, "Black and White Visions of Welfare Activism, 1890–1945," *Journal of American History* 78 (September 1991): 578, for a discussion of elitism among middle-class club women.

11.   Olive Blue interview; Aggregate statistics. For a discussion of working-class women's networks, see Carol B. Stack, *All Our Kin: Strategies for Survival in a Black Community* (New York: Harper & Row, 1974); Karen Brodkin Sacks, *Caring by the Hour: Women, Work and Organizing at Duke Medical Center* (Urbana: University of Illinois Press, 1987); Nancy Naples, "'Just What Needed to be Done': The Political Practice of Women Community Workers in Low-Income Neighborhoods," *Gender and Society* 5 (December 1991): 478–94; Nancy Naples, "Activist Mothering:

Cross-Generational Continuity in the Community Work of Women from Low-Income Neighborhoods," *Gender and Society* 6 (September 1992): 441–63.

12. Aggregate statistics; Johnson, *The Negro War Worker in San Francisco*, pp. 5, 7, 12; Johnson, *The Second Gold Rush*, p. 53.

13. Ethel Tillman interview.

14. Bertha Walker interview.

15. Lacey Gray interview.

16. Olive Blue interview.

17. Ethel Tillman interview; Aggregate statistics.

18. Bertha Walker interview; Lacey Gray interview.

19. Lacey Gray interview.

20. Bertha Walker interview.

21. Robert Wenkert, *An Historical Digest of Negro White Relations in Richmond, California* (Berkeley: University of California Survey Research Center, 1967), pp. 10–22; Brown, "Impact of the War Worker Migration," p. 41; U.S. Congress, House, Committee on Naval Affairs, *Investigation of Congested Areas*, p. 798; Harvey J. Kerns, *Study of Social and Economic Conditions Affecting the Local Negro Population* (Oakland, Calif.: Council of Social Agencies and Community Chest, 1942); France, "Some Aspects of the Migration," pp. 32–33; Oakland Council of Social Agencies, *Our Community: A Factual Presentation of Social Conditions* (Oakland, Calif.: Community Chest, 1945); Barbara Lou Sawyer, "Negroes in West Oakland" (Oakland, 1952) mimeographed, Black Social Conditions File, Oakland History Room, Oakland Public Library; Johnson, *The Second Gold Rush*, p. 116.

22. Lacey Gray interview; Aggregate statistics.

23. Johnson, *The Negro War Worker in San Francisco*, pp. 26–27.

24. Ibid.

25. Aggregate statistics.

26. Lacey Gray interview; Aggregate statistics.

27. Ethel Tillman interview.

28. Olive Blue interview; Lacey Gray interview; Ethel Tillman interview; Taylor Memorial United Methodist Church, *History of the Church, Founders and Ministers 1921–1988*, Church File, Northern California Center for Afro-American History and Life (hereafter NCCAHL); Progressive Baptist Church, *Twenty Years of Progress, 1935–1955*, Church File, NCCAHL; Downs Memorial Methodist Church, *A Brief History of Downs*, Church File, NCCAHL; Cooper A.M.E. Zion Church, *Souvenir Program 1898–1948*, Church File, NCCAHL.

29. Joseph W. Scott and Albert Black, "Deep Structures of African American Family Life: Female and Male Kin Networks," *Western Journal of Black Studies* 13 (Spring 1989): 22; St. Paul A.M.E. Church, *History of the Church*, Church File, NCCAHL; Oakland Institute on Human Relations, *Seminar Report on What Tensions Exist Between Groups in the Local Community* (Oakland, Calif.: n.p., 1946); Albert S. Broussard, *Black San Francisco: The Struggle for Racial Equality in the West, 1900–1954* (Lawrence: University Press of Kansas, 1993); Douglas H. Daniels, *Pioneer Urbanites: A Social and Cultural History of Black San Francisco* (Berkeley: University of California Press, 1990), pp. 170–80; Aggregate statistics.

30. Anderson, "Last Hired, First Fired," p. 84.

31. Record, *Characteristics of Some Unemployed Negro Shipyard Workers*, pp. 11–12; U.S. Department of Labor, *Labor Force in Durable Goods Manufacture in the*

San Francisco Bay Area, pp. 713–14; Brown, "The Impact of War Worker Migration," pp. 174–75.

32. Olive Blue interview.

33. Ethel Tillman interview; Bertha Walker interview.

34. Lacey Gray interview.

35. Faith McAllister, interview held in Richmond, California, May 2, 1991; *Selected Documents from the Records of the Committee on Fair Employment Practices*, Region XII, Reel 111, Richmond Prefabrication Plant File, 12-BR-108; Reel 111, Richmond Shipyard #1 File, 12-BR-81.

36. *Selected Documents from the Records of the Committee on Fair Employment Practices*, Region XII, Reel 110, Machinists Local 824 File; Reel 108, Complaints against Boilermakers File.

37. *Selected Documents from the Records of the Committee on Fair Employment Practices*, Region XII, Reel 109, California Manufacturing Company File.

38. Aggregate statistics; Ethel Tillman interview; Maude Green, interview held in Richmond, California, January 17, 1991; Canary Jones, interview held in Richmond, California, March 6, 1991.

39. U.S. Department of Labor, *Women Workers in Ten Production Areas and Their Postwar Employment Plans*, U.S. Women's Bureau Bulletin #209.

40. Earl R. Babbie and William Nichols III, *Oakland in Transition: A Summary of the 701 Household Survey* (Berkeley: University of California Survey Research Center, 1969), pp. 108–9.

41. Bertha Walker interview.

42. Olive Blue interview.

43. Lacey Gray interview. Postwar housing discrimination is described in detail by W. Miller Barbour, *An Exploratory Study of Socio-Economic Problems Affecting the Negro White Relationship in Richmond, California* (Pasadena, Calif.: United Community Defense Services and the National Urban League, 1952); Wenkert, *An Historical Digest*; Babbie and Nichols, *Oakland in Transition*; France, "Some Aspects of the Migration"; Johnson, *The Second Gold Rush*, pp. 224–33.

44. Ethel Tillman interview.

45. Olive Blue interview.

46. Lacey Gray interview; Bertha Walker interview; Ethel Tillman interview.

47. Babbie and Nichols, *Oakland in Transition*, pp. 104–11, 124, 162–63, 184–85.

48. Jacqueline Jones, "Southern Diaspora: Origins of the Urban 'Underclass,'" in *The "Underclass Debate": Views from History*, ed. Michael Katz (Princeton, N.J.: Princeton University Press, 1993), p. 38.

9

Catalyst for Change: Wartime Housing and African-Americans in California's East Bay

Delores Nason McBroome

Between World Wars I and II, African-Americans sought avenues for creating a political and economic voice in the white-dominated society of California's East Bay. The African-American population by 1940 in the combined East Bay cities — Oakland, Berkeley, and Richmond — totalled over 12,000. World War II dramatically increased that population to over 70,000.[1] In addition, the pressures of a swollen black population increased consciousness among the East Bay's black residents of discriminatory housing policies that severely constrained their ability to compete successfully for living quarters. In 1940, defense industries located in the Bay Area acted as magnets, drawing racial and ethnic minorities discouraged by the lack of employment opportunities elsewhere in the country. Although housing shortages for the East Bay's African-American population existed long before World War II, the urgent demands that both black residents and newcomers migrating for defense work after 1940 made upon housing created a climate for change in the East Bay's residential policies. The conclusion of World War II, however, did not bring about resolutions to the housing problems African-Americans faced as a result of de facto discrimination. In the postwar years, African-Americans in California's East Bay mounted a legislative campaign, finally resulting in the 1963 Rumford Fair Housing

Act prohibiting discriminatory housing practices based upon race. The catalyst for this legislative campaign stemmed from the increased awareness and militancy that World War II fostered in California's African-American communities.

Beginning with the Great Migration of African-Americans from southern communities to the North and West during the 1920s, Bay Area residents found housing difficult to buy, and most African-Americans remained tenants. Housing rentals were scarce, and competition for them increased in the 1930s. In West and North Oakland, the increasing need for housing was temporarily assuaged by homeowners and tenants taking in boarders. Blacks confronted the lack of available housing and restrictive ordinances based on race by organizing neighborhood improvement associations and by campaigning for equitable housing laws. These associations provided not only a political voice for African-American members but also a social network providing opportunities for meeting other black residents and sharing information.

These prewar efforts to address housing shortages for the East Bay's African-American population too often are minimized as insubstantial or ignored as historians focus upon the growth of public housing introduced in the mid-1930s.[2] The African-American newspaper, the *California Voice*, reported as early as 1922 that a "small number of Berkeley residents [were] trying to pass an ordinance that would prohibit the members of our group owning homes in the district."[3] Several restrictive ordinances were passed during the decades of the 1920s and 1930s. Investors in Wall's Addition, a new residential area for Richmond, advertised that restrictive housing covenants would be upheld there just as in Lakeshore Glen, South Lakeshore Glen, and Lakeshore Hills: "Savages running wild in a central African forest, living on wild nuts and fruit, sleeping in trees or caves, don't care much about a home — they don't want property because they can't take care of it. But white men, civilized men, twentieth century Americans should need no argument to make them see the beauty of owning property — real property — A HOME."[4]

These restrictive covenants plagued African-Americans coming to the East Bay in the prewar era.

Marilynn Johnson describes Oakland, North Richmond, and Richmond's south side as multiracial, working-class communities able to absorb "most of the migrant population into existing vacancies" during the early mobilization period in 1940.[5] Examples of de facto discrimination abound prior to 1940 and are not restricted to the greater area of Oakland. The office of the County Recorder for Alameda County lists many property agreements such as the one filed August 9, 1932. In that instance, four Berkeley property owners filed papers in which they mutually agreed that none of the property they owned "shall ever be used or occupied by any person other than of the Caucasian race."[6] This property agreement affected four contiguous lots on the north side of Carlton Street, stretching westward from the corner of Milvia toward Grove. The National Association for the Advancement of Colored People (NAACP) tried to break restrictions as well as encourage employment for African-Americans in housing construction trades. In 1938 an NAACP committee inquired why so few Negroes were used in the building trades only to find that most of the trades unions had color restrictions.[7] Not only did African-Americans find little employment working on housing projects encouraged by the New Deal, but restrictions also existed that excluded them from living in the newly constructed projects. Sheffield Village, constructed by the Federal Housing Administration (FHA), had a restrictive clause stating "For use only by persons whose blood is entirely of the Caucasian race, except strictly in the capacity of domestic servants."[8]

Federal law introduced during the New Deal provided opportunities for municipalities to adopt enabling resolutions and then set up housing authorities to construct low-cost projects for their areas.[9] Oakland's City Council would not consider an enabling resolution, so, Alameda's NAACP representative, C. L. Dellums, started leading demonstrations backed by labor's Non-Partisan League at city council meetings.[10] The Oakland League of Women Voters also supported low-cost housing and spoke in favor of it.[11] During the prewar period, African-Americans mounted protests regarding housing inadequacies through the NAACP and the Non-Partisan League. Mass protest at grass-roots levels would come about during World War II.

When Oakland's City Council finally passed an enabling resolution for low-cost housing, two businessmen (one dealing in downtown business properties and the other in residential properties in adjacent Piedmont) were placed on the housing authority. These businessmen never really looked at the insides of the houses they appraised. According to Dellums, they simply drove through an area in their cars and turned in their reports based upon only a casual glance at the neighborhoods. They then sent to Washington, D.C., a very low evaluation for homes in West Oakland. The FHA then cut this figure by 40 percent. People refused to sell for such low prices, and eventually a housing authority realtor sought Dellums's help. Asking the FHA to reexamine its appraisals and increase the values so they no longer represented a steal, Dellums encouraged homeowners to sell their properties.

However, few in West Oakland felt they would receive a "fair" price for their homes. Some people held out until their cases went to court.[12]

The second phase of the low-cost housing fight began with the housing authority's policy for selecting tenants. African-Americans demanded that Oakland's housing authority announce a public policy of integration. The housing authority refused to comply; however, it did select William P. Butler, an African-American realtor and friend of C. L. Dellums, to manage the newly constructed Campbell Village. Butler selected tenants to racially and ethnically checkerboard Campbell Village. Dellums said that "it became a showplace of the nation for public housing projects. He [Butler] checkerboarded every floor, every unit, and it lasted for years that way and the people got along just beautifully."[13]

Butler's checkerboard policy was not employed by Oakland's housing authority in its other projects. The second low-cost project to open, Peralta, did not follow the same pattern. According to Dellums, "One building would be all-white, the next building all-Negro. But there was no integration in the buildings, no checkerboarding, in various buildings. This is what we called integrated segregation."[14] The third project, Lockwood, was all white when it opened. Dellums criticized the housing authority in his statement: "You see how they went? From integration to integrated segregation to lily-whiteism."[15] Eventually, Butler also managed Peralta, although little change toward integration occurred there. Lockwood, in predominantly white East Oakland, did not offer proximity to black employment areas.

Adequate housing for African-Americans living in the East Bay deteriorated until a crisis was widely recognized during World War II. Between April 1940 and January 1944, California's population expanded from 6,907,387 to 8,450,000, an increase of 22.4 percent. This represented "the greatest numerical increase experienced by any state during this period."[16] For many East Bay areas, this meant that desperate housing conditions for the Negro population prevailed. "Population 'doubled up' with existing residents" of the area until a new Negro ghetto formed in Berkeley, bounded on the north by Dwight Way, on the west by Grove, on the south by the city limits, and on the east by San Pablo.[17] Thus, with the advent of World War II, African-American residents of the East Bay experienced tremendous pressures from restrictive housing ordinances, poorly integrated low-cost housing projects, and the needs of newly arriving black migrants.

Tensions built throughout the war period, often resulting in violent outbursts, such as the 1944 race riot near the Oakland intersection of Twelfth and Broadway. A local white newspaper proclaimed the race problem a phenomenon caused by "new socially liberated negroes who are not bound by the *old and peaceful understanding* between the Negro and the white in Oakland."[18] San Francisco and the East Bay finally experienced the "Chicago effect," which Allan Spear noted in his study of *Black Chicago*. Spear explained that when the black population is small, the white population does not fear it, but when numbers increase, conflict occurs. Citing the black population of Chicago as a very small component (0.9 percent) of its total population in 1860, Spear found an absence of racial conflict. However, when the black population increased in Chicago during the next two decades, the white antagonism toward African-Americans surfaced in discriminatory patterns affecting housing and employment.[19]

As more African-Americans came to the Bay Area after 1941, patterns of residential segregation increased, with the expanded use of occupancy clauses in deeds and leases that restricted racial minorities to certain areas of Oakland and the East Bay. This "Chicago effect" would continue to deny equal opportunity in housing to African-Americans long after the war had ended.[20]

Prior to World War II, African-Americans made up, at most, no more than 3 percent of the West coast's shipbuilding industries. By 1945 there were more than 700,000 workers in West coast yards, with approximately 7 percent (50,000 people) African-Americans.[21] Nearly 13 percent of the total workers among the four leading shipbuilding companies of the Bay Area were African-Americans by 1943. People seeking work could apply to the four shipyards of Henry J. Kaiser in Richmond, Marinship in Sausalito, the Moore yards in Oakland, or the Todd yard in San Francisco. Many black families from the Dustbowl states of the Southwest began to migrate to the Oakland area soon after the war began. Edward L. Coleman, a young African-American migrant to Alameda in 1943, said that a carload of men left his home in El Dorado, Arkansas, every week for California. Coleman's father went with one of the carloads at the urging of his wife, who saw the shipyard checks her neighbors' husbands sent home from their jobs in California.[22] The first money order that Coleman's father sent to his wife after a week away from home was for $100. This represented an incredible sum, because the Colemans had never been able to earn that much in one week in Arkansas. In El Dorado, Coleman was a barber and his wife worked in a cleaners. Together they would earn between $17 and $18 for a six-day workweek.

The high wage rate in the West coast defense industries drew even reluctant migrants to California. Coleman called his father "the ultimate pessimist," because the senior Coleman believed that the war would not last long enough for the men with whom he left El Dorado to find good jobs in the defense industries. Sometimes it would be six months to a year and a half later when the rest of the family followed the men who went west. The Coleman family came to Oakland in 1943 with no furniture and only their luggage. When they arrived in St. Louis en route to California, they found the typical pattern of wartime transportation. There was mass confusion as passengers boarded trains that often were delayed. Railway passengers were segregated; however, Coleman recalls that the segregation policy was meaningless, because the trains were packed with soldiers, and there were no seats left for black people. Coleman with his mother and sister stood up in the vestibule of the train and in the toilets practically all the way to Salt Lake City. He remembers his mother going to the bathroom just so she could sit down.[23]

Once the Colemans arrived in Oakland, they faced the same housing shortages that other black families found in the Bay Area. They lived for nine months in a housing project where six people occupied a one-bedroom apartment. An African-American social worker and NAACP activist, Tarea Hall Pittman, worked for the Richmond Travelers Aid Society, United Service Organizations, during the war and remembered working with transients and people who were moving into California: "We had a time opening up the Kaiser Industries, and we had a doubly hard time in trying to get some housing for those men. Some of the people were sleeping in 'hot beds.' So naturally, when their families came, you'd have a very difficult time finding them because all the landlady knew was that she had a stream of people going and coming. One man would work one shift and sleep in the 'hot bed,' then that one would be up and gone, and there would be another shift."[24]

California maintained a three-year residency requirement for public assistance during World War II, while southern states such as Oklahoma, Texas, and Louisiana had one-year residency requirements. This meant that people coming to California would lose their former residency while not qualifying for resident status in California. Nevertheless, the migration of African-Americans to the wartime defense industries reached staggering proportions by 1945, when approximately 152,000 blacks moved to the West coast.[25]

Dealing with the needs of migrants settling in the Bay Area posed special problems for the community. Robert E. Colbert noted in 1946 that: "So sudden was the deluge that not only was the majority group made conscious of this alien element, but the older Negro residents in this area were probably for the first time made aware of their place as a minority group. . . . Relationships between older Negro residents and whites changed. Many reactions by these older residents toward the newcomers — the sharecroppers — were experienced."[26] Assuming that World War II represented a watershed in African-American experience, comments such as Colbert's indicated to many that the black community splintered politically between older and more recent residents. However, this factionalism was overcome in California's East Bay, where the more settled black "pioneer urbanites" joined forces with the migrant newcomers in order to promote nondiscriminatory policies.[27]

For example, the East Bay community of Richmond transformed itself dramatically during World War II. From a population of 23,000 people living in one-family houses before the war, Richmond's population grew to over 100,000, encouraged by the construction of four Kaiser shipyards and a prefabrication plant built on its waterfront.[28] Activists such as Tarea Pittman and local African-American organizations united to monitor the housing situation and employment conditions of the shipyards throughout the war. Sprawling public-housing projects were built beside the harbor and town of Richmond to accommodate the new shipyard workers, who built one-fifth of all the Liberty ships constructed during the war. Shipyard workers in Richmond were drawn by the promise of a high wage, which averaged $61 a week. If a worker were lucky enough to find a three-room apartment in someone's private house, he would pay $120 a month for it, almost half his monthly wage.[29] By 1945 there were 14,000 African-Americans in Richmond, where fewer than 250 lived before 1940.

Richmond's acute housing shortage and also substandard construction predated entry of the United States into the war by several years. The 1940 census reported that of a total of 7,611 dwellings, 1,539 needed major repairs or had no private bath.[30] On January 21, 1941, the *Oakland Tribune* reported that Richmond's City Council adopted a resolution to form a five-person housing authority to investigate "unsafe, unsanitary and congested dwelling accommodations."[31] The housing authority was charged with making a citywide survey and reporting on housing units in the city of Richmond in order to initiate action designed to request the construction of low-cost housing units from the United States Housing Authority.

The resolution passed by the Richmond City Council in January 1941 claimed that: "Unemployment and the existence of unsafe, unsanitary and congested dwelling accommodations have produced an alarming economic and social condition. Emergency measures are necessary for the immediate preservation of public peace, health and safety."[32]

Council members expressed concern about the expected influx of workers who would seek housing in Richmond later in the year, after the Todd-California shipyard in San Francisco began its full production schedule. Many shipyard workers, unable to find housing in San Francisco, would commute by ferry from Richmond to their work at the Todd shipyard. By the end of 1941, two low-cost housing projects were completed, neither of which admitted African-Americans.

Three years later, many of the newly constructed shipyard housing units built in Richmond with the aid of the federal government were considered unfit by the Contra Costa's county coroner's inquest. In January 1944, eight unidentified African-American shipyard workers were killed in a fire at Dormitory "O," located at South Eleventh Street and Potrero Avenue. Richmond's fire chief, William P. Cooper, testified before the coroner's jury that various Richmond housing units were "totally unsafe, and built in violation of all state, local and national laws."[33]

Of the 24,000 housing units built during the war, only 750 were permanent dwellings, with the majority of African-Americans in Richmond living in temporary housing units. Cooper also testified that the Richmond Housing Authority was not to blame for the unsafe conditions. The Public Works Administration, the FHA, and other governmental agencies built these housing units and then turned them over to the housing authority to administer. Chief Cooper said: "I've written to the various authorities and commissions telling them about conditions in these housing units. I've told them they are unsafe. I've told them they are endangering the lives of shipyard workers and their families. I've pleaded with them to remedy the situation — I've ordered them to take steps to remedy these conditions. And they've told me to go to hell!"[34]

A survey following the January 1944 fire showed that of 9,000 units housing between 50,000 and 90,000 persons only 64 had fire protection including alarm systems and fire hydrants. Cooper revealed that in one section of the housing projects, fire hydrants were installed but were not turned on for three months because "none of the agencies knew which one had the authority to order the water turned on."[35]

The alarm caused by the hazards of inadequate fire protection in Richmond's shipyard housing exacerbated tensions already present within the city's African-American community. Representatives of local black organizations complained of illegal evictions and threatened a "rent strike" if the evictions did not cease. The city council recommended that the housing authority establish a definite policy concerning evictions and illegal tenancy. Charles Strothoff, executive secretary for the Richmond Housing Authority, released its policies and procedures to the public on January 21, 1944. The definition of eligibility for housing authority units and rooms included those persons working in certain unnamed war industries. Strothoff said complaints of illegal tenancy occurred when families moved into housing units without acceptance of a formal application: "Legal residents all must have signed leases with the authority. In cases of evictions for non-payment of rent, the authority must, and will, follow State and O.P.A. rules and regulations. . . . In cases where families are illegally occupying a unit, each case will be handled separately and those families who are working in eligible war industries [we] will try to place the families as rapidly as possible."[36]

In 1948, Richmond's housing crisis still went unresolved as the city's chamber of commerce declared a section of north Richmond a "blighted area" that was "hazardous to health and the public welfare."[37] African-Americans charged that the area's designation as "blighted" was an attempt by the city of Richmond to acquire more land at cheap prices for industrial development.

Wartime opposition by the white community in Richmond to the expansion of African-American residential areas followed the patterns and tactics used throughout the San Francisco Bay Area. Real estate agents and homeowners refused to sell property to African-Americans, and restrictive covenants were employed despite legal prohibitions. Banks and other lending institutions either refused to make loans to African-Americans or scrutinized minority applications so stringently that few succeeded. Occupancy criteria maintaining the previous racial composition of "neighborhoods" were upheld by government agencies that built new residential units or financed housing.[38]

Even before World War II, a real estate survey taken in 1936 for Oakland by local real estate appraisers showed very few African-American residents in the Oakland-Berkeley hills region. The survey stated that restrictive covenants were partially behind this de facto segregation.[39] The heavily concentrated African-American district of West Oakland attracted more industrial than residential growth, thereby increasing the housing shortage for black residents of Oakland. By 1938 a series of studies to determine the need for low-cost housing verified that Oakland did have substandard housing conditions and could qualify for federal funding. The studies recommended that areas in West Oakland should be demolished. The first projects were proposed for the heart of West Oakland, areas bounded by Eighth, Twelfth, Cypress, Union, and Poplar streets and by Eighth, Tenth, Campbell, and Willow streets. African-Americans residing in West Oakland used a community relocation service to find new homes in North Oakland and South Berkeley.

The city of Berkeley also experienced residential segregation during World War II. Having a higher proportion of African-Americans in its population than any other Bay Area city during the war, Berkeley's black population concentrated itself in "South Berkeley." This area's boundaries ranged from Oakland on the south to Dwight Way on the north and from Grove Street on the east to San Pablo Avenue on the west. Ashby Avenue provided the chief thoroughfare for this region of South Berkeley.[40] Most of the homes in this section were comfortable single-family dwellings. Another area in West Berkeley paralleling San Pablo Avenue to Dwight Way and extending toward the industrial area adjacent to Aquatic Park did not fare as well as South Berkeley. Housing in this section of West Berkeley was substandard and overcrowded.[41] During World War II, the internment of Japanese families living in South Berkeley offered African-Americans an opportunity for housing in areas already heavily populated by black families; nevertheless, Berkeley's housing shortage continued. Many white families began to move away from racially mixed neighborhoods, which opened up housing units but further exacerbated the residential segregation of Berkeley.[42]

The Federal Public Housing Agency began to consider the construction of an emergency war housing project on vacant lots in northwest Berkeley between San Pablo Avenue and the Southern Pacific Railroad tracks. White residents of Berkeley, concerned by this prospect, lobbied the Berkeley City Council in August 1943 to reject the proposed housing project. The vice-president and general manager of the Berkeley Chamber of Commerce, J. Delbert Sarber, expressed his concerns in a letter read at the council meeting of August 20, 1943. It stated the chamber's opposition to public housing and to federal construction of emergency housing projects that eliminated land from the city tax rolls. The chamber requested that the FHA administration make a thorough search for land elsewhere. It also urged that private enterprise be encouraged by the federal government to construct new housing. Among the chamber's arguments were the claims that land could be found closer to the worker's place of employment and that the federal government had not proven the failure of Berkeley's private sector to provide adequate housing. Berkeley's citizens did not desire change in their housing conditions.[43] The Berkeley Manufacturers Association also expressed caveats similar to those of the chamber of commerce.

The Berkeley City Council received these protests at that meeting. Opponents of the housing project claimed that the proposed project would take land needed for the future industrial development of Berkeley. Councilman Redmond C. Staats chaired a committee of the Berkeley Council that prepared the draft of a letter sent to Washington, D.C., opposing the housing project.[44] The FHA replied that it had considered other available locations and needed the proposed site in order to carry out its responsibilities to a defense area. The Berkeley City Council adopted a resolution to take the issue to the Truman War Investigation Committee; yet, all its efforts failed when the housing authority built Cordonices Village in early 1944. The council's reluctance to encourage a federal housing project that would introduce large numbers of African-American war workers into Berkeley did not go unchallenged. On January 19, 1994, W. Byron Rumford, a member of the Berkeley Interracial Committee, presented to the Berkeley City Council a petition, signed by 283 Berkeley residents, seeking nondiscrimination in the selection of tenants for Cordonices Village. The council responded that it was an issue for the federal government and that assignments had not yet been made. Yet, when the project opened in April 1944, the FHA assigned the least-desirable units, close to the Southern Pacific Railroad tracks, to African-Americans. It would not be until 1946 that continued demand by minority groups for housing ended de facto segregation in Cordonices Village through the introduction of a nondiscriminatory policy.[45]

By 1953 the federal government wanted to return the site of Cordonices Village to its private owners and to liquidate its investment in the Berkeley housing project. When eviction proceedings began in 1953, many African-American residents refused to leave. One year later, African-Americans comprised 88 percent of the inhabitants of Cordonices Village. Arthur Green acted as their spokesman and pointed to the large number of families who would have to be relocated. The council appointed a committee to study the housing problem. Finally, it resolved to relocate families and return the vacated land to industrial development.[46] Exclusive white neighborhoods remained intact during this relocation. Groups such as the Claremont Improvement Club prevented African-Americans from occupying housing in white neighborhoods by bringing legal suits against them.[47]

African-American protests against discrimination in housing and employment opportunities escalated during World War II. Veteran organizers within the black community joined both local and nationwide campaigns to promote equal opportunity. Although many

African-Americans believed that change was too sporadic and slow for real integration, they did experience a high level of mobilization for protest that did not exist before World War II began. Between 1956 and 1966, African-Americans in California's East Bay would recognize the efficacy of mass protest for equality and legitimacy within the East Bay community.

NOTES

1. United States, *Sixteenth Census, 1940: Population, I* (Washington, D.C., 1943); Davis McEntire, *The Population of California: A Report of the Research Study Made by the Authorization of the Board of Governors of the Commonwealth Club of California* (San Francisco: California Department of Justice, 1946).

2. Historical discussion focuses upon the wartime activities of the National Housing Agency. See John F. Bauman, *Public Housing, Race and Renewal* (Philadelphia, Pa.: Temple University Press, 1987), p. 70; Marilynn S. Johnson, "Urban Arsenals: War Housing and Social Change in Richmond and Oakland, California, 1941–1945," *Pacific Historical Review* 60 (August 1991): 290–91.

3. *California Voice*, January 7, 1922, p. 2.

4. *Wall's Addition to the City of Richmond*, Pamphlet 4599-45 (on exhibit at Oakland's Northern California Center for Afro-American History and Life).

5. Although Johnson sees World War II "as an agent of social change in American cities," it may be more accurate for the East Bay's African-American population to view the war as a catalyst for housing reforms recognized as necessary by black residents already living in the East Bay before 1941. Johnson, "Urban Arsenals," pp. 284, 288.

6. Cottrell L. Dellums, *Correspondence and Papers*, Carton 9, Folder: Orig. NAACP, 1948, Bancroft Library, University of California, Berkeley.

7. *California Voice*, October 28, 1938, p. 1.

8. *Restrictions by Federal Housing Administration for Sheffield Village*, March 10, 1939 (on exhibit at Oakland's Northern California Center for Afro-American History and Life).

9. The 1934 Housing Act created the FHA, which encouraged home construction. More important for African-Americans living in the East Bay, however, was the passage of the U.S. Housing Act of 1937. Under its program, the U.S. Housing Authority funded public housing projects and slum clearance.

10. Finding African-Americans reluctant to attend meetings when they were held in city hall, which also housed the county jail, Dellums appealed to the Labor League for help in the demonstrations. Joyce Henderson, *C. L. Dellums: International President of the Brotherhood of Sleeping Car Porters and Civil Rights Leader* (Berkeley, Calif.: Regional Oral History Office, Bancroft Library, 1973), pp. 26, 67.

11. At least 90 percent of the people demonstrating in city councils were white. Ibid., pp. 26, 68.

12. Ibid., pp. 26, 69–70.

13. Ibid., pp. 26, 70.

14. Ibid., pp. 26, 72.

15.   Ibid., pp. 26, 73.
16.   For population statistics, see a fine study of Bay Area shipyards in Katherine Archibald, *Wartime Shipyard: A Study in Social Disunity* (Berkeley: University of California Press, 1947), p. 81. For quote, see C. J. Haggerty, "Where Does California Go From Here?" *The American Federationist* 52 (April 1945): 27–28.
17.   Dellums, *Correspondence and Papers.*
18.   Lawrence P. Crouchett, Lonnie G. Bunch, III, and Martha Kendall Winnacker, *Visions Toward Tomorrow: The History of the East Bay Afro-American Community 1852–1977* (Oakland: Northern California Center for Afro-American History and Life, 1989).
19.   Allan Spear, *Black Chicago: The Making of a Negro Ghetto, 1890–1920* (Chicago: University of Chicago Press, 1967). Spear compares San Francisco's population with that of Chicago during the nineteenth century.
20.   In 1960, Tarea Hall Pittman, then acting director of the NAACP's West Coast Regional Office, gave testimony to the United States Commission on Civil Rights that "residential segregation based on race is the general rule in the towns and cities in the West." Joyce Henderson, *Tarea Hall Pittman: NAACP and Civil Rights Worker* (Berkeley, Calif.: Regional Oral History Office, Bancroft Library, 1974), pp. 55–56.
21.   "Explorations in Black Maritime History Exhibit," *Maritime Humanities Newsletter* 2 (Spring 1983): 2, 5.
22.   Edward Leon Coleman, interview by author, Eugene, Oregon, May 11, 1990.
23.   Ibid. Segregation restrictions blurred somewhat as the trains moved westward. Edward Coleman saw African-American servicemen take seats on trains once they left St. Louis.
24.   Henderson, *Tarea Hall Pittman*, p. 37.
25.   Alonzo Smith and Quintard Taylor, "Racial Discrimination in the Workplace: A Study of Two West Coast Cities During the 1940s," *The Journal of Ethnic Studies* 8 (Spring 1980): 35–36.
26.   Colbert goes on to say that "In the early days the in-migrant was considered as an evil that had to be endured because of the war. When these people began to purchase homes and to give all indications that they were here to stay the old-timers had to evaluate the influence their presence would have on the total picture." Robert E. Colbert, "Current Trends and Events [Section C]: The Attitude of Older Negro Residents Toward Recent Negro Migrants in the Pacific Northwest," *Journal of Negro Education* 15 (Fall 1945): 695, 701.
27.   The term "pioneer urbanite" is borrowed from the title of Douglas Henry Daniels' book, *Pioneer Urbanites*. The term is especially appropriate for those pre–World War II residents who led African-Americans in the struggle for racial equality throughout the Bay Area. Douglas Henry Daniels, *Pioneer Urbanites: A Social and Cultural History of Black San Francisco* (Philadelphia, Pa.: Temple University Press, 1980).
28.   "Richmond took a Beating: From Civic Chaos Came Ships for War and Some Hope for the Future," *Fortune* 31 (February 1945): 264. This account is accompanied by photos by Ansel Adams and Dorothea Lange.
29.   Ibid., p. 264.
30.   U.S. Bureau of the Census, *Sixteenth Census of the United States: 1940, Housing*, 1 (Washington, D.C.: United States Government, 1940), p. 143.

31.   "Shipyard Housing Units Branded Firetraps," *Oakland Tribune*, January 19, 1941, p. 1; *Oakland Tribune*, January 21, 1941, p. 1.

32.   Ibid.

33.   "Richmond Jury Hits Fire Trap Housing Units," *Oakland Tribune*, January 19, 1944, p. 1.

34.   Ibid.

35.   Ibid. Cooper's testimony was repeatedly used by African-American agencies to encourage reform and better safety for shipyard workers living in Richmond.

36.   *Oakland Tribune*, January 21, 1944, p. 1.

37.   *Oakland Tribune*, June 29, 1948, p. 1.

38.   Edward Everett France, "Some Aspects of the Migration of the Negro to the San Francisco Bay Area Since 1940" (Ph.D. diss., University of California, Berkeley, 1962), p. 33.

39.   Ibid., p. 43. The U.S. Housing Authority received appraisals from East Bay realtors serving the local Oakland Housing Authority. According to Dellums, "they appraised houses while sitting in their cars — never going indoors. The they sent to Washington a very low evaluation for West Oakland and which was cut down by 40% by Washington." Henderson, *C. L. Dellums*, pp. 69–70.

40.   France, "Some Aspects," p. 47. In 1940 Berkeley's total population of 85,547 included 3,395 African-Americans (almost 4 percent of Berkeley's total population).

41.   Ibid., p. 47.

42.   Ibid., pp. 48–49.

43.   Ibid., p. 49.

44.   Ibid.

45.   Helen Smith Alancraig, "Cordonices Village — A Study of Nonsegregated Public Housing in the San Francisco Bay Area" (M.A. thesis, University of California, Berkeley, 1953).

46.   France, "Some Aspects," p. 51.

47.   Ibid., p. 52.

10

The CIO: A Vanguard for Civil Rights in Southern California, 1940–46

David Oberweiser, Jr.

This chapter primarily examines the role of antidiscrimination committees within the Congress of Industrial Organizations' (CIO's) locals and state councils in southern California during World War II. Initially formed to abolish the "Mexican wage" and bring African-American workers into war industries, these committees later responded to challenges outside the workplace, such as the Sleepy Lagoon murder case, the Sinarquista movement, public housing, and discrimination against Asian-Americans.

Although Latinos greatly outnumbered blacks in southern California, the CIO usually focused on the conditions of African-Americans, because its Communist and left-wing leaders believed that unity between black and white workers was the key to union organization. In many CIO organizing drives, such unity had led to victory during the 1930s. At the same time, however, the CIO won considerable prestige in the Hispanic community because of its organizing efforts among this population.

Before the CIO was founded on the West coast, black and Mexican workers were used to break longshore strikes in 1916 and 1919. Soon after, waterfront workers found themselves at the mercy of the company "Blue Book" system, which gave employers complete control of the hiring process. After the 1934 Pacific coast maritime strike, longshore and warehouse workers established a nondiscriminatory hiring hall, with union dispatchers. In 1937, following the "march inland," which organized warehouses up and down the Pacific coast, longshore and warehouse workers founded the International Longshoremen's and Warehousemen's Union (ILWU) and affiliated with the CIO.[1] The ILWU had secured a beachhead for multiracial industrial unions on the West coast. In 1938, it was instrumental in founding the California CIO.

Unlike its rival, the American Federation of Labor (AFL), the CIO organized thousands of African-American workers in steel, auto, rubber, and meat-packing plants in the 1930s and began to educate white workers to admit black workers as equals on the job. However, existing seniority rules often excluded minority workers from skilled and semiskilled jobs in the first CIO union contracts.[2]

Off the job, workers of color typically lived in ghettos and barrios. During the 1930s, segregation was widespread in southern California. Water fountains, swimming pools, schools, and better housing were reserved for whites. People of color could swim in public pools only on Wednesday, when the pools were cleaned. Mexican youth were abused in "schools for juvenile delinquents" at Preston and Whittier, and in the barrios Mexicans were often the target of police harassment and beatings. When employed, they were restricted to menial jobs in construction and stoop labor in the fields and were paid "the Mexican wage" — less than Anglos doing the same work.[3]

In this climate, the Spanish Speaking People's Congress (SSPC), a civil rights organization, was organized in 1938. At first the congress banded together to overturn the "Mexican wage" system in the Southwest and end all forms of discrimination. Inspired by Luisa Moreno, a fiery organizer with the United Cannery, Agricultural, Packing and Allied Workers of America, the SSPC sought to protect the rights of all Hispanic peoples. The California CIO urged its affiliates to support the founding of the SSPC, which many unions did. Longshore and warehouse locals in Los Angeles, backed by the entire ILWU on the Pacific coast, were a bulwark supporting the congress.[4]

Early CIO antidiscrimination committees in southern California targeted the mistreatment of minority workers, especially Hispanics. The Committee to Aid Mexican Workers (CAMW) was organized within ILWU Local 26 (warehouse) union in Los Angeles in 1939. It supported strikes by Mexican workers in the fields of Orange, Riverside, Ventura, and San Joaquin counties, in the mines of Arizona, and among railroad track gangs in the Southwest. Striking miners often faced the shutting off of their utilities and eviction from company housing; many were attacked by vigilantes and police and ultimately deported. The CAMW appealed to unions in San Francisco and Los Angeles to bring food, raise money, and otherwise defend embattled strikers. The major tasks of the CAMW, however, were to organize the fight against the dual wage structure for Mexican workers (men and women), end their exclusion from skilled and factory jobs, and mobilize the ranks of labor against all forms of anti-Mexican discrimination by employers and society at large. Later, a new CAMW was formed by the Los Angeles CIO Council to fight discrimination in war industries, increase participation of Hispanics in trade unions, provide bilingual pamphlets, and encourage Mexicans to become U.S. citizens.[5]

On the eve of U.S. entry into World War II, the booming war industries quickly absorbed all available white labor. However, many employers who cried for more workers excluded workers of color. The number of nonwhite workers in some defense industries actually shrunk from 1940 to 1941. Nevertheless, the rapidly growing war economy was hungry for labor, and many blacks from the South migrated west to find work. The ILWU and other CIO unions mounted intense campaigns against employment discrimination in war industries. In December 1940, the Committee on Negro Employment in Defense Industries was formed after, among other catalysts, CIO organizer Wyndham Mortimer reported, "Out of 60,000 workers (in the aircraft industry in southern California), the one Negro employed is on probation."[6]

The California CIO was aided by national events. In 1941, following protests by black leaders to President Roosevelt, A. Philip Randolph, founder of the Sleeping Car Porters Union, called for a march on Washington by "loyal Negro-Americans." Almost immediately, FDR issued Executive Order #8802 banning discrimination based on race, color, creed, or national origin in government and defense employment. It also declared that employers and unions had a duty to provide full and equitable employment for all workers in the defense industry. The march on Washington was called off, and in July 1941, after considerable wrangling, FDR appointed some African-American members to a Fair Employment Practices Committee (FEPC). Dogged by a segregationist Congress and plagued by scant funding, in the fall of 1941 the FEPC opened hearings in Chicago, Los Angeles, New York, and Birmingham.[7]

A few months before the hearings, the first California CIO Anti-Discrimination Committee (ADC), chaired by autoworker union leader Jack Montgomery with Walter Williams, Frank Lopez, Jr., and others, fought against the exclusion of blacks from southern California's war industries. ILWU Local 26 president Bert Corona and assemblyman

Augustus Hawkins addressed a joint ADC-United Autoworkers Union meeting, protesting antiblack discrimination in the arms industry.[8]

Although Latinos greatly outnumbered African-Americans in southern California, the Los Angeles FEPC hearings in October 1941 focused on discriminatory hiring practices against blacks, especially in aircraft and shipbuilding. Only two witnesses gave brief testimony on behalf of Latino workers in the two days of hearings. Philip Connelly, secretary of the Los Angeles CIO Council, complained that the CIO was given only ten days to collect information and prepare affidavits of job discrimination against Latinos. Connelly also noted the "fear [by the victims] of being eternally blacklisted, [was] especially true of the Spanish speaking people." After the hearings, the FEPC issued recommendations to remedy discrimination but stopped short of criticizing practices of specific companies or unions, overlooked past discrimination, and failed to require proof of compliance.[9]

Given the scant attention paid to Latino workers by the FEPC hearings, the California CIO ADC and the SSPC called for a December 7 conference on the situation of Latin-American workers in Los Angeles. State SSPC president Rosendo Rivera of the electrical workers union (UE) and CIO organizers Luisa Moreno and Frank Lopez, Jr. joined Corona, Bill Taylor, and other unionists in the ILWU and CIO furniture, steelworker, and transport worker unions at the conference. Spanish-speaking workers packed the CIO hall on December 7. As soon as the meeting learned of the attack on Pearl Harbor, the crowd focused on the war effort.[10]

Latino organizers also helped defend African-American victims of discrimination. A burning issue at that time was the frame-up of a black man, Festus Coleman, for a rape in San Francisco. Corona took the Coleman case to the Los Angeles CIO Council, which set up a Coleman Defense Committee. Lopez was a sponsor of the Festus Coleman Defense Coordination Committee. Coleman was sentenced to death until a valid confession, incriminating a policeman, proved his innocence after he had served over four years in prison.[11]

Six months after FDR issued his executive order banning discrimination, a North American Aviation memo stated: "In most cases, women are preferable to Negroes. . . .[It is the] hope of this factory that it will never be compelled to use Negroes." The head of North American Aviation said hiring black mechanics or aircraft workers violated company policy. Furthermore, craft unions in defense plants would not admit African-Americans; therefore, employers with closed shops could not hire blacks, and training schools would not admit workers without job offers. Guy Nunn estimated that if blacks and Hispanics were hired in proportion to their numbers in the area by 1942, they would have 35,000 aircraft jobs; instead, they held only 1,500 jobs, with one black for every eight Hispanics.[12]

Exerting pressure on the U.S. Employment Service (USES) and the FEPC, the ADC obtained jobs for several hundred black and Hispanic workers. The ADC and United Automobile Workers (UAW) Local 887, with CIO and community support, won reinstatement of a black worker at North American with full seniority and back pay after he was fired for talking to a white woman worker. The ADC was partly able to counter the USES policy of discriminatory hiring that specified the race, color, and creed of prospective workers. As a result of the CIO's efforts, USES organized its own antidiscrimination committees in northern and southern California.[13]

In May 1942, the CIO ADC chair, Revels Cayton, from the Marine Cooks and Stewards Union, went before the Los Angeles Board of Education to propose a program for "immediate classes" in welding, aircraft sheet metal, riveting, shipfitting, and expanded machine shop at various high schools in the African-American and Hispanic communities. Cayton also requested that "Negro and Mexican teachers, advisors, fieldworkers, clerks and other staff be hired to help integrate the minority groups in defense (work) training" and that "defense classes be opened for women." After CIO ADC meetings with the Los Angeles Board of Education and USES, schools for training workers in the war industries opened in black and Mexican-American communities for the first time. In the latter neighborhoods, the ADC conducted a job registration campaign, and 4,000 workers applied. The California CIO also forged close relations with civic and religious groups and newspapers in the black community as it participated in and sponsored a mass meeting to protest the firing of a black worker from North American.[14]

In August, ADC secretary Cayton recommended changing the committee's name to the Minorities Committee (MC) to better reflect its activities. At the same time, the ILWU dispatched its organizers to other industries where Hispanics, blacks, and women were working. Phil Nash, Bert Corona, Ralph Dawson, and Alan Metcalf helped organize the Los Angeles shoe industry with Frank Lopez. Other ILWU organizers assisted the UAW organizing drives at North American and Vultee Aircraft, as well as the Los Angeles Municipal Railway with the Transport Workers Union and in electrical plants with the UE. Several ILWU organizers, including Corona, joined organizing campaigns with the Mine, Mill and Smelter Workers Union at Trona, Tehachapi, the San

Jacinto tunnel for the Metropolitan Water District, and at Monolith Cement. They also lent a hand organizing oil and rubber workers and technicians in the chemical industry.[15]

At North American Aviation, the number of minority workers grew from 25 to about 700 men and women in nine months, nearly all of whom joined the CIO. Vultee Aircraft and Ryan Aeronautical, which previously refused to employ blacks in any job, also hired African-Americans in large numbers with the committee's assistance. Almost all black and Hispanic workers joined the CIO.[16]

However, the CIO ADC did not have the same success in the Mexican-American barrio that it had in the African-American community. Essentially, the state CIO conceded that it had failed to carry out a "solid" trade union program. Moreover, it stated, a "strong and aggressive" community movement among the Mexican people was lacking. Finally, the committee had failed to "weed out the influence of a small but intensively active group of Fascist minded Mexicans" opposing the CIO program through their Sinarquista Union, a "Mexican counterpart of the treacherous Falange of Spain." Despite this, the ADC concluded, the great majority of Mexicans were not profascist and wholeheartedly backed the "joint war effort of the United Nations." The *Labor Herald* noted, "the twin circumstances of greater concentration on the Negro problem and the strongly anti-union influence of the fascist Sinarquist movement . . . dangerously strong in the Mexican community [which] resulted in the greater success of the CIO in the Black community."[17]

Some evidence suggests that the Sinarquista Union was not strong in Los Angeles, much less among the ranks of organized labor. Boosted by profascist priests, the Hearst press, Charles Lindberg, and the American Firsters, the Sinarquistas had a small following in some parishes. "They [the Sinarquistas] were windbags, more than anything," recalls East Los Angeles activist Joe Gastelum. However, U.S. and Mexican journalists revealed that the Sinarquista movement in Mexico was part of a secret Axis campaign to disrupt the Allied war effort in North America.[18]

Oscar Fuss, legislative director of the California CIO, told a Los Angeles Grand Jury that "a subversive group known as the Sinarquistas . . . exploit all the legitimate grievances of the Mexican people for their particular purposes. . . . The cause for unrest among Hispanic youth are not found in the unions but in the slums of Jim-town and Happy Valley where Latinos receive less relief than other Americans on the theory that Mexican-Americans are accustomed to a lower standard of living."[19]

In 1942 ILWU warehouse workers at California Mill Supply circulated a petition demanding more recreational facilities, more training schools, and more jobs for unemployed barrio youth. In addition, they called for a federal investigation of a group of Mexican and Spanish individuals "who call themselves the Sinarquista Union, preaching fascism, support for Franco's Spain, the disruption of our trade unions and hatred against the American people and government." Advised by Mexican unions, Gomez, Isidro Armenta, and other warehousemen active in the SSPC led ILWU Local 26 in mobilizing Latinos against the Sinarquistas in the Los Angeles area. As World War II spread, the focus of the CIO ADC and civil rights groups, such as the SSPC, turned from highlighting discrimination to campaigning for national unity against the Axis powers. The SSPC merged itself into the campaign to unite the Latino community behind the Allied war effort. Regardless of the degree of danger posed by local Sinarquistas, SSPC leader Josefina Fierro still believed unity behind the war effort was critical and the merger necessary.[20]

At the same time, the Hearst press began to whip up a frenzy against Mexicans. "Zoot Suit Crime Wave, Mexican Goon Squads and Pachuco Killers" headlines hit the streets of Los Angeles routinely in the summer of 1942. On August 3, the mysterious killing of a Chicano youth near Sleepy Lagoon exploded in the press. All Mexican youth became suspect "zoot suit killers." Police and civilian mobs roamed Los Angeles streets, beating such young men indiscriminately.[21] ILWU warehousemen condemned the Los Angeles police for its "mass jailings, un-necessary arrests and beatings of Mexican youth." Arguing that "iron-handed methods will only create a worse and more bitter feeling among the Mexican people," the unionists urged a conference of all "Mexican organizations." By November, the Los Angeles CIO Council had set up a Mexican Workers Committee, led by Cayton and Moreno, to coordinate the fight against racism in unions, develop an educational program on the Sleepy Lagoon case, support the Sleepy Lagoon Defense Committee, and launch a CIO membership drive throughout the Latino community. Los Angeles CIO Council secretary Philip Connelly blasted the "Gestapo tactics" of the Sleepy Lagoon prosecutors. According to testimony at the Sleepy Lagoon trial, several of the young defendants were abused, threatened, and beaten unconscious in handcuffs before they testified to the grand jury.[22]

Newly elected California CIO vice-president Moreno was assigned to the Sleepy Lagoon Defense Committee in April. Although Irish-Americans, Jewish-Americans, African-Americans, and others actively participated, the Mexican-Americans such as Josefina Fierro, Anthony Quinn, Corona, Lopez, and "other persons of Hispanic origin played an indispensable role in the Sleepy Lagoon Defense."[23] CIO unions throughout the state, including small locals like the San Pedro fisherman, donated to the Sleepy Lagoon cause. Joseph Marty, chair of the Los Angeles Sleepy Lagoon Defense Committee, won support from the 1943 UE convention. The national CIO also passed a resolution supporting the Sleepy Lagoon defendants at its sixth convention. The San Francisco CIO Council helped the Sleepy Lagoon victims financially and through an extensive petition campaign. Los Angeles CIO leader "Slim" Connelly urged his ally Attorney General Robert W. Kenny to push for the release of the "Sleepy lagoon youth." Finally, after the appeals court had ruled that charges against the defendants were "totally lacking," the youth were freed, after spending nearly three years in jail. The united effort by labor, religious, and civic groups won the battle.[24]

CIO activists also organized campaigns against housing discrimination. During the strikes in the scrap iron industry, ILWU organizers Lloyd Seeliger and Bert Corona went down to the "flats" along Los Angeles' East First and Third streets to mobilize pickets. There they found 10 to 12 families of Mexican workers living in each slum house. Before the United States went to war, the warehouse strikes and organizing drives stirred the community to demand better housing, and some low-income housing projects were built in neighborhoods where many ILWU warehouse members lived.[25]

As the war industry cranked into high gear, a housing shortage, especially severe for black and Latino workers, became a major issue for the CIO. In Los Angeles, a number of Mexican workers had given up their homes for a new housing project promised for them. However, when the project was completed, only war workers were accommodated. Union leaders Bill Taylor and Corona then moved into the housing projects at Ramona Gardens, organized the displaced workers, and picketed the Los Angeles Housing Authority, demanding housing for Mexican warehouse workers. Their tenant organizing coincided with the CIO organizing drives in the warehouse industry. Adopting an ILWU Local 26 resolution on housing, the Los Angeles CIO Council petitioned the housing authority to amend the Federal Housing Authority Act to permit "allied and friendly aliens" to occupy war housing projects. The Los Angeles Housing Authority then admitted "friendly aliens" in Ramona Gardens, Aliso Village, Estrada Courts, and Pico Gardens.[26]

In 1943, so-called race riots flared up in New York, Detroit, and Beaumont, Texas; the "zoot suit riots" tore up Los Angeles. The glitter of

Hollywood attracted many servicemen on furlough, and some of them were eager to "prove their manhood." "Zoot-suiters," demonized in the press, and Latinos in dance halls were a favorite target of servicemen. For over a week in June, sailors and soldiers rampaged in theaters, ballrooms, movies, bars, and streetcars, destroying property and attacking zoot-suiters — Chicano, black, and Filipino. The victims were arrested by the hundreds, and the servicemen usually were released. Finally, military authorities intervened and declared downtown Los Angeles off-limits. In a wire to the navy, federal, state, and local officials protested the servicemen's attacks on the zoot-suiters. CIO leader Harry Bridges said, "The past history of the L.A. Police Department does not lead us to believe that they are blameless or that they exercise the proper spirit of tolerance and treatment of Negro and Mexican people."[27]

The CIO MC called a conference on racial and national unity for August 8, 1943, in San Francisco, where signer Paul Robeson and Bridges addressed over 1,200 participants. Calling discrimination "Hitler's secret weapon," Bridges charged that "Hearst made the riots in Los Angeles." The California CIO also played a major role in the governor's committee established to inquire into the zoot suit riots under Attorney General Kenny. The committee condemned the "ghetto like conditions" under which 240,000 Hispanics lived in Los Angeles, with poor sanitation and recreational facilities for children. It also urged an end to segregation in public facilities and additional public housing projects for minority workers and recommended special training for the police in dealing with minority groups.[28]

The California CIO also fought discrimination by union members. AFL and CIO shipyard workers had circulated a petition in 1943 to remove four black families from a San Pedro housing project. The CIO Maritime Committee and a CIO shipyard local leader opposed the petition before the housing authority, and subsequently, the executive board of the Marine and Shipbuilding Workers Local 9 in San Pedro resolved that any member violating the union's constitutional provision for racial equality would be expelled and denied work.[29]

The state CIO urged Governor Earl Warren to condemn "propaganda directed against Jews, Negroes and Mexicans" and to counter actions "sabotaging the war effort," such as distributing circulars opposed to construction of housing for black war workers in Los Angeles or proposing the exclusion of "kikes or niggers" from neighborhoods where housing projects were planned. The MC denounced "Jim Crow, Jew-baiting, mob violence against Negro and Mexican people, exclusion of Chinese, denial of citizenship to Filipinos, the turning of Protestant against Catholic, Christian against Jew, native against foreign born" in its report to the 1943 state CIO convention. The MC report adopted Moreno's recommendation to emphasize the growing danger of anti-Semitism, and the state CIO declared "war against this weapon of Hitler, whether it appears in the form of dirty rumors, rhymes or slanders in any form against Americans of Jewish faith or origin."[30]

State CIO president Connelly said that the zoot suit riots "resulted because we in the labor movement failed to recognize the importance of the Sleepy Lagoon case as a trial balloon to see how far the people of this country would stand for Gestapo methods. . . . [T]his is the leading fight, as the Scottsboro fight and the Mooney case were." Arguing that racism was not "a minority problem" but a majority concern, Judy Dunks from the CIO's State, County, and Municipal Workers Union also told the 1943 convention, "If any union member thinks Negroes and Mexicans shouldn't live in the house next door to him, [or] . . . that the L.A. riots were caused by 'pachucos' and 'zoot suiters' and even uses these names, the union has failed." The 1943 state CIO convention concluded that discrimination was not just a union issue but also a "community problem" to be met "with community forces, under union leadership." During the war, CIO unions "have moved from the narrow field of wage and hour struggles to the broader field in which their interests and those of other elements of the population are one — price control, health, housing, etc."[31]

Responding to discrimination on the job, the CIO conducted successful organizing drives in war industries and opened training programs for female and minority workers for the first time. This was bitterly resisted at times by both workers and employers. However, a Lockheed Aircraft spokesperson, noting that 80 percent of the Mexican-Americans working in detailed assembly, general assembly, and riveting were women, testified in Senate hearings, "Mexican-American women workers have shown themselves especially adaptable . . . to difficult job conditions more readily than other groups." An officer from California Shipbuilding Corporation added, "the variety of jobs at which they can be utilized is limitless if . . . management simply will make a point of using them. Production records indicate they have an equal aptitude with other groups."

As war production peaked, the employment of minority and women workers in 1943 increased, on the average, by two and a half times over 1942. The proportion of women working in California war industries doubled from January 1941 to comprise 26.6 percent of the work force in July 1943 in all manufacturing. The California CIO, during the war years, had demanded training for women in war industries, better pay and conditions for clerical workers, pregnancy leaves as well as child care, protective legislation for working women, and equal pay for comparable work. Lithuanian-born Sonia Baltrun of the Textile Workers Union and Guatemalan-born Luisa Moreno of United Cannery, Agricultural, Packing and Allied Workers of America served as two outstanding leaders on the California CIO executive board. Calling for a halt to discrimination in federal appropriations, the MC report to the 1946 CIO convention also proposed special attention to the problems of women workers, specifically nondiscriminatory hiring, promotion, and equal pay for equal work.[32] Working women not only contributed to war production as "Rosie the Riveter" but also joined some of the massive job actions as the war ended. For example, in Los Angeles, UAW women strikers shut down General Motors' Southgate plant with 24-hour picket lines for many weeks during the bitter 1945–46 strike.[33]

By the end of 1943, the CIO MC countered attacks on Jews, blacks, and other minorities by changing its focus from antidiscrimination activities to campaigning for racial unity on behalf of the war effort. As a result of meetings between CIO MC leaders and Los Angeles financiers, Hollywood producers, Kiwanis clubs, rabbis, and church leaders in 1944, Los Angeles Mayor Fletcher Bowron appointed the Council for Civilian Unity, which arranged for movie stars to broadcast calls for multiracial unity on the radio. CIO MC chair Cayton urged his committee to coordinate with the CIO Political Action Committee to unite the 225,000 black voters with Latinos and all people of color in California to build "a certain spirit of liberation, an enthusiasm which will spread to the white workers as well."[34]

Except for the campaigns on the Sleepy Lagoon case and on the zoot-suit riots, CIO leader Moreno complained in 1943 that the work of the CIO in the Latino community was "practically nil (even though) we have thousands of CIO members who are Mexican." However, a year later, Moreno reported that the Mexican community was united and anxious to participate in the CIO Political Action Committee.[35] Because of CIO organizing drives and training programs for war industries in the Latino community and its resolute defense of the Sleepy Lagoon case and zoot suit victims, the CIO won considerable prestige in the barrio. Even after the war, the CIO enhanced its prestige in the Latino community by fighting police brutality and promoting Mexican cultural events, and it attracted Mexican-Americans in the Independent Progressive Party campaigns.

Overshadowing the campaign for national unity behind the war, racists stubbornly resisted FDR's policy of equal opportunity. For example, the Ku Klux Klan (KKK) opened a headquarters in Los Angeles. The CIO MC continued to push the federal government to implement nondiscrimination programs in the War Manpower Commission and in the USES by working closely with the FEPC and civic and labor organizations. It also demanded that the state of California establish its own FEPC and that affirmative steps be taken to halt growing anti-Semitism.[36]

In Los Angeles, the Spanish-speaking division of the FEPC, led by steelworker Jaime Gonzalez, began organizing in late 1944. Its main task was to coordinate activities with other groups in sympathy with the proposed FEPC (Hawkins Bill) in California. Assemblyman Hawkins wrote Hispanic leaders for action in support of his own bill to establish a California FEPC, covering all employees, including government, employment agencies, and labor organizations. "Bulldog" Hawkins, the first black elected to the California Assembly in 1934, had worked in the San Pedro shipyards during the war and was legislative director of the California CIO. Recognizing the faults of the wartime FEPC, Charlotta Bass, publisher of the *California Eagle*, noted, "weak as it was, the Fascists in America were quick to strangle it." Citing recent police attacks on picket lines, the burning of the O'Day Short family home in Fontana, the Festus Coleman case, and restrictive covenants on housing, she argued that an effective state FEPC was a basic step in the defense of minority rights. For years, the state CIO MC continued to fight for FEPC laws at all levels of government and condemned the Truman administration for stalling on civil rights legislation.[37]

As the war began to conclude, postwar conversion threatened to undermine the employment gains made by female and minority workers. In California, the "two war babies" — aircraft and shipbuilding — accounted for nearly 500,000 of the 850,000 employed in manufacturing. A cutback to prewar levels of employment would throw about 1.5 million out of work. Practically all women, blacks, and Latinos would be laid off. Therefore, the CIO lobbied for conversion bills that promised to retrain and relocate workers; provide unemployment bonuses, full education, and mustering out pay for veterans; and protect small businesses and farmers from land speculators.[38]

The California CIO proposal for an economic conversion council run jointly by corporate, labor, and civic groups was sidetracked until after V-J Day. Then, the chamber of commerce set up a Citizens' Reconversion Council (CRC) in Los Angeles that shut unions out of decision making. Eventually, organized labor was invited to join the CRC. However, the CRC launched a drive to convince workers to accept low-paying jobs (which consigned blacks to domestic service), to abolish the National Housing Agency, and to begin a minor public works program.[39] Meanwhile, layoffs began to multiply, hitting women and minority workers first. The housing shortage in Los Angeles grew critical as thousands of veterans and workers lived in overcrowded, unsanitary, unsafe dwellings, made worse each day by accelerating demobilization and the return of 35,000 Japanese-Americans from the relocation centers. More than 100,000 adequate family units were needed. Freeway construction projects exacerbated the housing problem. Noting the serious plight of minority groups, who were prevented from living in large sections of the city by restrictive housing covenants and discrimination by landlords and speculators, the Los Angeles CIO council demanded the continuation of rent control, emergency housing construction, and anti–housing discrimination legislation.[40]

In one week of September 1945, 37,000 workers were laid off in Los Angeles. The War Manpower Commission estimated over 100,000 production workers had been idled since V-J Day. Still ahead were 45,000 layoffs in aircraft and 10,000 more in shipbuilding and repair. Los Angeles manufacturing jobs declined to the prewar total of 152,000. From 1940 to 1944, the working population of Los Angeles County had increased by 400,000. The Haynes Foundation estimated that at least 500,000 war workers would be dislocated in the county, while returning veterans would be hired for over one-third of the prewar jobs. The report of the MC to the 1945 CIO convention declared: "Negro, Mexican and all minority groups in California are rapidly becoming the first postwar casualty." Insuring full CIO support for the state FEPC bill became a legislative priority. To reduce massive layoffs of the last-hired, some unionists proposed "super-seniority" for minority and women workers, whereby more-senior workers would be laid off first. Los Angeles CIO furniture worker union leaders Oscar Castro and Gus Brown unsuccessfully insisted on "super-seniority clauses" in the 1945, 1946, and 1947 master contracts. Nevertheless, they did convince several employers not to fire recently hired black workers. However, the idea of "super-seniority" died in the scramble for jobs after the war, recalls former ADC leader Cayton.[41]

The postwar period witnessed a chilling upsurge of racist terror across the nation. Shootings and assaults on black and Hispanic war veterans in the Southwest who protested segregated public facilities coincided with the desecration of synagogues and with blatant anti-Catholicism.

Ideologies of hate began to corrode the spirit of wartime unity. The Los Angeles CIO, spurred by San Pedro longshore Local 13 (ILWU), petitioned CIO members to rescind any action taken by CIO locals to stop members from working with returning Americans of Japanese ancestry. The state CIO called upon government officials to do "everything in their power . . . to assist in the readjustment of those loyal Japanese-Americans to our community life." The California CIO also fought discrimination against other Asian peoples. It backed bills to legalize the naturalization of Filipinos. Earlier, after the attack on Pearl Harbor, ILWU president Harry Bridges had urged the CIO executive council: "Don't jump on anyone who happens to be Japanese. Plenty of Japanese are just as anxious as we are to have Japan lose the war." In 1943, the state CIO supported the bill to repeal the Chinese Exclusion Act of 1882 and advocated normal immigration and citizenship policies toward the Chinese.[42]

It was not only private citizens and hate groups but also some police officers who perpetrated racist attacks. For example, in San Pedro, the ILWU fought to keep women and blacks employed on the waterfront as it organized the National Metals Company, which cut up warships into scrap iron. However, the police chief tried to move blacks and Spanish-speaking people out of San Pedro by ticketing their vehicles and selectively enforcing minor infractions. The Los Angeles ILWU Harbor Committee exposed such racist harassment by local police departments. Furthermore, by unionizing scrap metal and other peacetime conversion jobs, it won back some jobs lost to postwar layoffs. The Los Angeles CIO Council pressed for investigations of police shootings of minority peoples, called upon the sheriff's department to discharge a deputy sheriff for his KKK activities, and commended state Attorney General Kenny for investigating the KKK. In addition, the council urged each of its affiliate unions to expel KKK members from their locals and asked the mayor and police department to take action against KKK terrorist acts.[43] In the face of a racism deeply rooted among employers, government agencies, some labor unions, and workers, the California CIO recognized that the "fight against discrimination is the fight for the very existence of our unions," and with its allies, it proved that the contagion could be contained and even forced to retreat. For all its shortcomings, the CIO record on equality during World War II was "a shining star" compared with that of the AFL, which proclaimed education the way to eliminate racism among white workers but did little to educate its members. Father George Dunn praised the CIO's work: "The CIO in this fight is far superior to the role of the clergy in the U.S. . . . . We must look to labor unions and I mean the CIO." A leader of the AFL boilermakers and iron shipbuilders union, which excluded blacks throughout the war, admitted, "The AFL for years didn't care about taking Negroes in. It was only when the CIO came in that Negroes got into the unions."[44]

NOTES

1. Bruce Nelson, *Workers on the Waterfront* (Urbana: University of Illinois Press, 1988), pp. 259–60; Harvey Schwartz, *The March Inland: Origins of the ILWU Warehouse Division, 1934–1938* (Los Angeles, Calif.: Institute of Industrial Relations, 1978); *The ILWU Story: Three Decades of Militant Unionism* (San Francisco, Calif.: International Longshoremen's and Warehousemen's Union, 1963), pp. 20, 24–25.

2. Philip S. Foner, *Organized Labor and the Black Worker 1619–1973* (New York: International Publishers, 1978), pp. 215, 221–33.

3. Rodolfo Acuña, *Occupied America, A History of Chicanos* (New York: Harper & Row, 1981), p. 323. On discrimination against Mexican-Americans in southern California, see also Ricardo Romo, *East Los Angeles: History of a Barrio* (Austin: University of Texas Press, 1983); George J. Sanchez, *Becoming Mexican America: Ethnicity, Culture and Identity in Chicano Los Angeles, 1900–1945* (New York: Oxford University Press, 1993); interview with Bert Corona, Los Angeles, May 26, 1986.

4. Interview with Josefina Borboa Fierro, Los Angeles, July 26, 1982; "The Case of Luisa Moreno Bemis," (San Francisco, Calif.: Labor Committee for Luisa Moreno Bemis, n.d.); interview with Bert Corona and Lloyd Seeliger, Los Angeles, April 3, 1986; *Proceedings of the 2nd Annual Convention California State Industrial Union Council*, October 6–8, 1939, p. 26.

5. Stuart Jamieson, *Labor Unionism in American Agriculture* (New York: Arno Press, 1945), pp. 172, 176; interviews with Bert Corona, May 26, 1986, and Lloyd Seeliger and Bert Corona, April 3, 1986; *Labor Herald*, November 7, 1941.

6. *Executive Board Sessions California State Industrial Union Council*, December 7–8, 1940, p. 10; interview with Bert Corona, May 26, 1986; Foner, *Organized Labor and the Black Worker*, pp. 238–39.

7. Foner, *Organized Labor and the Black Worker*, pp. 239–42.

8. *Labor Herald*, June 27, 1941.

9. Cletus Daniel, *Chicano Workers and the Politics of Fairness: The FEPC in the Southwest 1941–1945* (Austin: University of Texas Press, 1991), pp. 6, 10–12.

10 *Labor Herald*, November 28, 1941; interview with Lloyd Seeliger and Bert Corona, April 4, 1986.

11. *People's World*, January 17, 1942; letter from Elaine Black Yoneda, Coleman Defense Co-ordinating Committee, San Francisco, May 1945; interview with Lloyd Seeliger and Bert Corona, April 4, 1986.

12. *People's World*, January 31, 1942; *Reports Executive Board Session, California Industrial Union Council*, February 28–March 1, 1942, p. 11.

13. *Report of the State Executive Board California CIO Council to the 5th Annual State Convention California CIO Council*, October 9–11, 1942, p. 11.

14. Ibid.; *Labor Herald*, February 27, 1942, and May 1, 1942.

15. *Executive Board Sessions*, California State Industrial Union Council, August 1–2, 1942, pp. 14–15; interviews with Lloyd Seeliger and Bert Corona, April 4, 1986, and with Bert Corona, May 26, 1986.

16. *Report of the State Executive Board California CIO Council to the 5th Annual State Convention California CIO Council*, October 9–11, 1942, pp. 10–12.

17. Ibid., pp. 12–13; *Labor Herald*, October 9, 1942.

18. Interviews with Joe Gastelum, Los Angeles, August 2, 1982, and Bert Corona, May 26, 1989; Mario Gil, *Sinarquismo: Su Origen, Su Esencia, Su Mision* (Mexico: Club del Libro, 1944), pp. 135–42; Allan Chase, *Falange: The Axis Secret Army in the Americas* (New York: G. P. Putnam and Sons, 1943), pp. 158–75.

19. *Labor Herald*, October 9, 1942.

20. *Labor Herald*, October 16, 1942; interview with Josefina Borboa Fierro, Los Angeles, July 26, 1982, and Bert Corona, May 26, 1986.

21. "A Statement on the Sleepy Lagoon Case," unpublished, (Los Angeles, 1943), p. 2; Guy Endore, *The Sleepy Lagoon Mystery* (Los Angeles, Calif.: The Sleepy Lagoon Defense Committee, 1944), p. 12.

22. *Labor Herald*, October 2, 1942, October 16, 1942, November 19, 1942, and June 25, 1943; Endore, *The Sleepy Lagoon Mystery*, pp. 15–17.

23. George E. Shibley to editor, *Los Angeles Times*, September 25, 1978.

24. *Proceedings of the 6th Annual Convention California CIO Council*, October 21–24, 1943, p. 128; *Proceedings of the 9th United Electrical, Radio and Machine Workers Convention*, September 13–17, 1943, pp. 128–30; "Resolution on the Sleepy Lagoon Case Adopted at the Sixth Constitutional Convention of the CIO, Philadelphia, 1943," Los Angeles CIO Sleepy Lagoon Defense Committee, December 13, 1943; Philip Connelly to Robert W. Kenny, October 7, 1944; Guy Endore, *Sleepy Lagoon: Victory for Democracy* (Los Angeles, Calif.: Sleepy Lagoon Defense Committee, 1945), pp. 1–2.

25. Interview with Lloyd Seeliger and Bert Corona, April 4, 1986.

26. *Labor Herald*, October 16, 1942, and November 20, 1942; telephone interview with Bert Corona, Los Angeles, June 18, 1986.

27. Acuña, *Occupied America*, pp. 326–28; *Labor Herald*, June 18, 1943.

28. *Labor Herald*, June 18, 1943, and August 12, 1943.

29. *Proceedings of the 6th Annual Convention California CIO Council*, October 21–24, 1943, p. 128; *Labor Herald*, August 12, 1943.

30. Gus Hawkins to Governor Earl Warren, November 2, 1943; *Proceedings of the 6th Annual Convention California CIO Council*, October 21–24, 1943, pp. 23, 146.

31. *Proceedings of the 6th Annual Convention California CIO Council*, October 21–24, 1943, pp. 24, 128–30.

32. *Labor Herald*, May 11, 1945, p. 6; *Proceedings of the 9th Annual Convention California CIO Council*, December 12, 1946, p. 49.

33. "To All CIO Unions," United Automobile Workers circular, December 17, 1945.

34. Revels Cayton, "Minorities Report Given at California CIO Council Meeting Executive Board," January 16, 1944, pp. 1–3.

35. *Proceedings of the 7th Annual Convention California CIO Council*, August 31–September 3, 1944, p. 7; *Report on Political Action and Executive Board Meeting California CIO Council*, July 1, 1945, pp. 12A–13A.

36. *Proceedings of the 7th Annual Convention California CIO Council*, August

31–September 3, 1944, pp. 96–97.

37.   Agenda, "Meeting of the Spanish Speaking Division FEPC," January 11, 1945; Gus Hawkins to Manuel Ruiz, Jr., January 18, 1945; *Labor Herald*, July 2, 1943, March 15, 1946, and August 3, 1946; *Proceedings of the 10th Annual Convention California CIO Council*, November 20–23, 1947, p. 105.

38.   *Proceedings of the 7th Annual Convention California CIO Council*, August 31–September 3, 1944, pp. 98–113.

39.   Ibid., p. 21.

40.   "A Resolution Regarding the Housing Shortage in Los Angeles," Los Angeles CIO Housing Committee, November 2, 1945.

41.   "The Facts on Unemployment in Los Angeles," California CIO Research Department, October 1, 1945, pp. 1–4; *Proceedings of the 8th Annual Convention California CIO Council*, December 5–9, 1945, pp. 111–13; Luis L. Arroyo, "Industrial Unionism and the Los Angeles Furniture Industry, 1918–1954" (Ph.D. diss., University of California, Los Angeles, 1979), p. 244; interview with Revels Cayton, San Francisco, April 26, 1983.

42.   "Resolution submitted by ILWU Local 13 Delegation," adopted by Los Angeles CIO Council, May 18, 1945; "Return to California of Americans of Japanese Ancestry," resolution adopted by the Executive Board of the California CIO Council, January 14, 1945; *California Industrial Union Council Executive Board Session*, February 10–11, 1940, p. 4, and December 13–14, 1941, p. 10; *Report of the Executive Committee Meeting of the California CIO Council*, April 3–4, 1943, p. 5.

43.   Interview with Lloyd Seeliger and Bert Corona, April 4, 1986; *CIO Minutes Digest, LA CIO Council*, April 5, 1946, p. 4, April 19, 1949, p. 3, and June 21, 1946, p. 2.

44.   *Proceedings of the 10th Annual Convention California CIO Council*, November 20–23, 1947, p. 108; interview with Revels Cayton, April 26, 1983; *Labor Herald*, March 15, 1946; Foner, *Organized Labor and the Black Worker*, p. 237.

Index

About the Contributors

James B. Atleson is professor of law at the State University of New York at Buffalo. He is the author of *Values and Assumptions in American Labor Law* (1983).

Richard P. Boyden is a supervisory archivist at the San Francisco Federal Records Center. His book *The Militant Tradition and the Liberal State: The San Francisco Machinists from Depression to Cold War, 1930–1950* is forthcoming.

Daniel A. Cornford is associate professor of history at San Jose State University. He is the author of *Workers and Dissent in the Redwood Empire* (1987) and editor of *Working People of California* (1995).

Alan Derickson is associate professor of labor studies and industrial relations at Pennsylvania State University. He is the author of *Workers' Health, Workers' Democracy: The Western Miners' Struggle, 1891–1925* (1988).

Marilynn S. Johnson is assistant professor of history at Boston College. She is the author of *The Second Gold Rush: Oakland and the East Bay in World War II* (1993).

Gretchen Lemke-Santangelo is assistant professor of history at Saint Mary's College. She is the author of the forthcoming *Long Road to Freedom: African-American Migrant Women and Social Change in the San Francisco East Bay Area, 1940–1950.*

Delores Nason McBroome is associate professor of history at Humboldt State University. She is the author of *Parallel Communities: African-Americans in California's East Bay, 1850–1963* (1993).

Sally M. Miller is professor of history at the University of the Pacific. She has published *Victor Berger and the Promise of Constructive Socialism, 1910–1920* (1973); *The Radical Immigrant, 1820–1920* (1974); *Flawed Liberation: Socialism and Feminism* (1981); *Kate Richards O'Hare: Selected Writings and Speeches* (1982); *The Ethnic Press in the United States* (1987); and *From Prairie to Prison: The Life of Social Activist Kate Richards O'Hare* (1993).

Shirley Ann Moore is assistant professor of history at California State University, Sacramento. She is the author of the forthcoming *To Place Our Deeds: The Black Community in Richmond, California.*

David Oberweiser, Jr., is an independent scholar who has presented several papers on the Congress of Industrial Organizations in California.

Nancy L. Quam-Wickham is assistant professor of history at Long Beach State University. She is completing her dissertation, "'Proletarians' and 'Petroleocrats': Work, Class, and Politics in the Southern California Oil Industry, 1917–1935," at the University of California, Berkeley.

Robert H. Zieger is professor of history at the University of Florida. He is the author of *Republicans and Labor, 1919–1929* (1969); *Madison's Battery Workers, 1934–1952: A History of Federal Labor Union 19587* (1977); *Rebuilding the Pulp and Paper Workers' Union, 1933–1941* (1984); *American Workers, American Unions, 1920–1985* (1986); and *John L. Lewis: Labor Leader* (1988).

ISBN 0-313-29074-1

90000>

EAN

9 780313 290749

HARDCOVER BAR CODE